39

*The Struggle for Social Security, 1900–1935*

A Publication of *The Center for the Study of The History of Liberty in America,* Harvard University

# The Struggle for Social Security

## 1900–1935    by Roy Lubove

---

Harvard University Press

Cambridge, Massachusetts

1968

Library of Congress Catalog Card Number 68-14265
Printed in the United States of America

This monograph was prepared with the assistance of a grant to the
author provided by the American Philosophical Society.

The work of the Center for the Study of the History of Liberty
in America has been supported by grants from the Carnegie Corporation
of New York and the Lilly Endowment, Inc.

*to Diane*

# *Foreword by Oscar Handlin*

"Three decades after its appearance, the federal social security system has become an accepted feature of American life. It is difficult, in retrospect, to understand the acrimony of the debate that preceded the enactment of the New Deal legislation in this field. Long after the European countries, at comparable stages of industrial development, had developed such protection against dependency, the issue in the United States was still open.

There were complex reasons for the delay and for the bitterness of the struggle. Federalism complicated the whole issue in the United States. Yet Imperial Germany had also been a federal state and had nevertheless moved rapidly toward government provisions for security. There was an immense gulf between the potentially dependent proletariat and the rest of the population in the United States. But American employers were no more heartless or ruthless than their European counterparts.

Political and social factors contributed to the lag in the United States. But the ideological element was unique in the American situation. By the opening decade of the twentieth century, the concept of individualism had become so well entrenched that any social action seemed a threat to personal liberty. A rival pattern of voluntary effort was regarded as more appropriate and more in accord with national character. Social security proposals, therefore, were not considered simply in the light of the needs they served, but as an entering wedge in the process of extending state power that would ultimately curtail individual freedom.

Previous studies have shown the relation to liberty of both individualism and voluntarism. Yehoshua Arieli's *Individualism and Nationalism in American Ideology* (Cambridge, Mass.: Harvard University Press, 1964) traced one pattern to its roots in the American past. Morton Keller's *The Life Insurance Enterprise, 1885–1910* (Cambridge, Mass.: Harvard University Press, 1963) showed the importance of voluntarism in another context. Roy Lubove's present book analyzes the factors which influenced the development of welfare legislation in the United States.

In the end the issue was not as clear-cut as it seemed to those who fought over it. The social security system neither damaged the liberty of the citizen nor eliminated the voluntary aspects of community action. Instead, it provided a support that invigorated both. This book is a useful contribution to the understanding of the whole process.

# Contents

*The Struggle for Social Security, 1900–1935*

# I  The Constraints of Voluntarism

The idealization of voluntary institutions is deeply rooted in the United States. As early as the 1830's Tocqueville was impressed by the number of "intellectual and moral associations" which flourished. He saw a close connection between the principle of equality and the proclivity for voluntary association. Compared to aristocratic societies citizens of a democracy were independent, but they were also feeble and powerless unless they combined to achieve their ends. The American association served as the counterpart of the "wealthy and powerful" citizen of an aristocracy with his disproportionate leverage and influence. Americans have often interpreted the character of their society in the rhetoric of "individualism," but Tocqueville recognized that voluntary association was the real key to social action and organization in the United States.

Along with equalitarianism, mobility and heterogeneity were prominent features of American society in the nineteenth century. These elements of the social system, combined with the absence of a well-defined class and institutional structure, produced anxieties and tensions. Individual role and status were ambiguous, behavioral and cultural norms confused. Voluntary associations performed the strategic function of mediation between Tocqueville's feeble individual, on the one hand, and the mass society and government, on the other.

Private charitable, philanthropic, and mutual-aid societies flourished in this context of voluntary association. They were often tied to sectarian and ethnic group aspiration. As mediators between the immigrant and a strange, often hostile American environment they served as buffer and interpreter. In short, voluntary association for benevolent ends functioned as an instrument of acculturation and a source of individual or group identity.

In the broadest sense voluntary association provided an alternative to politics and governmental action. It enabled groups of all kinds to exert an influence and seek their distinctive goals without resort to the coercive powers of government. It led to the assumption by private groups of responsibilities for collective action delegated to government or elite groups in other countries. "What political power," Tocqueville asked, could carry on the "vast multitude of . . . undertakings which the American citizens perform every day, with the assistance of the principle of association?" [1]

Prior to the twentieth century voluntary association was a dynamic, progressive influence in American life. It not only played a mediating role between the individual and society, but made limited government possible by diffusing power and responding to collective needs. Yet, by the twentieth century the ideology of voluntarism and the vast network of institutional interests which it had nurtured had become retrogressive in many respects. Assumptions about the self-sufficiency and superiority of voluntary institutions obstructed adaptation to changing economic and social conditions. And nowhere did the rigidities of the voluntary creed prove more disastrous than in the area of social welfare legislation, as demonstrated by efforts to enact a comprehensive economic security program before the 1930's. In other areas as well — low-cost housing, medical care and urban planning — voluntarism became, as I. M. Rubinow put it, the great American substitute for social action and policy. What occurred was the creation of socio-economic no-man's-lands; voluntary institutions failed to respond to mass needs, but thwarted governmental efforts to do so.

The social insurance movement, launched in the early twentieth century, was a decisive episode in the history of American social welfare. In contrast to the middle-class reform tradition of the past, with its emphasis upon economic independence and mobility, the sponsors of compulsory social insurance addressed them-

selves to problems of security in a wage-centered, industrial economy. They maintained that neither public welfare nor private
social work nor voluntary insurance sufficed to provide "indemnity against financial losses from . . . ordinary contingencies in
the workingman's life." [2] Charitable assistance, moreover, subjected the individual to the indignities associated with pauper
status.

Social insurance was proposed as an alternative to the existing,
but inefficient, system of economic assistance. Operating independently of the poor laws, it would respond predictably and
adequately in the event of an individual's exposure to the long-
and short-term risks which interrupted income flow: accident,
sickness and maternity, old age and invalidity, unemployment, or
death resulting in impoverished dependency. The social insurance movement was a thrust toward rationalization of the American welfare system; it aspired to centralization, the transfer of
functions from the private to the public sector, and a new definition of the role of government in American life.

Paralleling the social insurance movement was a self-conscious
effort, identified mainly with the private sector, to establish
social work as a profession. Professionalization was associated
with the quest for a skill monopoly, the creation of an occupational subculture to formulate standards and channel career opportunities, and the establishment of an appropriate administrative setting. In these respects, professionalization altered traditional assumptions about the role of the volunteer.[3] The social
insurance movement had a similar, though more profound, effect.
Its commitment to rationalization posed an unprecedented challenge to treasured assumptions concerning the role of voluntary
institutions in a democratic society.

Voluntarism\* was closely linked in American thought to a
cluster of political, social, and economic principles. These included individual liberty, limited government, self-support, and

\* By "voluntarism" I mean organized action by nonstatutory institutions.
Although the term has been widely used in this sense throughout the United
States, until recently only the word "voluntaryism" has been so used in
dictionaries.

an economic incentive system which distributed rewards on the basis of merit in a competitive market. The inherited political and economic order made possible a "functional income distribution," or an allocation of payments to "employed factors of production" according to efficiency criteria. Charity or social insurance, representing systems of "secondary income distribution," were suspect.[4] They allocated goods or services on the basis of need rather than participation in the labor force. In providing a form of guaranteed income, they undermined incentive and work discipline.

This book focuses upon the clash between social insurance goals and the ideology and institutions of voluntarism. As a rule, historians have not appreciated the significance of the social insurance movement, which launched a national debate over fundamental issues of liberty, the role of the state, and the dimensions of security in a wage-centered, competitive economy. My secondary theme concerns the influence of voluntarism upon the social insurance movement. Social insurance was introduced into an incongruous, inhospitable environment. The voluntary framework determined the limits of achievement, and even shaped social insurance theory and programs. In workmen's compensation, for example, private insurance companies were authorized to serve as carriers (in competition with each other or state funds), and merit-rating systems were introduced as a stimulus to accident prevention. Thus, a collective public institution was partly administered through voluntary organizations and competitive pressures. By the 1920's one group of social insurance experts, influenced by the compensation model, proposed a generalized "American" approach which emphasized prevention rather than benefits as the main purpose of social insurance.

Social insurance has been described as a "social invention which was brought into being to perform a specific function in a specific economic and social environment." It emerged, in the context of the late nineteenth and early twentieth centuries, as an "ideal instrument for effecting a significant break in the deterrent treatment of insecure workers, because its apparent analogy with private insurance made the change acceptable to a society which was dominated by business ethics and which stressed individual economic responsibility." [5] This interpretation, accepted by most authorities, is accurate but limited. The progress of social insurance in the United States would have been swifter if it simply had to demonstrate its compatibility with equity principles of private insurance. The sponsors of social insurance had to legitimize their innovation in terms of the broader idealization of voluntarism (which encompassed the conventional economic doctrine). Americans assumed that their country was unique in assigning to private, voluntary institutions a wide range of responsibilities which in other nations were relegated to government or elite groups. Voluntarism, the right of citizens to define and pursue their goals in free association, resulted in limited government and maximum liberty. Democracy and voluntarism were for all practical purposes synonymous. Compulsory insurance, however dignified by analogy with private insurance, seemed hostile to American traditions. Critics of social insurance interpreted the real issue as paternalism and statism versus personal liberty and voluntarism.

Each man in a democracy controlled his own destiny. If he entered into social relationships based upon voluntary cooperation he did not compromise his autonomy; he substituted a "social discipline" for a "democratic discipline." Both differed from the "paternal discipline" embodied in compulsory social insurance.[6] Paternalism, in the form of income guarantees, undermined the other disciplines and thus the foundations of a free society. State insurance and pension programs diverted wealth from the industrious and efficient to the idle and incompetent members of society. If the American people countenanced any such "system of morals or law which justifies the individual in looking to the community rather than to himself for support," men would no longer fear the consequences of dependency. This fear served as a "chief discipline in the interest of wholesome living." [7]

Men were at all times as lazy as they dared to be. If they became accustomed to public support when earning capacity diminished, what inducement would they have to "make provision for the future"? How could society maintain the "necessary degree of production and of economy"? The working classes would provide for themselves and their families if an "unwise charity" did not "offer a bonus to incompetence." [8]

Voluntary income-maintenance institutions, in contrast to state insurance, nurtured the democratic and social disciplines. They served as a "persistent reminder of the necessity that lies on every man to provide for his own future needs." They taught the worker that "future gratification" was contingent upon "present denial." [9] Social "order and harmony" depended upon awareness of this truth — an incapacity to restrain desire for immediate physical gratification typified the drunkard, prostitute, criminal, glutton, and other degenerates. Because voluntary thrift institutions instilled "obedience to the accepted laws and canons of righteous living as prescribed by the best tone of the community," they provided a foundation for labor legislation. Of what value were improved living and working conditions if men were not educated to use their time and money wisely? The eight-hour day, for example, "might prove the ruin of a people unless there had been an adequate growth in moral restraint." [10]

The sponsors of social insurance found themselves embroiled in a violent cultural conflict. The issue from their viewpoint was predominantly economic, administrative, and actuarial. Yet critics of social insurance invariably shifted the plane of debate, stressing the unique educational and social functions of voluntary institutions, their compatibility with American traditions, and the subversive implications of compulsory insurance. What social insurance experts regarded as technical issues were converted into moral issues and a sweeping defence of the American way of life.

Social insurance was condemned as an alien importation, if not a foreign conspiracy. Commercial insurance representatives perfected this stratagem in their campaign against compulsory health insurance. Proposed health insurance legislation, which provided for government contributions to local funds, even outdistanced the "state socialism" of Germany and propelled the

nation toward "Marxian socialism." Such proposals were sympto-
matic of a "reckless advocacy of hopeless panaceas of social and
political reforms." Democracy, "the perpetuity of our . . . fundamental conceptions of personal and political liberty," was at stake.
Social insurance was perhaps the most dangerous form of radicalism. More subtle than anarchism or nihilism, it duped Americans,
by means of a "cleverly disguised propaganda," into accepting a
"needless enlargement of the sphere of the state." The path to
"internationalism and racial decay," social insurance heralded the
decline of private enterprise and private life, "lived in accordance
with rational ideas and legitimate desires, free from undue restraint and interference." [11]

Some critics described social insurance as a German plot,
hatched by Bismarck to counter the growth of socialism and
insure the stability of the imperial throne. Otherwise, the ruling
classes could not proceed in their designs for "world conquest and
imperial aggrandizement." German autocratic militarism rested
squarely on the "social control of the wage-earning element and
the establishment of permanent class distinctions." Unfortunately,
the military elite discovered a flaw in the design. German industry
had been burdened with crushing costs which undermined its
competitive strength. It was necessary, therefore, to "induce other
countries . . . to adopt the same system, so as to equalize the
cost of production." [12] In developing this second phase of the
conspiracy, the German government published a mountain of
documents lauding the achievements of the social insurance system. It prepared elaborate exhibits for the St. Louis Exposition
of 1904, launched the International Association for Labor Legislation, and never lost an opportunity to sponsor international social
insurance congresses.

The fact that a number of American economists, and other intellectuals, were trained in German universities or influenced by
German social theory enabled social insurance to gain a foothold
in the United States. Confronted with indifference and opposition,
this small group of American propagandists had responded with a
"clever manipulation of public opinion." [13] Frederick Hoffman

and others who pursued this line of attack usually failed to cite the comprehensive English social insurance program, and its influence on American thought.

Controversy raged around the term "compulsory." Social insurance experts interpreted it in a technical, instrumental sense — as simply a device to maximize coverage and cost distribution, a means to protect those who most needed but could least afford insurance. Critics, however, invested the term with moral attributes. It was condemned as antithetical to the tradition of voluntary association, which had found its "chosen habitat" among the Anglo-Saxon race. Americans not only prized their liberties, but made a "fetish" of individualism.[14] Citizens discerned and responded to need on their own initiative. They formed organizations, if necessary, which competed for support in the benevolent marketplace. In lieu of income guarantees through compulsory insurance, Americans coped with social problems through a charitable free enterprise system.

This sharp distinction between "voluntary" and "compulsory" obscured the emergence of the modern organizational society — the structural similarities between public and private institutions which had developed.[15] Voluntary was equated with any form of "free," nongovernmental enterprise or association. Defined so broadly as to include virtually all private institutions, the term lost connection with reality. It encompassed private mutual-aid agencies ranging from the neighborhood burial group to the Metropolitan Life Insurance Company. Yet many institutions defended as expressions of American voluntarism were more comprehensible as large-scale bureaucratic systems with their characteristic features of great size, specialization, hierarchy, and routinization. The nature of private, voluntary institutions in an industrial-urban society had changed, giving rise to an essentially bureaucratic phenomenon. But the ideology of voluntarism lagged. It viewed public institutions as generically different from private; the latter, presumably, were neither bureaucratic nor coercive.

Private bureaucratic institutions in a wage economy did possess coercive power. They served as the individual's source of livelihood, mobility, and status, and could impose the most extreme sanctions. The rhetoric of voluntarism confused the real issue in the social insurance controversy. This issue centered on the division of labor between two bureaucratic systems, public and private, and their respective capacity to deal with the specific problem of income maintenance.

The ideology of voluntarism, which equated private and voluntary with nonbureaucratic and noncoercive, was not the only obstacle to social insurance. A large number of private vested interests viewed it as a threat to their survival. Critics of social insurance cited industrial establishment funds, trade union benefit funds, and fraternal, mutual, and commercial insurance as evidence that voluntary action in America precluded the need for government intervention. If government had any significant role, it was to create a favorable legislative climate for the continued growth of these private institutions. The mere fact that voluntary insurance funds existed, irrespective of how efficiently they performed, created two nearly insuperable obstacles to social insurance. How was it possible to refute the claim that voluntary income-maintenance institutions would suffice? Who could prove that existing arrangements would not expand and gradually include the entire population in their protective sphere? Reference to European precedent only reinforced the conviction that social insurance was an alien concept inappropriate to American circumstances. There existed one definitive test of the validity of the argument, impossible to apply: time alone could demonstrate whether voluntarism was equal to the challenge.

Defenders of the status quo had a second advantage. The elaborate rationale for social insurance was based almost exclusively on objective economic need. Social insurance experts maintained that voluntary programs reached only a small fraction of the population, and usually did not include those who needed protection most. They cited European experience, where autonomous voluntary funds were superseded by state subsidies to voluntary carriers, and ultimately by compulsory insurance. European nations recognized that voluntary insurance lacked rationality with its attribute of predictability. A given worker might or

might not be protected against one or more risks. His protection was not necessarily adequate to the need. In the event of temporary disability, for example, a worker might conceivably be eligible for benefits from an establishment fund or a labor union fund, a fraternal society or a commercial insurance company, or from some combination of these resources, or from none. It was necessary, therefore, to create a centralized public welfare machinery which could respond predictably and adequately in the event of income deprivation. Income maintenance could not be left to the vagaries of private initiative when access to goods and services was predominantly a function of wage continuity.

Critics of social insurance argued that voluntary institutions were adequate, but the ultimate justification for their primary role did not hinge on questions of economic efficiency. In discharging their economic function, voluntary institutions also served a number of indispensable educational, social, and moral ends. Public welfare bureaucracies, abstract and remote, could not duplicate their role. Social insurance had to be judged by noneconomic criteria.

Voluntary benefit funds first emerged on a significant scale toward the end of the nineteenth century. Available statistics provide a general picture of their evolution, but it is difficult to determine their precise scope. It is clear that little was accomplished before the 1890's, and that some provision for death (funeral) and temporary disability benefits was the major achievement of the voluntary system up to the 1920's.

Company establishment funds reflected a broader interest in the possibilities of welfare capitalism. Whether organized and maintained by employer or employee or through some cooperative arrangement, they expressed new ideals of "industrial statesmanship" and "service." The establishment fund substituted for the loss of personal relationship between employer and worker in an era of large-scale production units. "Beneath all other causes of trouble and conflict in the labor world, making them seem superficial only," was this "personal alienation of the employer from his fellow-men whom he engages to work for him in large numbers." Welfare capitalism demonstrated that the employer had assumed responsibilities "commensurate with his real power." [16]

The worker's quest for security testified most poignantly to his sense of alienation. An "intelligent employer" had to recognize that fear of the consequences of disability or old age demoralized the average worker. Lack of security acted as an "incubus to his efforts and progress." [17] Permanent industrial peace depended upon the employer's understanding that it was "just as important to furnish security for the job as it is to furnish security for the investment." Enlightened capitalism surely was preferable to "governmental initiative," which Americans scorned.[18] Louis Brandeis, who described business as a potential profession based upon academic training and service ideals, pointed to the welfare work of Boston's Filene family as a model. The Filenes had demonstrated that the "introduction of industrial democracy and of social justice is at least consistent with marked financial success." [19]

In the first flush of enthusiasm welfare capitalism seemed to have many advantages. It enabled the employer to discharge at minimal cost any personal sense of moral or social responsibility for his workers, while demonstrating to the community at large that business had evolved beyond the predatory stage. A secure, contented labor force was, in the end, more loyal and efficient. It was also more disciplined and compliant. Welfare capitalism provided "strong inducements for good behavior." The employee realized that "unsatisfactory conduct" might result not only in dismissal, but in loss of an asset like an old-age pension.[20]

A report of the United States Commissioner of Labor, published in 1908, examined establishment benefit funds.[21] Only 26 of the 461 funds surveyed had been instituted prior to 1880; 335 were created after 1890. The funds affected 342,578 employees out of a total labor force of 750,000. They represented 126 industries, but 241 funds were concentrated in 14 industries,[22] most notably transportation, coal mining, and metals production. The 6 largest funds, all in the Pennsylvania mining, iron, and steel industries, included 83,634 persons or almost one-quarter of the total. Establishment funds, on the eve of the social insurance movement, apparently enrolled only a percentage of the labor force in a limited range of industries. They were faulty also by the standard of risk coverage. Benefits applied mainly to temporary disability and death. Of the 461 funds, 429 provided a disability benefit, and 419 a death benefit. Both risks were covered in 390 funds, 54 made some provision for invalidity, and only 5 paid any form of superannuation benefit. The death benefit, usually fifty or one hundred dollars, amounted to little more than burial expenses. The temporary disability benefit was usually limited to five or six dollars a week for a period of thirteen weeks in a year.

If one ignored transportation, metals, and selected "model" employers, there would be little point in discussing establishment funds in the early twentieth century. The railroads were especially prominent in the evolution of this phase of welfare capitalism. Their benefit plans, which served as examples to other employers, "made . . . the most important contribution to the promotion of industrial insurance." [23] Railroad relief funds, as well as those in the iron and steel industry, were significant for another reason: they demonstrate that theories of welfare capitalism and the creation of relief funds were stimulated by the urgent, concrete problem of industrial injury. Establishment funds progressed furthest not only in large industries, but in dangerous ones, and were closely related to the origins of industrial medicine and prepaid medical care programs. This industrial accident problem also launched the social insurance movement, which centered originally on workmen's compensation.

Five large rail systems established relief departments as early as the 1880's: the Baltimore and Ohio; Pennsylvania; Pennsylvania West of Pittsburgh; Chicago, Burlington and Quincy; and Philadelphia and Reading.[24] These companies owned or operated one-eighth of the total mileage in the United States, and their labor force included one-sixth of all rail employees. These relief funds provided benefits mainly for death and temporary disability. The conditions of railroad work — its hazardous nature, mobility of the labor force, and extensive construction in isolated areas — led to pioneering efforts in the administration of medical services, as a supplement to cash benefits. Beginning with the Southern Pacific in the 1860's, railroads established precedents for pre-paid and contract medical care. In some cases the railroad owned hospitals and related facilities, staffed by company doctors. Or the company might contract, particularly in the densely populated East, with private hospitals and physicians to care for injured employees. These arrangements were frequently combined with the maintenance of emergency company hospitals in charge of salaried surgeons.[25]

Railroad relief departments experienced a twofold expansion after 1890. Additional companies introduced relief plans (fifty departments administered by thirty-seven rail systems existed by 1908), and provision for superannuation became more common. Of the five original relief funds, only the Baltimore and Ohio had included an old-age benefit.[26] By 1908 at least fourteen railroads provided old-age pensions. Most industries or firms adopted the railroad pension formula. The beneficiary received 1 percent of his average monthly pay for the ten years preceding retirement, multiplied by the number of years of service.

The steel industry, following the establishment of the United States Steel Corporation (U.S.S.) in 1901, emerged as a second prototype for welfare capitalism. Industrial accident problems again provided the immediate stimulus, but the long-range goal was labor discipline. Steel officials viewed the welfare programs as a substitute for trade unionism, aiding in the stabilization of a heterogeneous labor force and securing the loyalty of the skilled worker.[27] According to board chairman Elbert H. Gary, unions might have been necessary in the past because "workmen were not always treated justly." Enlightened management policies now made unions superfluous; they benefited none except the "union labor leaders." [28]

Steel industry accident relief and prevention (Safety First) programs were widely publicized and acclaimed. A gift of four million dollars from Andrew Carnegie led to the establishment of the first accident relief (and old-age pension) plan in 1902.[29] It was reorganized in 1910 following a U.S.S. donation of eight million dollars to the original endowment.[30] Systematic accident prevention had begun even before the criticism inspired by the Pittsburgh Survey of 1907–08. The Survey included John Fitch's vivid portrayal of the steelworker's oppressive way of life, and Crystal Eastman's grim recital of death and dismemberment in the industries of Allegheny County, Pennsylvania. In 1906, however, officials of subsidiary companies had already been charged with the responsibility of developing an effective safety program, and in 1908 a central Committee of Safety was organized. With the support of Judge Gary, it was given sweeping powers to devise and enforce safety regulations throughout the U.S.S empire. The Committee of Safety appointed inspectors for the subsidiary companies, served as a general clearinghouse on safety matters, studied the most serious accidents at its quarterly meetings, and assisted in the administration of the relief plan. Under its supervision, two kinds of safety committees were organized in most plants of subsidiary companies. The first was a permanent or central committee, made up of superintendents, master mechanics, and department heads, who reported directly to the plant manager. The other consisted of rank and file workers, who were allowed time to inspect plants once or twice a month. Their recommendations went to the permanent committee.[31] The relief and safety programs, along with an employee stock subscription plan instituted in 1903, were consolidated in 1911 into a Bureau of Safety, Relief, Sanitation and Welfare.[32]

Other employers accepted the new ideals of welfare capitalism in the early twentieth century. The International Harvester Corporation, for example, established a pension plan and an employees' benefit association in 1908. Like U.S.S. it eventually created a central welfare department to deal with safety and relief, as well as "educational work, charities, recreation, savings and loans, and civics."[33] Westinghouse Air Brake, Westinghouse Electric, General Electric, and National Cash Register were among the firms frequently cited in surveys of industrial welfare programs.[34]

Labor leaders agreed with businessmen that the "American 'way out' would seem to be through . . . improving voluntary organizations and systems."[35] Consensus disintegrated when it came to choosing the appropriate voluntary medium. Organized labor considered welfare capitalism no less objectionable than social insurance. One implied an industrial feudalism, the other a labor movement subordinate to the state.

John Mitchell of the United Mine Workers complained that company pension allowances "forestall union effort by binding the employe to his job, are economically a detriment to society in destroying the mobility of labor, in closing the labor market to men nearing a possible pension age, and in tending to suppress the activities of trade unionism." [36] The faults of voluntary pension programs derived partly from their status as a moral rather than a legal obligation. An employee had no vested rights. If he left, or was forced to leave a company, he lost all claims. Union leaders viewed corporation relief plans as another form of coercion. Membership in establishment funds might be made a condition of employment. More objectionable was the frequent clause requiring an injured employee to choose between a legal suit against the company, or acceptance of the fund benefit.

Although labor recognized that a voluntary institution could be coercive, the principle of voluntarism as exemplified by the trade union movement remained inviolate. Samuel Gompers' unbending hostility to social insurance proved a serious liability. Insurance companies and other private interests frequently quoted him to prove that the American worker preferred freedom to paternalism. Gompers' views on social insurance were influenced by his suspicion of "intellectuals" and other "saviours of Labor" who threatened to "dominate the labor movement with their panaceas or destroy it." He described them as "understudies to Providence" and "barnacles," who aspired to serve the workers in every way except the most essential — "get off their backs and give them an opportunity to do things for themselves." [37] These barnacles were not so altruistic as they seemed. All their proposals curiously hinged upon their employment as government "experts." Apparently the intellectual's "enthusiasm for human welfare" varied in proportion to his employment opportunities.[38]

Gompers interpreted social insurance in terms of a broader struggle for control over the labor movement. The wage-earner, he insisted, had to lead himself; he welcomed cooperation, but not outside direction or domination. Responsibility could not be delegated to employers or bureaucrats.[39]

Gompers translated the issue of power and influence into a defence of personal freedom and voluntarism. Compulsory social insurance would solidify class distinctions and destroy the wage-earner's voluntary institutions, which made possible their "complete control over their labor power." [40] The wage-earner prized his liberty more than his health. Unaccustomed to obey the dictates of authority, Americans differed fundamentally from Germans in "race psychology." After a long struggle to "get the tentacles of governmental agencies from off the throats of the workers," the labor movement now had to protect itself against the Socialists and their cohorts.[41] Rather than permit the entry of government agents and spies into the "homes and the lives of the workers," Gompers vowed to assist in the "inauguration of a revolution against compulsory insurance." [42]

He took violent exception to the claim that social insurance was necessary because existing institutions had failed to meet the economic needs of the wage-earner. Such views were a personal insult to himself and others who had devoted their lives to the labor movement. If conditions were as bad as alleged, then the "organization of trade unions extending over more than three-quarters of a century" had been in vain. The intellectual ignored not only the general contribution of trade unions to improved working conditions, but their distinctive emphasis upon adequate wages. The worker, if paid enough, could provide for all his needs. Social insurance was a superficial response to problems of poverty compared to trade unions. It provided jobs for "professional microscopic examiners," but did nothing to raise wages.[43] Social insurance would, however, undermine trade union benefit funds, which attracted men to unions or strengthened their allegiance.[44] Gompers favored old-age pensions through voluntary action by workers, assisted perhaps by government contributions. Similarly, he approved of unemployment insurance and exchanges, but only if administered by trade unions.

The social insurance expert considered it "somewhat naive . . . to discuss the question whether voluntary systems are better than compulsory systems." Voluntary mutual-aid had been "tried and found wanting." [45] But was it less naive to underestimate the resiliency of voluntary institutions, which gained strength from their identification with American social and economic values? Equally important, they often provided personal gratifications which compensated for their economic limitations. Although voluntary institutions like trade unions or fraternals were themselves evolving into large-scale bureaucratic systems, they still aroused a sense of personal loyalty and reverence. An abstract social insurance bureaucracy could not compete with the trade union in terms of individual identification with a cause and a tradition. Criticism of the economic limitations of voluntary institutions only reinforced the tendency to exalt their social functions. These were diminishing, but the bureaucratic attributes of voluntary institutions were obscured by emotion and a national ideology which equated voluntarism with democracy and freedom. The social insurance movement, consequently, experienced great difficulty in bridging the gap between demonstration of economic need and remedial social legislation.

Statistics substantiate the criticism that trade union benefit funds were defective by rational economic criteria. The majority of wage-earners were not even organized.[46] Not all unions maintained benefit funds. Local rather than national unions carried the main burden, an arrangement conducive neither to actuarial controls nor sound management. Limited financial resources severely restricted the range and level of benefits.

Trade union funds, like establishment funds, existed in the 1880's and experienced a more rapid expansion after 1890. Local unions usually assumed the initiative. National and local funds concentrated almost exclusively upon the risks of temporary disability and death. The Commissioner of Labor's survey of 1908 revealed that if a national union provided any kind of benefit, it was for death. Only nineteen had a temporary disability benefit, and the same number made some provision for permanent disability (usually equivalent to the sum allotted for death). The majority limited the sickness benefit to approximately five dollars a week for thirteen weeks in a year. Four unions had some arrangement for superannuation, but only one — the Cigarmakers' Union — paid a weekly unemployment benefit.[47]

Local benefit funds, in the early twentieth century, were more important than those established by national unions. Of the 530 included in the Commissioner of Labor's study, the earliest was a death benefit instituted in 1815; the second did not appear until 1852. It was not until the 1880's that benefit funds were commonly established at the time a local union was organized. The 530 local funds, which affected 173,690 persons, exhibited the usual faults of limited-risk coverage and inadequate benefit level. Only 304 of the local funds provided a benefit for temporary disability resulting from accident and sickness (another 42 paid benefits for one or the other). Death benefits ranging from $20 to $375 ($100 or less in a majority of cases) were distributed by 401 funds. Ten had some arrangement for permanent disability, and the same number provided some kind of unemployment benefit.

Along with those of the railroad brotherhoods, the benefit programs of the Cigarmakers' Union and German-American Typographia were probably the best American trade unionism had to offer.[48] The Cigarmakers' instituted sickness and death benefits in 1881 (supplemented in 1887 by a benefit for death of a member's wife, and one after 1891 for widowed mothers of deceased single members). Unemployment benefits were instituted in 1889, and provision for permanent disability in 1902. The Typographia provided an old-age annuity in addition to disability, death, and unemployment benefits.

The sponsors of social insurance emphasized its historical inevitability. They noted that Great Britain had adopted compulsory unemployment insurance in 1911, even though British trade unions had developed a far superior system of unemployment benefits. Great Britain, similarly, had enacted national compulsory health insurance the same year, despite the elaborate voluntary program of the fraternal or friendly societies.

British friendly societies in the nineteenth century played a role comparable to the trade unions and cooperatives. These movements fulfilled a longing for status and security. They represented "ways in which those without political power sought to protect themselves in an increasingly industrialised society." [49] The British fraternal system was significant also in establishing precedents for regulatory and supervisory legislation later applied by the government to other working-class institutions. Not least important, the disability insurance administered by the affiliated English fraternals proved instrumental in the development of actuarial science and the extension of medical services to workers on a prepaid basis.

British fraternal membership increased from approximately one million in 1815 to more than four million by the early 1870's. Dominant in numbers and influence were the great affiliated orders like the Manchester Unity of Oddfellows and the Ancient Order of Foresters. These organizations attracted better-paid workers, small businessmen, and even professionals. Men employed in agriculture, mining, and railroads tended to associate in independent societies because of their peculiar occupational risks. [50]

It had been discovered, by the late eighteenth century, that insurance benefits alone failed to attract new members to fraternal societies. Local lodges began to brighten the monthly meetings with ceremonies, entertainments, and other social activities, supplemented by occasional excursions, picnics, and sports events. Toward the end of the nineteenth century, social fraternalism experienced a decline in comparison to the societies' insurance functions. The change was most apparent in the case of the affiliated orders, which imposed increasing controls over local lodge autonomy in the interests of sound business management. Competition from commercial insurance companies provided one stimulus to rationalization at the expense of primitive social gratification. The emergence of commercial recreation and entertainment facilities also contributed to the decline of the local lodge's social role. Friendly societies, particularly the affiliated orders, thus evolved from primary-group mutual-aid societies into bureaucratic insurance mutuals.

Fraternalism in the United States differed in several respects from the British prototype. American fraternals usually provided a death rather than a sickness benefit. In England administration of the medical benefit by the affiliated orders, notably the Manchester Unity of Oddfellows, was based upon the use of sophisticated actuarial principles. Study of the "probability of sickness among working men had not been undertaken systematically until the needs and experience of the orders made it both necessary and possible." [51] Even the fondest admirers of American fraternalism conceded that business management was often amateurish. Yet proposals for state supervision encountered "violent opposition." [52]

The national fraternal system emerged after the Civil War. John G. Upchurch of Pennsylvania, a Freemason, established the Ancient Order of United Workmen in 1868; and fraternal growth was encouraged in the 1870's by the "extraordinary mortality among the legal reserve old-line insurance companies." [53] A National Fraternal Congress, organized in 1886, enrolled 85 out of some 200 national orders by 1914. Members of the Congress were described as "true fraternal orders," the rest being "mere assessment orders which maintained no genuine lodge system." [54] The affiliated societies claimed a membership of 5½ million in 1914, and a total of $7 billion of insurance in force. Benefits distributed that year, mostly for death, reached nearly $75 million. [55]

Presumably the affiliated orders differed from the assessment societies because they maintained a lodge system. But a committee of the NFC complained that the "vast majority of these local bodies" were "inactive — doing nothing." [56] In the United States as well as in England it proved increasingly difficult for fraternals to reconcile their social and business functions. The original tendency to appeal to the "spirit of fraternalism without due regard to mathematics of mortality experience" subjected them to sharp criticism from state insurance officials, and increased their vulnerability to competition from commercial insurance companies.[57] Older fraternals, which had underassessed their membership, encountered difficulties in discharging their accrued liabilities; but if they raised assessments they could not attract new, younger members. Reform entailed the introduction of sound business management at the expense of democratic autonomy and spontaneity.

Despite bureaucratic encroachments, fraternalism was defended as an invaluable expression of voluntary cooperation in American life. In contrast to social insurance, which embodied the "onward march of a paternalistic theory," fraternalism served educational and character-building purposes. It demonstrated the "value and the importance of the saving habit in the form of small amounts."[58] Once again the argument was raised that voluntary institutions precluded the economic need for social insurance and, more importantly, fulfilled individual and group aspirations.

In the immigrant community at least fraternals often did perform an important social function. The conditions of immigrant life in the early twentieth century minimized for a time the inherent conflict between bureaucratic rationalization and small-group association. Organized along religious and ethnic lines, fraternal institutions served as mediators between the individual immigrant and the incomprehensible, often alien, society which surrounded him. Like his church, they provided him with a measure of identity, worth, and security. Nowhere perhaps was the fraternal order more prominent in the immigrant's life than in isolated mining and mill towns where few social and recreational alternatives existed. The anthracite coal communities of eastern Pennsylvania were pervaded by a "plethora of orders of all sorts."[59] The fruits of the Pittsburgh Survey included Margaret Byington's detailed survey of working-class life in Homestead, a nearby steel town. Using a sample of ninety family budgets, she found that a majority of men paid lodge dues, and that fraternal association was especially important in the lives of Slavic families. Homestead's hundred-odd lodges aroused a measure of "fraternity and common interest which otherwise finds little stimulus in the town." Though their sponsorship of excursions, dances, card parties, and other social activities, the fraternals provided "some of the good fun which Homestead craves." They offered the women of the community an opportunity to escape from household drudgery, if not "almost their only chance to meet other people." [60]

Commercial insurance representatives took delight in criticizing the "gloomy record" of cooperative and mutual-aid associations which furnished protection "in defiance of life-insurance principles." They nonetheless exhorted the fraternals to join in the crusade against the "paternalism that is trying to inject itself into the body politic of this country and take away enterprise, destroy individual initiative, tear down American ideals." [61] Voluntarism, ironically, found no more spirited champion than the vast commercial insurance enterprises.

The Prudential Insurance Company of England had first instituted workingmen's or industrial insurance in 1854. Following a careful study of Prudential (and the British friendly societies), John F. Dryden, founder of the Newark Prudential, introduced industrial insurance for American workers in the 1870's.[62] The 11,000 Prudential policies in force by the late 1870's had risen to 3,500,000 by 1900. The eleven principal companies writing industrial insurance that year reported over 10,000,000 policies in force, representing an insured value of more than a billion dollars.

Industrial insurance differed in several ways from ordinary level-premium life policies. A company agent collected the small, weekly industrial premium at the home of the insured. The amount of industrial insurance was adjusted to the unit premium; whereas the premium in ordinary life was adjusted to the amount of insurance stipulated. Ordinary insurance covered the head of a family for a large sum; an industrial policy might insure every member of a family for a small amount. Most important, the nickel and dime premiums collected under industrial insurance provided little more than funeral expenses.

Social insurance experts charged that industrial insurance was exceptionally expensive and inefficient. Administrative overheads and profits consumed an inordinately large percentage of the premium dollar. Insurance executives reached an entirely different conclusion. They claimed that these overheads were not economic waste, but the cost for a distinctive social service. Once again the defence of voluntarism was based upon noneconomic criteria. Commercial companies placed such great emphasis upon the social advantages of workingmen's insurance that profit considerations seemed almost incidental. Industrial insurance, described as the "most effective . . . education in thrift which has yet been developed," acquainted the masses with the "first principles of saving." Small, but regular insurance payments were more likely than occasional savings bank deposits to result in "foresight, frugality, and abstinence from needless expenditures." [63] The insurance agent was not merely a salesman, whose commissions increased administrative overheads, but a prophet of the "gospel of thrift," a "true friend" who assisted the worker in attaining security and independence. He might even be compared to a social worker, "striving to keep away from the wage-earners the necessity of charity." [64] Voluntary thrift, embodied in industrial insurance, nurtured character, but social insurance was merely a glorified form of poor law legislation. To concede a need for public insurance or pension programs was "to concede that the social and economic development of the nation has been in the wrong direction, that the education in thrift has been defective, and that the virtues of intelligent self-denial and self-sacrifice have been replaced by considerations of selfish indulgence and indifference to the welfare of others." [65]

The social insurance movement aspired to rationalize the income-maintenance system in the United States. Such rationalization hinged upon centralization and the transfer of responsibilities from the voluntary to the public sector. The need for social insurance was rooted in the individual's precarious status in a wage-centered, money economy. Any interruption of income-flow reduced or destroyed entirely his ability to command goods or services.

Efforts to establish a comprehensive social insurance program in the early twentieth century took place in an incongruous ideological and institutional framework. It was difficult, if not impossible, for social insurance advocates to disprove the argument that voluntary institutions could expand and provide universal economic security. The historical experience of Europe served as the only counterargument, but it was dismissed as invalid because of the uniqueness of American civilization and was used to discredit social insurance as an alien importation. Voluntarism, with its manifold political, economic, and social implications, was lauded as the distinctively American method of collective action. Voluntary charitable, insurance, and savings institutions were not only sufficient for purposes of economic security, but performed indispensable educational and character-building functions. Centralized government bureaucracies could not serve as substitutes.

The constraints of voluntarism prevented the enactment of most social security legislation until the 1930's. Equally important, a successful program like workmen's compensation demonstrated that social insurance had to be adapted to voluntary values and institutions. These acted as a filter which rejected outright or refined any social insurance proposals.

## II  Social Drift and Social Planning

Before the establishment of the American Association for Labor Legislation in 1906, social insurance was not a serious subject of debate in the United States. Most Americans were uninformed about European programs, and the whole issue seemed as irrelevant as life on some distant planet. The mainstream of American social work, with little interest in techniques of income security, emphasized the stimulation of work incentives among the poor on an individual case basis. The ideal public welfare system, eternally on guard against pauperization, minimized relief expenditures. Public welfare should serve two categories of dependency: the impotent poor who required long-term institutional care, and the recalcitrant able-bodied poor who could not, or would not, be rehabilitated by private agencies. For these, the public system would serve as the ultimate deterrent. Social insurance, or any welfare policy which implied a right to maintenance on the grounds of presumptive need, was wholly objectionable.

The earliest studies of European social insurance programs were sponsored by federal and state labor bureaus in the 1890's. Workmen's compensation provided a major stimulus. In 1893 the United States Commissioner of Labor published John Graham Brooks's account of German social insurance. The annual report of the New York State Bureau of Labor Statistics for 1899 included Adna F. Weber's examination of the German accident insurance system. William F. Willoughby of the United States Bureau of Labor published the first comprehensive study of European social insurance in 1898. In 1909 the annual report of the

Commissioner of Labor consisted of an exhaustive, two-volume survey of European insurance and compensation.[1]

Brooks, in his pioneering study, claimed that compulsory insurance could achieve ends which Americans equated with voluntary institutions. He maintained that German social insurance was less important for its economic benefits than for related "moral and educational influences." The most important of these included the "sense of solidarity which the very attempt to make the laws succeed will intensify and increase." Compulsory insurance, he conceded, put traditional institutions of self-help to "much risk," but European experience demonstrated that "society is unwilling to wait for the self help institutions to deal with social ills." [2]

Willoughby reached a different conclusion. In his estimation the central issue of social insurance was the role and power of the state. A fierce contest already raged in Europe between the "principles of state action and private initiative," even though social insurance had barely entered the "stage of discussion in this country." [3] Using a continuum from compulsory state insurance to voluntarism, Willoughby divided European programs into four categories. Compulsory insurance, at one extreme, was best represented by Germany and Austria. Insurance against accident, sickness, and old age was obligatory upon the entire wage-earning population. The second category, voluntary state insurance, was best exemplified by France, Belgium, and Italy. In France state insurance institutions for accident, death, old age, and invalidity had existed for many years. Voluntary insurance societies — regulated or aided by government — comprised the third category. The most important examples included the friendly societies of England, the *Sociétés de Secour Mutuels* on the Continent, and the numerous trade union benefit funds. Finally, a large number of private, unregulated funds had been established by employers, particularly in the mining and railroad industries.

Willoughby favored the French system as a model for the United States. Its "remarkable collection" of public (but noncompulsory) and private insurance institutions seemed most suitable for this country, where "voluntary insurance is of far greater importance than compulsory insurance, which rests upon principles of state action foreign to American thought." [4] In the three-tiered French system, government played a positive, but noncoercive role. The first tier included the three national insurance departments for old-age annuities (established in 1850), accident (1868), and death (1868). These were supplemented by the local mutual-aid societies which concentrated upon sickness benefits. And French establishment funds had developed "to an extent, and of an excellence, that is found in no other country in the world." A recent innovation which had impressed Willoughby was the formation of central insurance associations by employers in the same trade.[5]

The French system never exerted much influence in the United States. Social insurance experts consistently objected that voluntarism, even when subsidized, provided limited benefits for a select minority of the population. Willoughby's own evidence suggested that the three state insurance departments were failures.[6] Critics of social insurance, on the other hand, proved equally consistent in their suspicions of state insurance, regulation, or subsidies.

Willoughby's evaluation of the French system was hopelessly outdated within a decade. After 1900 a general trend toward compulsory insurance, state pensions, or subsidized voluntary programs emerged in Europe. These foreign social insurance programs provided the only fund of experience and technique for American reformers. Equally important, the rapid transition from voluntarism to state insurance or pension systems in Europe produced an unwarranted optimism in the United States. Sponsors of social insurance underestimated the resiliency of voluntary institutions.

Germany, in 1884, was the first nation to establish workmen's compensation on a national scale.[7] Employers had to carry insurance through mutual trade associations. Other nations, including Austria, Hungary, Norway, and Luxembourg, adopted the same method of compulsory insurance, but differed as to the specified carrier. The Austrian legislation provided for territorial rather than trade associations of employers; and Norway created a monopoly state fund. Under the system adopted by Italy, Finland, and the Netherlands the employer's financial liabilities were defined by law, but the method of insurance remained optional: employers could choose self-insurance, a private company, or a state fund, if one existed. A third system, established by England in 1897, required compensation but not insurance; Belgium, Denmark, France, Greece, Russia, and Spain adopted this scheme. American state legislatures, beginning in 1911, had a choice of models. Questions of economic or administrative efficiency would prove less influential than the prerogatives of voluntary institutions.

German national health insurance had been established in 1883, a year before workmen's compensation. Compulsory programs followed in Austria (1888), Hungary (1891), Luxembourg (1901), Norway (1909), Great Britain (1911), Russia (1912), and the Netherlands (1913). Several nations, including Sweden, Denmark, Belgium, France, and Switzerland, provided subsidies to approved voluntary societies which administered sickness benefits. The compulsory health insurance legislation proposed in the United States after 1915 was an amalgam of German and English practice, which differed in cost distribution, benefits, and administrative arrangements.[8]

By the time the American social insurance movement was launched in 1911, Germany, England, and Austria had progressed furthest from purely voluntary arrangements to compulsory insurance. Using a risk rather than a territorial classification, workmen's compensation ranked highest, followed by health insurance, and then protection against old age and invalidity. Compulsory, contributory old-age insurance was established in Germany (1889), Austria (1909), and France (1910). Other nations, including Russia, Belgium, and Italy, had limited compulsory programs which applied to workers in selected industries. In the 1890's Denmark, New Zealand, Australia, and France had inaugurated tax-supported old-age pension programs. After many years of investigation and debates, England in 1908 adopted a pension rather than an insurance scheme for the aged.[9]

Compulsory unemployment insurance ranked lowest on the continuum. An early experiment in the Swiss town of St. Gall in the 1890's was abandoned after a year. The first national program, applicable to a selected group of industries, was launched in Great Britain in 1911.[10] In Europe as a whole, by that date unemployment insurance had reached the second stage in the evolution from voluntary to voluntary subsidized to compulsory insurance. The "Ghent system" of government subsidies to labor union unemployment funds spread rapidly after 1901. Named after the Belgian city where it originated, the Ghent system was adopted by communities in Belgium, Holland, Italy, Germany, and Switzerland. Larger French and Belgian jurisdictions, such as provinces or departments, sometimes supplemented the municipal subsidies. The same nations, as well as Norway and Denmark, added a small national subsidy.[11]

Contributory old-age insurance or tax-supported pension programs usually made some provision for invalidity benefits. Maternity and funeral benefits were often included in health insurance programs. Sponsors of American social insurance complained that the worker in the United States spent over $180,-000,000 a year for funeral benefits alone. An equivalent sum in Germany, to which employers or the state contributed, protected the worker against accident, sickness, old age, invalidity, maternity, and burial expenses. The comparison between Germany and the United States illustrated the "frightful difficulties in the way of making universal insurance possible under a voluntary system, and the insignificant results obtainable notwithstanding the high cost." [12]

The American Association for Labor Legislation (AALL) created and sustained the organized social insurance movement in the United States. Established in 1906 as a section of the International Association for Labor Legislation, the AALL testified to the emergence of the social scientist as an influence in social legislation and reform. University economists and political scientists such as Henry Farnam (Yale), J. W. Jenks (Cornell), Henry Seager and Samuel McCune Lindsay (Columbia), and John R. Commons and Richard Ely (Wisconsin) were among its original leaders, and nonacademic economists including John B. Andrews, Isaac M. Rubinow, and Adna F. Weber played a major role.[13]

Ely and Weber served as the president and secretary of the new Association. At the first annual meeting, held in December 1907, Farnam was elected president, and Commons became secretary. Ely described Farnam as the real founder of the AALL. As publicists, fund-raisers, and advisers, he and Commons were instrumental in insuring the survival of the AALL, which in 1908 claimed a membership of only two hundred.[14] Commons was responsible for the appointment of Andrews as executive secretary in December 1908, and of Irene Osgood (later Mrs. Andrews) as assistant secretary.[15] Andrews' key advisers included Farnam and Joseph P. Chamberlain of the Columbia University Legislative Drafting Service. Chamberlain prepared, or was consulted in the preparation of, most legislative proposals emanating from the AALL.[16] Commons exerted the greatest influence over Andrews, who had been his student at Wisconsin.[17]

Under Andrews' leadership (which continued until his death in January 1943), the AALL concentrated upon the issues of accident compensation and industrial safety, unemployment, and social insurance. The AALL assisted in the drafting and enactment of many early compensation laws; subsequently, it goaded states to improve their existing legislation. Andrews labored diligently to broaden the definition of industrial accidents to include occupational disease, and to secure mandatory reporting of work-related illness.

The AALL's first major effort, following Andrews' appointment as secretary, centered upon this issue of industrial hygiene. Inspired by the International Treaty of 1906, which banned the use of poisonous white phosphorus in the manufacture of matches, Andrews prepared a report for the United States Bureau of Labor. His vivid portrayal of the horrors of "phossy jaw" and other forms of phosphorus poisoning helped launch the industrial hygiene movement in the United States.[18] The AALL assumed the initiative in negotiations with the Diamond Match Company, which controlled the patent for a safe substitute. Ultimately, the patent was assigned to a group of three trustees, paving the way for federal legislation in 1912 banning the use of poisonous phosphorus in the manufacture of matches.[19] The Association's crusade against industrial disease led to investigations of lead, brass, and anthrax poisoning. It organized a National Commission on Industrial Hygiene in 1908, and in 1910 sponsored the First American Conference on Industrial Diseases.[20] During the 1920's Andrews led a campaign for legislation to prevent mine explosions.[21]

The AALL's efforts extended beyond the enactment of state compensation and safety legislation. It worked on behalf of occupational groups not covered by state laws. An improved federal employees' compensation law in 1916, and the Longshoremen's and Harbor Worker's Compensation Act of 1927, were attributable to AALL pressure. The Association devoted considerable attention to the responsibilities of state compensation boards for vocational rehabilitation following the enactment of federal grant-in-aid programs in 1918 and 1920.[22] It stressed the need for efficient administration of labor legislation, especially the advantages of commission rather than court administration of compensation laws.

Debate over workmen's compensation and the wave of state legislation beginning in 1911 transformed social insurance from an abstraction into a live public issue. Rapid enactment of compensation laws roused hope that other forms of social insurance would follow. After the appointment of an expert Committee on Social Insurance in 1912, the AALL assumed leadership of the second, broader phase of the movement.[23] Emphasis now fell upon health insurance and, to a lesser extent, unemployment insurance. The Social Insurance Committee published a standard health insurance bill in 1915, which served as the basis for proposed state legislation from 1916 to 1920. The AALL also established a Committee on Unemployment, which acted as the American section of the International Unemployment Association; it sponsored two national conferences on unemployment during the depression year of 1914, and published surveys of the national employment situation in 1914–15 and 1920–21.

The AALL heralded the opening of a new era in "scientific

social betterment." It marked the beginnings of a "revolution in our thinking regarding industrial legislation." This revolution took the form of "scientific organization" to secure "greater care and greater uniformity in protective labor legislation." [24] The AALL exemplified ideals of social engineering which emerged in the early twentieth century. The efficient organization of human affairs in a complex industrial society presumably required the same degree of planning and expert administration which prevailed in the business sector. Human conservation depended upon a greater decision-making role for social workers, social scientists, and other experts.

According to Commons, the AALL's unique function was the sponsorship of scientific investigations by experts to provide a basis for effective labor legislation. The "trained expert" had to replace the "amateur" because welfare legislation had become a critical factor in the "preservation of the race and maintenance of its quality." The work could no longer be left by default to narrow interest groups. In contrast to any other segment of society, the fraternity of experts combined knowledge of and allegiance to the broad community interest. AALL experts sought to "apply to legislation the same study of causes, of processes, and of effects, that lies at the basis of our modern science." They introduced into legislation the "best results of the work done in medicine, hygiene, economics, sociology, and jurisprudence." [25]

Ideals of scientific social engineering were associated with the new public service functions ascribed to university experts after the turn of the century. This development was foreshadowed in the 1880's by the involvement of college faculty and students in settlement work and charity organization. In the same period, the introduction of courses in Applied Christianity in seminaries and divinity schools provided a link between universities and the service ideals of the Social Gospel. The emergence of professional training for social work after 1898 provided another tie between social problems and institutions of higher education. After 1900 the close relation established between the University of Wisconsin and the State House during the La Follette regime, and the concentration of social scientists in the AALL, exemplified the new service role of university faculties.

The bond between Commons and Andrews insured that the Wisconsin approach to labor legislation would exert a profound influence upon the AALL. This method implied not only scientific investigation and the employment of experts, but a favored system of administration — the collective expertise embodied in the industrial commission idea. Commons described the industrial commission as a "fourth branch of government," a necessary "extension of the police power required to meet the rapidly changing and widely varying conditions of modern life and business." [26] Established in 1911, the Wisconsin Industrial Commission absorbed the office of the commissioner of labor, the board of arbitration and conciliation, the public employment offices, and the newly formed Industrial Accident Board designated to administer the workmen's compensation act.[27] The Industrial Commission's legitimacy as a new tool of government derived from its unique capacity to discern and execute the "general will." It arrived at an understanding of the "general will" through its constructive powers of "investigation and research." [28] The statutory authority of the commission, and the data accumulated through research, provided the foundation for sound labor legislation. Commons emphasized, however, that the best results could be attained if the Commission enlisted the cooperation of business and labor in the preparation or enforcement of its regulations. The Commission thus drew upon the expert knowledge of special interest groups to promote the broader community interest.[29]

Labor leaders were not inspired by the Commons-Andrews vision of scientific labor legislation "under the leadership of the universities." Their views had not been "affected appreciably by university thought regarding the social status of the laboring classes." [30] Gompers admitted the usefulness of intellectuals, but only in an advisory capacity; leadership belonged to the workers through their own organizations. Abstractions like "disinterestedness" and "general will" puzzled the labor leader, who was more concerned with the appointment of union members to administrative agencies than with impartiality of administration or civil service regulations (which might disqualify union men).[31] The rhetoric of disinterested benevolence, in his eyes, disguised a struggle for power between himself and self-proclaimed friends of the working-class. The labor movement had already suffered a good deal of repression in the name of a superior community interest.

Isaac Max Rubinow (1875–1936), the outstanding American theoretician of social insurance, assumed early in his career that "compulsory State insurance" would prove attractive to trade unionists if "properly presented." He would discover that unions were less anxious than he thought to relieve their treasuries of the "burden" of relief benefits. Prophetically, his "old teacher," Benjamin Seligman of Columbia University, turned down his first article on unemployment insurance in 1903 because the idea was too "un-American and revolutionary" for the *Political Science Quarterly*.[32]

Rubinow had emigrated to the United States from Russia in 1893. His educational preparation enabled him to enter an advanced class in Columbia College, and, after graduating in 1895 he devoted a year to advanced work in biology. He then entered the University Medical College (New York University), and received an M.D. degree in 1898. Medical practice among the New York poor aroused his interest in social and economic problems. Awareness of the "horrible circumstances" under which women fulfilled their maternal functions in working-class districts proved a decisive influence, resulting in years of "continuous and obstinate agitation" for social insurance.[33]

Between 1900 and 1903 Rubinow took courses in political science at Columbia. He then abandoned medical practice entirely to occupy a series of posts with the federal government (Civil Service Commission, Department of Agriculture, Department of Commerce, and Bureau of Labor). He was chief actuary and statistician for the Ocean Accident and Guarantee Company from 1911 to 1916, during which time he established his reputation as a leading social insurance authority. The monumental two-volume study of workmen's insurance systems in Europe, which Rubinow directed, was published by the Commissioner of Labor in 1911; Columbia awarded him the Ph.D. degree for the sections on Italy, Russia, and Spain, submitted as his dissertation. He published an outstanding interpretive text on social insurance in 1913,[34] and in 1914 founded the Casualty Actuarial and Statistical Society of America, which he served as president for two years.

After 1911 Rubinow became a consultant to state compensation boards, and chairman of the rate committee of the Workmen's Compensation Service Bureau (a joint organization of casualty companies).[35] His major technical achievement in this field was the preparation of a standard accident table to assist in rate computation. One of the original members of the AALL's Committee on Social Insurance, Rubinow believed that health insurance was the inevitable sequel to workmen's compensation, and he helped draft the AALL's standard health insurance bill. He resigned his insurance company position in 1916 to become secretary of the newly established Social Insurance Committee of the American Medical Association, and spent part of that year in California as consultant to the State Social Insurance Commission, investigating the possibilities of establishing a compulsory program. Also in 1916 he published a book on health insurance.[36]

No one exemplified better than Isaac Rubinow the challenge to voluntarism posed by the social insurance movement. His socialist convictions and encyclopedic knowledge of European welfare legislation made him an impatient, if not contemptuous, critic of American commitments to collective action under voluntary auspices.[37] He was convinced that social insurance was as inevitable in the United States as in Europe, and that much needless suffering occurred while Americans resisted their historical destiny in the name of anachronistic institutions and beliefs.

Rubinow viewed social insurance as a logical response to income-maintenance problems inherent in a wage-centered, industrial economy. The wage-earner had become the victim of an institutionalized insecurity. His ability to command goods and services varied with the amount of money in his possession, but money was acquired principally through labor force participation. The worker, however, was subject to a variety of risks which at any time might eliminate him from the labor force. His wage flow could be interrupted, yet his material needs and financial obligations remained constant.

Insecurity led to widespread destitution, and public and private charities emerged to perform the relief functions handled by the extended kinship or peer group in pre-industrial societies. Rubinow dismissed charity as an objectionable expedient — the antithesis of social insurance, which embodied a protest against charity and "its insufficiency, both extensive and intensive, against its degrading character, and against its social injustice." At best, charitable relief provided the "necessary minimum for a physiological existence, and only that." [38] Social insurance, which intervened at an early stage of dependency, prevented destitution and the need for relief.

Insurance, Rubinow explained, substituted "social, co-operative provision for individual provision"; it reduced or eliminated economic risk by distributing losses.[39] The main burden of cost was transferred from the individual to the group. Insurance made possible a budgeting or premium system through which a small, calculated sacrifice of current consumption protected the individual against much severer contingent losses. Rubinow defined social insurance as the "policy of organized society to furnish that protection to one part of the population which some other part may need less, or needing, is able to purchase voluntarily through private insurance." [40] It differed from private insurance in introducing compulsion, cost participation by employers or the state, and public insurance institutions. Technically, any two or even one of these three innovations sufficed "to bring the system within the sphere of social insurance." [41] If a program was fully tax-supported, like mothers' pensions or old-age pensions, it became an assurance more than an insurance system.

Rubinow maintained that the redistributive purposes of insurance could not be attained on a voluntary basis. Adequate protection against the many contingencies which affected participation in the labor force — accident, illness, unemployment, old age, invalidity, maternity, or dependent motherhood — would require too great a sacrifice of current consumption levels. The worker inevitably had to compromise on benefit levels or risk coverage. European experience proved, to Rubinow's satisfaction, that the required degree of redistribution could not be achieved even through subsidized voluntary insurance. It failed to accommodate those who most needed protection, but could least afford it, and provided inadequate benefits for the minority who belonged to the plans. Before the National Insurance Act of 1911, he observed, the registered Friendly Societies of England offered sickness benefits to 6,000,000 persons, or 13 percent of a population numbering 45,000,000. French mutual-aid societies provided sickness benefits for 4,000,000 persons, or 10 percent of the population. Belgian societies in 1908 covered 388,000 persons, or 5 percent of the population. Danish societies enrolled 550,000 persons in 1907, or 27 percent of the population. These were the most advanced voluntary programs in Europe.[42]

In the area of unemployment insurance, Rubinow pointed to English experience as an object lesson. The hundred principal unions, between 1898 and 1907, had distributed nearly $20,000,000 in unemployment benefits — more than 20 percent of their total budgets. Yet unemployment benefits affected less than 1,500,000 out of a total union membership of 2,500,000 and a total wage-earning population of almost 15,000,000. The number of insured under the Ghent subsidy program around 1910 ranged from a high of 95,000 in Denmark to 40,000 in Belgium and France.[43]

Voluntary, noncompulsory insurance was based upon the contractual, equity principles of private insurance. Social insurance differed fundamentally in providing a "social guarantee against the results of emergencies and accidents." Equity principles were tempered by considerations of need and ability to pay. Social insurance alone made possible "those standards which due consideration for national vitality makes immediately imperative." Instituted through the coercive power of the state, it represented a "powerful object lesson of the reality of the new concept of the state as the instrument of organized collective action, rather than of class oppression."[44]

An innovation like social insurance could be defended on ethical grounds: the community and employer were partly responsible for the existence of substandard living and working conditions, and should share part of the cost for the worker's protection. But Rubinow emphasized social expediency. The state used social insurance to help raise the "standard of living of the neediest and productive classes, or to prevent destitution among them." He admitted that social insurance was "true class legislation" which presumed to "readjust the distribution of the national product more equitably." [45]

If Rubinow challenged the myth of the classless society, he was equally outspoken in dismissing the prerogatives of voluntarism. Social insurance resulted in the "extension of social activity at the expense of private activity." [46] Rubinow belittled claims that the United States was unique in the role assigned to voluntary institutions, and that these, rather than the state, marked the limits of collective action. He never took seriously the argument that voluntary institutions performed distinctive educational, social, or character-building functions. Resistance to social insurance, cloaked in the rhetoric of voluntarism and Americanism, was a tactic which enabled "private group interests" to camouflage themselves "by arguments based upon public considerations." [47]

From Rubinow's economic and actuarial perspective, efforts to defend voluntarism in terms of work incentives and national moral fiber were absurd. Social insurance might lead to malingering or fraud on the part of some individuals but, Rubinow pointed out, private insurance offered the same opportunities. He challenged the conventional wisdom in America which attributed work incentive and discipline to fear. The idea that social progress depended upon the "despair of unemployment, disease, and underfeeding" was, to say the least, "misanthropic." [48] It was rooted in a deterrent psychology which had no foundation in science or human nature.

The moral issues raised by old-age pension proposals offered Rubinow unparalleled opportunities to display his pungent, irreverent wit. Katherine Coman, an economist, concluded after a survey of European old-age pension programs, that the "ultimate test of the wisdom of the various forms of public provision for destitute old age must be, not merely the comfort and gratification of the individual concerned, but the influence on the moral fibre of the community . . . Thrift is an old fashioned virtue, but it is still an essential element in race efficiency." [49] Rubinow wondered whether Miss Coman had not confused the issues of the "moral regeneration of the working class" and the "practical problem" of aged destitution. He did not think she favored restoration of the medieval practice of purification by fire, but "old ideas of asceticism still clamor for recognition." The social reformer feared injury to the soul in helping the body, but why did the moral dangers lurking behind efforts to satisfy elementary physical wants seem "especially great in the case of the poor and needy"? Rubinow could not detect any singular "virtue in practicing self-denial," when human progress was based upon efforts to "get the things which man wants."

The application of ascetic principles to old-age dependency bore no relation to psychological or social realities. Deviance or conformity to "recognized moral precepts" by the young would hardly "be influenced by the chance of getting an old-age pension at seventy." [50] The fears expressed by a Massachusetts Commission and others that old-age pensions would weaken family solidarity were altogether ludicrous. There was, Rubinow reflected, a "good, old-fashioned, atavistic nobility of sentiment" in the argument that pensions would undermine the incentive of children to love and care for their aged parents. The logic appealed irresistibly to all "except those who have to be supported by their children, and those who have to support their parents and also their own families on a wage-earner's budget." Apparently "we love our burdens, and . . . when parents cease being burdens the children cease loving them." The status of the aged spinster aunt troubled Rubinow; it could not be maintained that the "support of all spinster aunts is also a fundamental principle of American family solidarity." Perhaps all public assistance should be terminated "because of the demoralizing effect upon said children and relatives." [51] Criticism of old-age pensions, Rubinow concluded, rested upon ideals of a patriarchical family structure which had disappeared in every industrial country and never had existed in the United States.

Social insurance, Rubinow generalized, had nothing whatever to do with morality. Maternity insurance raised the problem of illegitimate birth. But social insurance "has or should have no official point of view on matters of sexual morality," for it was designed to correct economic difficulties, not to shape personal behavior or attitudes. Birth out of wedlock was neither rare nor a sign of "eternal damnation" and "hopelessly incurable moral decrepitude." [52]

Rubinow felt that social workers held many conventional views on the relation between voluntary institutions, economic incentives, and the preservation of moral standards. Private relief agencies vehemently objected to widows' (mothers') pension legislation as another form of public outdoor assistance with all its pauperizing tendencies. Their criticisms of public assistance, and obsession with individual responsibility for protection against economic adversity, provoked Rubinow: "The progressive social worker must learn to understand that a sickness insurance law, even in one state, can do more to eradicate poverty, and is, therefore, a greater social gain, than a dozen organizations for scientific philanthropy with their investigations, their sermons on thrift, and their constant feverish hunt for liberal contributions." [53] The contempt for public welfare added to the prevailing confusion over the role of public and private institutions in an industrial society. Many social workers did not recognize that economic security was necessarily the responsibility of the public welfare sector. As Rubinow argued until the Depression of the 1930's proved him correct, private social work lacked the resources.

Rubinow's criticisms of private social work were based upon personal experience. After the dissolution of the AMA's Social Insurance Committee in 1917, he directed a Bureau of Social Statistics in the New York City Department of Public Charities; he had hardly launched studies of children's institutions and the dependency index in New York when the Bureau was abolished.[54] He then directed investigations of grain exchanges for the Federal Trade Commission, and served as economic consultant to the

Commission on Conditions of Peace. Rubinow left for Palestine in 1919, at the urging of Henrietta Szold, to direct the American Zionist Medical Unit (later Hadassah Medical Organization).[55] Upon his return in 1923, he became director of the Jewish Welfare Society of Philadelphia, and from 1929 until his death in 1936, served as secretary of B'nai B'rith.[56]

Rubinow had been disturbed by the claim that private social work could "substitute for community action through the duly constituted governmental authority." The trend toward professionalization in the 1920's added to his dismay. A psychiatric, clinical orientation had become popular in social work practice. Interest in environmental problems had receded in favor of "adjustment and modification of personality." Social workers of the 1920's, he complained, "almost dread to admit that they deal with poverty — only with maladjustment, which, we are glibly told, may just as frequently arise in any economic stratum." [57] The objective causes of poverty — illness, injury, unemployment, death of the breadwinner, old age — nonetheless continued to operate. Dependency caused by objective environmental circumstances demanded economic solutions, not casework. A vacuum had been created in the American welfare system. Private social work was indifferent or opposed to extension of public assistance programs, but professional social workers had lost interest in the relief of destitution.

The efforts of social workers, psychiatrists, and others to increase scientific understanding of personality were legitimate, but the pendulum had swung too far. The helping professions had forgotten how much the individual remained "subject to the conditions of social organization." [58] Equally pertinent, the concept of poverty was changing. In "dynamic industrial societies," any definition of poverty had to be based upon "comparative scales and standards of living." [59] The need for social insurance and assistance programs increased rather than diminished as living standards rose. Private, voluntary institutions and casework could not cope with poverty in the older, static sense of inability to obtain *"those necessaries which will permit . . . a state of physical efficiency."* [60] The new, dynamic definition would require an even greater redistributive effort, one based upon the resources and coercive powers of the state.

The rapid development of community chests in the 1920's had important implications. They testified to the fact that "philanthropy and social work were not fads for individuals and small groups to play with, but a community liability." Yet all forms of "voluntary, non-governmental communal organization," including the chest, were insufficient in ordinary times and broke down entirely in periods of "great economic distress." One could not "sweep away the ocean of human misery with a charitable broom." [61]

Rubinow personified the challenge to voluntarism posed by the social insurance movement. His principle of a "social guarantee" clashed with the inherited belief which stressed individual responsibility for maintenance and cooperative action under voluntary auspices. Social insurance implied the establishment of a secondary income distribution system geared to need, rather than incentive and efficient participation in the labor force. Rubinow was involved in a second conflict, one within the social insurance movement. It centered on prevention as a legitimate social insurance function. Prior to the 1920's the issue did not produce a serious split in social insurance ranks. It was not entirely clear that the two objectives were incompatible; moreover, the overwhelming task of propaganda and education diverted attention from internal divisions of opinion. Most important, reform ideology in the early twentieth century stressed the need for widespread environmental changes which prevented dependency. It is not surprising that preventive ideals influenced the social insurance movement. They were an answer to critics who argued that social insurance was a remedial measure, one whose trivial benefits were not worth the sacrifice of American liberties and institutions. [62]

By the 1920's a distinctive conception of social insurance had emerged, stressing prevention as the primary goal. From the beginning, Commons and Andrews had viewed prevention as something more than an expedient or secondary objective. "Prof. Commons and I," Andrews explained, "in all of the work we have done together have thought first of prevention and second of relief in dealing with each form of social insurance in this country. I firmly believe that the success of social insurance in the long run must rest upon this second use of the method every bit as much as upon the first." [63] The Safety-first campaign and merit-rating techniques associated with early compensation legislation furnished the model. The "American" approach to social insurance, compatible with individual economic incentive and responsibility, was to provide financial inducements for prevention. An unemployment insurance scheme devised by Commons in the 1920's brought into focus the hitherto latent conflict between the Rubinow and AALL theory of social insurance.[64]

Economic maintenance was the primary purpose of any social insurance or assurance program, according to Rubinow, not a trivial function which treated the symptoms rather than the causes of distress. No matter how efficient our social institutions, there would remain a residue of need, best handled by a social insurance machinery which responded predictably, promptly, and adequately. Any preventive role assigned to social insurance evolved from this primary responsibility of economic maintenance — a well-designed social insurance system prevented destitution.[65]

Rubinow questioned the validity of comparisons between prevention and insurance. Prevention deals with the "social factors of accidents, unemployment, etc., while insurance deals with the individual victim of these conditions." They were "two distinct social efforts." [66] Reviewing the early social insurance movement, he charged that it was the "casualty companies, in union with employers fighting compensation and fearful of the danger of state insurance, who suddenly grew sentimentally eloquent about accident prevention. It was life insurance companies, anxious to kill the health insurance movement, who spoke of sickness prevention; it was chambers of commerce which loudly mouthed about regularization of industry." [67] No one, least of all the insurance companies, proclaimed that fire prevention should substitute for insurance; the argument would undoubtedly have been used, Rubinow suggested, if anyone had proposed state fire insurance.

Rubinow thought originally that emphasis on prevention was a defensive tactic, an understandable response to the exaggerations and misrepresentations of the opposition. The "proselytes of health insurance," for example, were provoked into making "extravagant promises that the cost would be entirely shifted upon the consumer; that the increased efficiency of a healthy labor force would increase the profits of the employer; that health insurance would almost magically improve health conditions and reduce the rate of illness; or even that health insurance, coming after compensation, would entirely, or almost entirely, eliminate the necessity for private charity." [68] He did not anticipate that a tactic would become a principle.

The trouble with preventive social insurance was that it achieved neither economic maintenance nor prevention. It blew "hot and cold," striving to "create a force for prevention by making industry responsible" for accidents or unemployment, while trying to "calm the employers' opposition by holding the cost within narrow limits." The "American Plan" produced results which were "nearly absurd." [69] It exerted a downward pressure on employers' costs, resulting less in prevention than in reduced benefit scales.

The differences between the Rubinow approach and the Commons–Andrews approach to social insurance were rooted in their interpretations of the workmen's compensation experience. Rubinow did not believe that its stimulus to accident prevention, if any, justified the subordination of maintenance to prevention. European experience offered little proof that compensation had reduced accident rates, absolutely or relatively. The theory of compensation (or any social insurance) was based upon "frank recognition" of the fact that all accidents (or other risks) could not be prevented. They were, statistically, an "inevitable accompaniment of economic activity." The maintenance purpose of social insurance was neither a "makeshift" nor an "apology," but an indispensable need in modern economic relations.[70] Rubinow's viewpoint did not prevail. Even before World War I, workmen's compensation cemented a tie between social insurance and risk prevention which would conflict with economic security or redistribution objectives.

# III  *The Origins of Workmen's Compensation*

Workmen's compensation was the earliest social insurance program in the United States, and the only one in operation before the 1930's. A major influence in the evolution of the broader social insurance movement, it was closely associated with preventive goals. In this respect and others it illustrated the manner in which a collective welfare program was adapted to the prerogatives of voluntarism and to a society which prized economic incentive above economic security, even under the extenuating circumstances of work-injury.

Social insurance experts mistakenly assumed that the rapid spread of compensation legislation after 1911 would lead to other compulsory programs. They thought that the compensation debate had performed a broader educational service when it embodied a specific response to the specific issue of industrial accident. Far from providing an entering wedge, it solidified the opposition of private interests to any further extension of social insurance. Workmen's compensation did not signify the emergence of new convictions about the role of the secondary income distribution system in a capitalistic society; it was accepted as an expedient by voluntary interest groups.

Several developments in the early twentieth century aroused national interest in problems of work-related disability. The Safety-first program of the U.S. Steel Corporation had a major impact. Studies lauding the preventive efforts of the German trade associations which administered workmen's compensation helped arouse indignation over American accident rates. The American

Association for Labor Legislation focused considerable attention upon industrial injury and disease. Publicists like William Hard condemned the "industrial juggernaut" for its waste of life and indifference to the consequences of work-injury.[1] Not least important was the classic indictment prepared by Crystal Eastman for the Pittsburgh Survey of 1907–08. Years afterward Isaac Rubinow described it as "perhaps the strongest single force in attracting public opinion and arousing public conscience concerning this one aspect of wage workers' rights in this country."[2]

Allegheny County in 1907–08, the period of Miss Eastman's field work, contained a population of one million. The 250,000 wage-earners included 70,000 steel workers, 50,000 railroad employees, and 20,000 miners. These represented the leading industries, and main accident groups. In the period surveyed, July 1, 1906 to June 30, 1907, fatalities totaled 526, including 195 steel workers, 125 railroaders, and 71 miners. Nonfatal accidents, based only upon an examination of hospital records for a three-month period, totaled 509. No wonder, she remarked, "that to a stranger Pittsburgh's streets are sad."[3] Saddest of all perhaps was the youthfulness of the killed and maimed: 84 percent of the dead were under forty years of age, and nearly 60 percent were under thirty.

Miss Eastman focused upon two questions: who was responsible for work-injuries? What were the economic consequences? The conventional wisdom in Pittsburgh attributed 95 percent of the accidents to employee carelessness. The case for workmen's compensation would be strengthened if it could be proven that personal negligence played a subordinate role. Unaccustomed by law or values to the doctrine of liability without fault, Americans had to be convinced that the conditions of industry, not the worker, were primarily responsible for work-injuries. It would then be possible to judge the "equity of the present system of distributing the accident loss."[4]

Miss Eastman obtained details concerning the cause of 410 fatalities. Since the responsibility was divided in some cases, the causal factors totaled 501. She attributed 132 fatalities to the victim, 56 to a fellow worker, 49 to supervisory personnel and 147 to the employer; the remaining 117 were attributable to none of these. Extenuating circumstances had to be considered, even when the worker was technically at fault. The victim was "green" or unaccustomed to the job in 22 out of the 132 cases; 13 were young boys; 12 deaths were caused by events over which the victim had no immediate control. Miss Eastman concluded that only 21 percent of the fatalities was attributable to carelessness. Yet carelessness had no absolute connotation; the term had to be understood in the context of modern economic life. Men would be injured or killed "even with the most perfect equipment, human and mechanical." The law of averages could not be abrogated. Human error and mechanical defect, as well as fatigue arising from long hours of arduous work, made accidents inevitable. And, if men were often "heedless," "inattentive," or "reckless," whose fault was it? A relentless pressure for speed, productivity, and efficiency permeated the industrial system. The foreman in the steel industry was continually driven by "bonus schemes, emulation, fear of discharge or desire for preferment." "Back of all" in the railroad industry was the "pressure for speed in handling the fast-increasing tonnage. The public demands it, and the whole railroad, from the president down to the yard brakeman, feels the demand. There can be no doubt that this accounts for much indifferent inspection, and for much of what is called carelessness." [5] The worker, for all practical purposes, had a choice between safety or employment.

Others also recognized that the "unreal abstractions of an antiquated psychology" controlled legal thought on the subject of work-accidents. The principle of no liability without fault dominated, although human nature was "imperfectly fitted for the strain put upon it by mechanical industry." The combination of speed, noise, long hours, fatigue, and monotony exerted pressures upon the "industrial operatives which makes occasional inadvertance on their part as inevitable as it is disastrous." The "reasonable man" of the common law, as portrayed by E. H. Downey, existed only as a legal absurdity: he was the man who "never relaxes his vigilance under the influence of monotony, fatigue, or habituation to danger, never permits his attention to be diverted, even for a moment, from the perils which surround him, never forgets a hazardous condition that he has once observed, and never ceases to be on the alert for new sources of danger." [6] By shifting the burden of responsibility from the individual to industry, those who favored compensation could defend a new principle of loss distribution. Equity demanded that the economic loss (or part of it) be transferred from the worker to the employer and, ultimately, to the consumer.[7]

Crystal Eastman's first achievement was to demonstrate the equity of workmen's compensation; her second was to formulate a rationale based upon social expediency. The employers' liability system was not only unjust, but "makes out of a largely necessary loss an absolutely unnecessary amount of privation." [8] At a later date, E. H. Downey similarly measured compensation by the test of "minimum social cost": "that distribution of unavoidable losses is to be preferred which imposes the least hardship upon individuals and results in the smallest diminution of the community's economic assets." [9] Miss Eastman's examination of the "social economy" of work-accidents covered 467 of the 526 fatalities, including 235 of the 258 married men. She found that 59 of the 235 families received no compensation from the employer; 65 received $100 or less; 40 got $100–$500; another 40, $500–$2000; and 20 families, less than 10 percent, received more than $2000. Combining data on fatalities and injuries, she found that in a majority of cases "the employers assumed absolutely no share of the inevitable income loss." The economic cost of work-accidents fell "directly, almost wholly, and in likelihood finally, upon the injured workmen and their dependents." The widow frequently had to seek employment, resulting in "hard work, long hours, poor pay, and in most cases children neglected." [10]

Considerations of equity and social expediency legitimized workmen's compensation, which would provide a powerful stimulus to the prevention of accidents. As matters stood, the employer had no incentive to prevent them. Competitive pressures made "economy and rapidity of production his controlling motives." If a "uniform and unescapable penalty" was affixed to each accident, "one economic motive would be set off against another." [11] In linking equity, social expediency, and prevention, Miss Eastman anticipated the main theoretical justifications for workmen's compensation.

Other social insurance proposals were justified in similar terms. Problems arising from unemployment or sickness were as widespread, chronic, and costly as those originating in work-accidents. Why did compensation alone succeed? One decisive factor by the early twentieth century was the growing discontent of employers over the operation of the liability system. Equally important, workmen's compensation was the only social insurance which did not entail an entirely new payroll cost. It involved an increase in an existing overhead. Even if the cost of compensation was higher than liability protection for some employers, it had a striking advantage. Compensation substituted a fixed but limited charge for a variable, potentially ruinous one.

Many employers carried liability insurance, and all were faced with the contingency of expensive lawsuits in the event of an employee's injury. In contrast to other risks, work-injury involved the employer in distinctive legal and financial problems. Workmen's compensation proved acceptable to employers, in part, because essentially it meant a transfer of costs, and a gain in their predictability. The social reformer may have justified workmen's compensation in terms of equity and social expediency, but the decisive consideration was that major voluntary interests anticipated concrete, material advantages through the substitution of compensation for liability. This circumstance was absent in the case of the other social insurances.

The employers' liability system, based upon the law of personal fault, was widely condemned by 1911 as one which "satisfies neither employers nor employees and is irregularly unjust and burdensome upon both; it does not fairly distribute either the burden of income loss or the contingent expenses of disability; it is economically wasteful and cruelly slow; as a whole it is a disgrace to our business intelligence, our sympathies, and our sense of justice." [12] The common law required employers to use reasonable care to safeguard workers. Liability was confined to negligence in exercising such care. In practice, "reasonable care" meant compliance with "statutes expressly enacted for the protection of employees." Even so, proof of negligence did not insure recovery for an employee; the negligence had to be the *"proximate cause* of the injury in respect of which recovery is sought." [13] The plaintiff had to demonstrate both negligence and proximate cause.

If the plaintiff overcame these obstacles, the employer still retained three potent common law defences. The assumption of risk doctrine relieved him of liability if an employee knew of a dangerous condition but continued at work; and the related burden of risk relieved him of liability for risks inherent in the industry. The fellow-servant rule protected the employer if a coemployee's negligence contributed to another's injury. The rule of contributory negligence absolved the employer if the injured party was at fault in any way. No one, at common law, could "hold another liable in damages for an injury to which his own want of ordinary care in any degree proximately contributed." The employer did not have to prove contributory negligence; freedom from it had to be "pleaded and proven by the employee to justify recovery." [14]

Despite their favored position under the common law, many employers were dissatisfied, a fact fundamental to their receptivity to workmen's compensation. Isaac Rubinow, evaluating the status of compensation after several years experience, noted that "there would have been a more critical attitude toward the compensation laws if the actual working out of the employers' liability laws through the medium of liability insurance had been better known to the laity." The much-despised "right to action" had acquired a "market value of its own, because of the necessary cost of litigating the action in court and also because of the ever-present chance of a larger or smaller verdict." Many claims, consequently, never reached court but were settled "by the sale, as it were, of that right to action to the insurance company for some substantial consideration." [15] The market value of the right to action had increased by the early twentieth century because of statutory modifications of the common law which improved the employee's position. Employers and insurance officials also complained about the tendency of lower-court juries to favor the plaintiff, necessitating appeals and further litigation. The employer confronted a practical choice between compensation and continued erosion of his common law advantages.

Six states by the mid-1890's had abrogated the coservant rule for railroad injuries; by 1908 the number had increased to sixteen. A handful of states had modified the assumption of risk doctrine by the turn of the century; their statutes provided that an employee's knowledge of safety violations constituted no bar to recovery. Nearly twenty states had enacted such legislation by 1908. Several states after 1906 modified the contributory negligence rule to allow recovery under the law of "proportional negligence." [16] The volume of employer liability insurance premiums rose steadily from the 1890's on. First introduced in England after the Employers' Liability Act of 1880, it spread to the United States. Premiums rose from about $200,000 in 1887 to more than $35,000,000 by 1912.[17]

When the compensation issue first emerged in the United States, the efforts of commercial insurance companies to discredit the concept of state insurance made it seem that they opposed any change. They issued sweeping condemnations of German social insurance, which had allegedly produced "simulation and fraud . . . combined with a decided lowering in the moral standards of the working classes." [18] In reality, the insurance companies perceived advantages in a shift from liability to compensation if state monopoly was avoided; it would increase their business and relieve them of virulent criticism from labor, the public, and even employers.

The universal complaint was that the casualty companies collected large sums in liability premiums, but distributed only a small portion to injured workers. Much of the premium dollar was consumed in profit and administrative overhead. The companies allegedly would exhaust every legal resource rather than award claims to accident victims. The legalistic orientation of the casualty companies did not lack justification. Liability insurance was, in essence, a "contract of indemnity to reimburse the policyholder for loss which he may sustain by reason of the liability imposed by law." This necessitated the "measure of all claims from the legal point of view."[19] Insurance companies could not adjust premiums to contingent legal liabilities of employers, and award benefits according to the victim's needs or some automatic compensation scale.

Social reformers exposed the magnitude of the work-injury problem, and its socio-economic consequences. All parties agreed upon the desirability of prevention, and most felt that compensation would stimulate it by attaching a definite cost to each accident. Most important, perhaps, employers and insurance companies anticipated advantages in substituting a fixed, but limited, cost for a variable, unpredictable one. Compensation promised to relieve employers and insurance companies of much bitter litigation and mitigate public indignation over the treatment of injured workers. Workmen's compensation was thus a program designed to meet the needs of private business groups as much as those of injured workers. Far from being a triumph over voluntarism, it was devised, in large measure, by voluntary interests. Its origin helps explain why compensation succeeded while the other social insurances failed, why it proved disappointing to many of its original, more disinterested sponsors, and why organized labor often opposed the substitution of compensation for the old liability system.

Sporadic efforts had been made to institute compensation before 1911. Miles M. Dawson, a consulting actuary and subsequently a leading compensation expert, prepared a bill for the Social Reform Club of New York as early as 1898. Inspired probably by the British Act of 1897, it was referred to a state legislative committee where it promptly died.[20] Maryland, in 1902, became the first state to enact a compensation law which provided benefits without proof of fault, and a cooperative insurance fund was established for workers in a few industries. The measure was declared unconstitutional in 1904 on the grounds that judicial functions were vested in an insurance commissioner and that individuals were deprived of the right to trial by jury.[21] That same year a Massachusetts committee reported in favor of a compensation act because "neither employers nor employees are satisfied with the present law." Nothing was accomplished until a second committee, appointed in 1907, recommended an optional act; this was passed in 1908, but had no perceptible results.[22] A Connecticut committee, appointed by the governor in 1907, could not agree upon a bill. In Illinois an industrial insurance commission, appointed in 1905, reported two years later in favor of an optional measure which failed to pass. Montana, in 1909, enacted a compulsory compensation law which applied only to the coal-mining industry, established a state insurance fund, and required contributions from employers and employees. It was soon declared unconstitutional.[23] Another optional, but futile measure enacted in Maryland in 1910 provided for a cooperative insurance fund limited to two counties.

Considerable impetus to the compensation movement came from the enactment of the 1908 federal law, which President Theodore Roosevelt strongly endorsed. Unfortunately, the benefit scale it established for serious injury was described as the worst ever known. Even the Spanish compensation act, the most illiberal in Europe, was superior to that "passed by the richest of the republics for its own servants." [24] The federal act was amended and greatly improved in 1916 through the efforts of the AALL.[25]

The era of employer liability commissions, resulting in rapid enactment of state compensation legislation, opened in 1909.[26] Minnesota, Wisconsin, and New York assumed the initiative, followed in 1910 by eight states: New Jersey, Montana, Washington, Ohio, Illinois, Maryland, Missouri, and Massachusetts. Similar commissions in 1911 were appointed in nine states: Colorado, Connecticut, Delaware, Iowa, Michigan, North Dakota, Pennsylvania, Texas, and West Virginia. Indiana, Louisiana, and Vermont were added to the list in 1913. By that year, twenty-one states had enacted compensation legislation (not including the optional New York law of 1910). The number increased to thirty-nine by 1917, and forty-three by 1920.[27]

The liability commission reports provide ample evidence that many employers favored compensation, assuming that a minimum economic burden was imposed upon industry. This implied a fixed but limited cost. No compensation system was acceptable, therefore, which retained the employee's right to sue for damages. Employers insisted upon the elimination of this right as a key to industrial harmony as well as a means to control costs. An end to litigation over industrial injury would remove a central source of labor bitterness and unrest. The existing liability laws produced "distrust and strained relations between employer and employee." Under the present law, one employer objected, "you may help a man and his family over some period and after that time he turns around and sues you, not perhaps of his own volition, but because someone has stirred him up and told him that is the thing to do." Another employer condemned the liability system as one of the "greatest evils of the present time in the social system, judging it simply from the standpoint of the relation of an employer with his employee." If compensation was fixed in advance, then "employer and employe would know just what was coming and therefore disputes could be largely avoided." [28]

Employers frequently criticized insurance companies and contingent-fee lawyers for contributing to labor unrest. Casualty companies had "no direct interest in the injured employee or in his harmonious relations with his employer." The latter spent four times as much for insurance as the worker received in benefits. Even if an employer wanted to assist an accident victim, he was constrained by fear of prejudicing his status with the insurance company. Employers also sharply condemned attorneys who pursued injured workers, discouraged them from accepting a settlement, and aroused hopes of munificent jury awards. "A lawyer will go to these ignorant men," a company representative testified, "and he will hold out high hopes of the amount to be realized as a result of that accident." [29] The occasional large verdict "loomed in their minds as the grand prizes of the lottery." [30]

The National Association of Manufacturers was a leading advocate of workmen's compensation. Its Committee on Industrial Indemnity Insurance sponsored an investigation of European compensation. Published in 1911, the report lauded the German achievement; and that same year the NAM endorsed workmen's compensation at the annual convention.[31] According to its president, the substitution of compensation for employers' liability would remove "perhaps . . . the most fruitful source of worry, dissatisfaction and friction to the employers and wage-workers of the United States." The principle of liability without fault was fully justified because accidents arose from "unavoidable risks inherent in the nature and circumstances of modern production." But the NAM did not suggest that the entire cost should be shifted from the worker to industry — what appealed about compensation was the idea of a determinate, predictable cost, "thus making certain the relief of the employe without unduly burdening the employer." [32]

Nothing impressed the NAM more than the preventive efforts associated with German compensation. The cause of accidents required "consideration equally with its consequences." [33] Responsibility for prevention in Germany rested with the employer mutuals which administered the compensation system, and penalized employers for violation of safety rules. The associations hired specialists to enforce a scientific inspection program. American employers, no less than social reformers, accepted accident prevention as a central goal of compensation. Compatible with American doctrines of competition and individual incentive, it became an additional means to reduce costs.

Like most employers the NAM found little to admire in the British compensation system, which allowed the worker to choose between compensation and a legal remedy. If he lost his case, he would apply for the compensation benefits. This amounted to a "gigantic scheme of poor relief," defective in its failure to "meet the causes as well as the effects of work accidents," or to remove "elements of personal antagonism" and "resort to the courts." [34] Labor groups in the United States, if they favored compensation at all, expressed a preference for the English system. Both employer and employee shared a dissatisfaction with employers' liability. Both wanted revision. The employer wanted a compensation system which eliminated the disadvantages of liability, but kept his costs low. Labor wanted one which insured the greatest leverage in terms of cash awards. The critical issue was whether the injured worker could retain his right to sue. From labor's viewpoint, this would result in an upward pressure upon compensation scales, and insure that a compensation system was adapted to the needs of the injured as well as those of the employer.

"I think," a representative of the Brooklyn Central Labor Union declared, "that our organizations are looking to the English Act as a model." The Joint Conference of the Central Labor Bodies of New York State and the Workingmen's Federation of the State of New York demanded that the "rights now guaranteed by common law and Employers' Liability acts shall be maintained, as is the case under the British Act." Ohio labor organizations favored a "just system" of workmen's compensation, but were "unqualifiedly opposed to any plan which does not give the widow or cripple the right to elect whether to accept a compensation, provided by a workingmen's compensation act, or rely upon the rights extended under the employers' liability acts now on the statute books." Railway workers were "unalterably opposed" to any substitution of a "general compensation act for the present employers' liability laws." Under compensation, injury awards could not be "sufficiently large to be an adequate substitute for the present rights." They opposed any plan which said to the worker, "we will compel you to accept the compensation plan or nothing." [35]

Where labor had a major voice in shaping compensation legislation, as in Arizona, injured workers were allowed a choice of remedy after injury. Employers, especially mineowners, had been "satisfied with their liability under the common law, but in view of the fact that the common law defenses of employers were being greatly reduced, they preferred to pay damages under a system of workmen's compensation, which would provide definite rates of compensation and avoid law suits." [36] A liberalized employers' liability measure, endorsed by the Arizona State Federation of Labor, and a compensation act, favored by the corporations, were voted into law in 1912. The railroads and mineowners had succeeded in their drive for a compensation law with "low rates and illiberal provisions," but failed to abolish the worker's right to election after injury. In the following decade, "most of the injured workmen used the Employers' Liability remedy, under which there was no legal limit to the damage recoverable." [37] Employers continually fought for amendment, and succeeded in 1925 when workers were required to elect a remedy before injury.

Business imperatives proved more influential in shaping workmen's compensation than considerations of equity and social expediency. The injured worker, rather than the employer or industry, continued to bear most of the costs. "What wonder," I. M. Rubinow observed, that a "few years of experience created a greater enthusiasm for the compensation system among the employers than among employees?" [38] "In no state," E. H. Downey maintained, "is the rate or the total amount of compensation at all sufficient either to replace the lost earnings of the deceased breadwinner or to provide reasonable maintenance and education for the widow and children." He estimated that compensation, after a decade, accounted for no more than "one-fourth of the pecuniary cost of those injuries which the compensation laws profess to cover." [39]

Compensation awards were lowered by a variety of devices, the most important being the low cash benefit schedule expressed as a percentage of wages. The benefit level also was affected by waiting periods, aggregate and maximum weekly cash allowances, time limitations, skimpy medical requirements, and the exclusion of occupational disease. A major legal decision may have contributed indirectly to the chronic inadequacy of compensation benefits. The opinion of the New York Court of Appeals in the Ives case, delivered in March 1911, declared a compulsory compensation act of 1910 unconstitutional. As a result, most states attempted to avoid possible constitutional objections by using the fiction of "elective" laws. If an employer failed to elect compensation, he surrendered his common law defenses; he retained them if the worker refused to elect. The implicit threat of employer rejection, combined with the reluctance of state legislatures to place local firms at a competitive disadvantage, resulted in low costs and benefits.[40]

All the shortcomings of early compensation legislation were embodied in the New Jersey statute of 1911, among the first to take effect.[41] As amended in 1913 it provided, after a two-week waiting period, a maximum of 50 percent of weekly wages in the event of total disability. The weekly maximum cash benefit was set at ten dollars, and the allotment for permanent total disability was limited to four hundred weeks. Victims of permanent partial disability were allowed 50 percent of wages up to ten dollars a week for three hundred weeks. The death benefit ranged from 35 to 50 percent of wages, according to the number of dependents, but could not exceed ten dollars a week for three hundred weeks. Although compensation had been instituted to minimize litigation, New Jersey and several other states provided for court administration. And, although compensation had been designed to provide a limited but guaranteed work-injury benefit, employers were not required to insure.

Despite its gross defects — low benefit scale, court administration, and absence of insurance requirement — the New Jersey statute was frequently "recommended as a model in non-compensation states by groups of insurance men and employers."[42] An investigation undertaken by the AALL in 1915 revealed that this model measure produced lengthy delays because of court adjudication of disputes. Injured men and their families carried the full burden of disability "when they are least able to bear it." Fifteen out of fifty-three awards for temporary disability in one year applied to disabilities that had ended. The low compensation scale worked "unwarranted hardships." And the absence of a compulsory insurance requirement had deprived some workers of "every penny of indemnity."[43]

The compensation laws of other states differed from New Jersey's in detail rather than substance. Some were superior in administrative arrangements, providing for the establishment of industrial accident boards or commissions. Others required employers to insure through private companies, mutuals, state funds, or self-insurance. All were defective by the critical standard of benefit levels. A one-to-two week waiting period was almost universal. Provision for medical treatment was limited in time, money, or both. Fifteen of the twenty-one compensation states in 1913 allowed 50 percent of wages for total disability, but subject to weekly and aggregate dollar maxima.

The inadequacy of the compensation laws was revealed most starkly in their provision for long-term disabilities — total and permanent partial. Rubinow described the latter as the "most important class of injuries from a social point of view," but the "least satisfactorily handled in American legislation." In contrast to European practice, which allowed partial benefits for the length of the disability, American states usually relied upon the dismemberment schedule, a product of guesswork and "crude bargaining." [44] Total disability benefits were similar to those for death, and terminated abruptly after a specified period of time. E. H. Downey also complained of the dismemberment schedules which governed benefits for permanent partial disability, but still "less excusable" was the "well-nigh universal failure to provide adequate medical, surgical, and hospital care, to say nothing of such re-training as might benefit the crippled worker." Employers, he noted, had no "incentive" to "rehabilitate industrial cripples." [45] Few states covered industrial disease in their compensation legislation; as late as the mid-1920's only ten made such provision.

Workmen's compensation never overcame its original structural deficiencies, rooted in benefit schedules adapted more to business imperatives than to the objective needs of injured workers. By the mid-1920's, a fourth of the compensation states still retained a benefit scale limited to 50 percent of wages; the maximum in any state was 65 percent. Victims of total permanent disability might receive from $3000 to $6000 in aggregate benefits over a period of weeks ranging from 260 to 1000. Most states retained the dismemberment schedule for permanent partial disability. Medical benefits improved, but the majority of states still imposed time and dollar limits (two weeks to a year, and $100 to $800). Only a few jurisdictions had eliminated the waiting period.[46]

By the early 1930's, "after twenty years under compensation laws but a small fraction of the burden of industrial accidents had been shifted from injured workers and their dependents."[47] The best legislation, in some half dozen jurisdictions, stipulated 65 percent of wages, subject to a weekly maximum of twenty dollars. A study of the compensation system in Pennsylvania confirmed that the economic cost of work accidents had only nominally been shifted to industry. Compensation's "robes of virtue" cloaked "many of the familiar patterns of the old liability system." Injured workers still suffered the "blow of an industrial accident by sacrificing hard won surpluses, by accepting privations and hardships, or are forced, if they cannot absorb the cost, to fall back upon the resources of the community."[48] The employer's liability for medical treatment in Pennsylvania was limited to thirty days following injury, though the average need for medical care was eighty-one days, and 42 percent of the cases required treatment for three months or more. Compensation payments, on the whole, equaled only half the wages lost. Defective administrative arrangements contributed to the worker's burden. The Bureau of Workmen's Compensation depended upon information supplied by employers or insurers as a basis for approving settlements, but accident victims signed agreements "under a sense of compulsion, upon the advice of employers or insurers, with no understanding of what is involved."[49] Litigation costs and hardships had not been eliminated. In contested cases the plaintiff's benefits were reduced because of legal and medical fees, and delays were "inordinate." Compensation was supposed to insure prompt, if limited benefits, but the average worker in Pennsylvania received no compensation for nearly a month, and 20 percent had to wait two months or longer.

Workmen's compensation continued to suffer from faults which had typified the program from the start. Of 54 compensation jurisdictions in the 1950's, 26 remained elective, a condition which "served as a formidable weapon in the hands of employers against liberalization of benefits." [50] Medical requirements had been raised considerably, and most states had added coverage for industrial disease, but if the estimate that compensation payments did not total more than one-third of income loss was correct, there was little improvement in cash benefits.[51] Nominal schedules ranged from 50 to 80 percent of wages; the largest number of jurisdictions, 22, established a two-thirds schedule for temporary disability. In 39 jurisdictions, however, the real maximum dollar totals (including dependent allowances) were set at $25 to $35 a week. Most jurisdictions applied further restrictions through time and aggregate dollar formulas. The wage percentages and weekly maximum were similar for permanent total disability. In cases of permanent partial disability, which Rubinow had described three decades earlier as the epitome of irrationality, the pattern remained "almost as inconsistent and chaotic as the jury awards for such injuries in precompensation days." [52] Widows' benefits averaged 50 percent of wages, but fell as low as 30 percent in Delaware. Including allowances for dependents, the most common figure was 66⅔ percent.

Workmen's compensation had been interpreted by reformers as an equitable, socially expedient innovation. The main object was to transfer the economic burden of work-injury from the victim to industry and, ultimately, to society. Compensation, thus formulated, was compatible with social insurance goals. It implied a rationalized income maintenance program achieved through centralization, an enhanced governmental role, and the transfer of functions from the private to the public sector. But employers often assumed the initiative in sponsoring workmen's compensation and the program ultimately was shaped by their objectives rather than the needs of the injured. Equally important was the influence of the private insurance companies.

Insurance companies claimed to prefer compensation to the liability system. They had "nothing to lose and everything to gain by the enactment of a workmen's compensation law containing a schedule of benefits to be paid in the event of the employer being liable for the injury." Compensation would eliminate many criticisms directed against their practices under liability. It also was preferable from the technical insurance viewpoint, for "if the extent and nature of a risk to be known an approximately correct premium can be computed." It was difficult to calculate loss reserves under liability, given the tendency of juries "to render verdicts for larger and larger amounts in personal injury cases." The cost of "disposing of the litigated cases" was becoming "much larger than had been originally contemplated." [53]

The commercial insurance companies were uncompromisingly hostile to the establishment of state compensation funds.[54] The Workmen's Compensation Publicity Bureau, an association of stock companies, published numerous critiques of state insurance in Europe and of the operation of American state compensation funds.[55] Workmen's compensation, according to insurance officials, was a "world movement, and in the eyes of the community the employers' liability system stands condemned by both justice and humanity." [56] But this did not justify the sacrifice of private enterprise. State bureaucracies never could cope with the "fraud, malingering, and simulation so characteristic of numerous claimants." Politics, rather than considerations of economy and efficiency, would control the administration of state funds. To the detriment of the community welfare, a "great political machine" might be established and disburse "huge sums of money practically without check." Government, in any case, had no right to usurp the prerogatives of private enterprise. Only Socialists denied the impropriety of state involvement in any activity which "interferes with or in any way curtails legitimate individual enterprise." History exhibited ample proof of the "deleterious effect upon a people's virility and prosperity inevitably following upon paternal government."[57]

Insurance officials expressed a dour view of human nature. Only private institutions were compatible with its "imperfections," implying the "organization of society on a competitive instead of on a socialistic basis." Socialists regarded altruism as the dynamic force in life, though progress was rooted in individual initiative, competition, and self-interest. These were the mainsprings of human action; to society's advantage they "let the fittest survive." They produced a "strong and self-reliant people," and nurtured the "active exercise of men's talents and energies."[58]

The most efficient administrative techniques in workmen's compensation would emerge from competition. Insurance companies stressed the many services they provided the employer and the superiority of private companies over state funds in encouraging accident prevention. They conceded that monopolistic state funds provided the cheapest insurance, but not the "best or more economical."[59] State fund officials, on the other hand, charged the private insurance companies with misrepresentation and unfair tactics. They emphasized that the state had no "moral right" to interpose "between its sovereignty and its distress a private agency to make money out of distress," nor did it possess the "economic right" to impose the "vast burden upon the industries of the state" which grew out of premium competition in workmen's compensation.[60] To presume, as did the stock companies, that a compulsory, collective welfare program should be the prerogative of private enterprise was "sheer effrontery." Private companies had "secured admission into this field only in the face of vigorous protests on the part of labor and persons sincerely interested to secure the best possible administration of compensation insurance."[61]

The stock companies maintained that they "had no objection to workmen's compensation as such, in fact they were ready to welcome it, but they naturally did not like its fellow, state insurance."[62] They had several strategic advantages in their crusade against state funds. Apart from the general American preference for private enterprise and voluntary endeavor, they were already in the field and could "reach employers directly and easily through their agents and brokers." Employers were deterred by "misinformation instilled into them by their brokers," such as allegations of state fund insolvency and the liability of employers in the event of bankruptcy.[63] Stock companies possessed another competitive advantage in their ability to provide package arrangements — reducing rates for other kinds of insurance if compensation was carried through their organization. The controversy was resolved in favor of the private companies: seven states established monopolistic funds; another ten competitive funds. Only two of these, both competitive, were established after 1920.[64]

From the beginning of the compensation movement, it was widely believed that a "compensation law adds a tremendous incentive for the promotion of safety as a business proposition and makes it easy for the officers of the state to meet the manufacturers on a common ground in the work of reducing accidents."[65] John Andrews described accident prevention as a "problem more interesting to me even than compensating the victims."[66] The compensation movement was accompanied by a vast amount of safety discussion and organization, including the establishment in 1913 of the National Council for Industrial Safety.[67] Insurance companies acclaimed the value of merit rating in creating a safety consciousness among employers. Few dissented from the proposition that accident prevention was "as much a part of the principle of workmen's compensation as is the paying of indemnity."[68]

The compensation movement undoubtedly stimulated industrial safety consciousness, but it is difficult to determine the precise relation between merit rating and prevention. According to John Commons, "experience with workmen's accident insurance shows the business-like way of prevention." Businessmen had done more for prevention in ten years of compensation than "all of the trade unions, all of the charities, all of the legislatures and state factory inspectors could possibly do, simply because they make money by doing it and the others do not."[69] This claim was stated rather than proven. Critics, in later years, maintained that the "operating forces" since 1911 which affected industrial injuries were numerous, but workmen's compensation as such had "little effect upon the result." [70] During the 1930's schedule rating, which adjusted premiums to plant physical conditions, was abandoned. Accident rates remained inordinately high in small enterprises.[71] Most important, prevention fell far "short of what would be attained under an adequate scale of benefits." If they were high enough, E. H. Downey suggested, "much would become practical which is now deemed visionary." [72] The exponents of prevention never fully appreciated that its potential in a social insurance program hinged ultimately upon benefit levels. If compensation costs, expressed as a percentage of payroll, were low because of benefit inadequacy, then rate differentials through merit rating provided only a limited inducement to employers. Equally important, since a "low loss ratio may be achieved by successful denial or reduction of compensation liability as well as through a low accident rate," employers or insurance companies had as much "incentive to fight claims or indulge in other practices injurious to the basic objectives of workmen's compensation." [73]

The emphasis upon prevention in workmen's compensation testified to the American belief in the salutary effects of economic incentive and competition. These same elements pervaded the administration of the program in the form of competing insurance carriers. Considerations like the right of private insurance companies to participate, low payroll costs, and the idea of prevention took precedence from the beginning over the objective economic needs of injured workers. Voluntarism proved incompatible with the social insurance ideal of predictable and adequate income guarantees.[74]

# IV  Health Insurance: "Made in Germany"

Workmen's compensation demonstrated the ability of voluntary interest groups to adapt a collective welfare program to private ends. The energetic but futile campaign for compulsory health insurance demonstrated their power to thwart completely a welfare measure from which they anticipated no material advantages. Health insurance was overwhelmed by an extraordinary mobilization of political resources by voluntary groups. The issues transcended the distribution of cost or tax burdens. Health insurance entailed innovations in the financing and organizing of medical services, changes in the status and social responsibility of the medical profession, and a substantial enlargement of the power and welfare role of government. Medical practice, an entrepreneurial endeavor tempered by charity, would be reorganized on a new semi-utility basis; it would be provided as a function of need rather than of ability to pay.

Opponents of health insurance objected that it would demoralize the medical profession and result in a deterioration in the quality of service. Beyond this generalized solicitude for the physician, the employers, fraternals, insurance companies, and other groups had concrete interests of their own to protect. The workmen's compensation experience intensified the determination of physicians and insurance companies to contest any further extension of social insurance. When the health insurance movement was launched around 1914, the insurance companies were still engaged in efforts to prevent the establishment of monopoly state funds, and the medical profession was bitter over alleged exploitation and growth of contract practice under the auspices of workmen's compensation. Thus, powerful voluntary groups were already critical of the first social insurance program and were determined to prevent the establishment of a new one.

Between 1915 and 1920 compulsory health insurance was one of the most controversial, widely debated social issues in the United States. Identified primarily with the American Association for Labor Legislation, and its Committee on Social Insurance, it reached an advanced legislative stage in New York and California.[1] The AALL published tentative standards for health insurance in the summer of 1914, followed in November 1915 by the first draft of a bill.[2] Versions were introduced into the New York, Massachusetts, and New Jersey legislatures in 1916, and into those of fifteen other states in 1917. California and Massachusetts commissions delivered reports on health insurance in 1917, when additional investigating commissions were authorized in Connecticut, Illinois, Massachusetts, New Hampshire, Ohio, Pennsylvania, and Wisconsin.[3]

The AALL program favored the German more than the English model.[4] Instituted in 1883–84, German health insurance provided for local administration of medical and cash benefits through a variety of autonomous funds. The most important were the local sick-funds, which grouped workers in a locality on the basis of occupations or industries. These were supplemented by establishment funds, building trades funds, miners' funds, guild funds, aid funds (comparable to British friendly societies), and communal sick-insurance funds for those not belonging to any other.[5] Up to 1911, the law included industrial, transportation, and construction workers (covering about 20 percent of the population). The Insurance Code revisions of 1911 extended coverage to agricultural and domestic workers. Employees contributed two-thirds of the cost, employers one-third. Each fund had to provide a minimum range of benefits, which could be extended if financially feasible. The employee contribution in 40 percent of the funds was 2–3 percent of wages; it infrequently rose beyond 4½ percent.[6]

Local funds were required to provide benefits for a minimum

of thirteen weeks until 1903, when the minimum was raised to
twenty-six weeks. Medical benefits included physician and surgical care, drugs, eyeglasses, and other supplies; funds could
arrange for hospital care if necessary. The cash benefit was
generally 50 percent of wages, although 12 percent of the funds
provided more.[7] Female wage-earners, in maternity cases, received the regular medical benefit and a cash benefit lasting six
weeks; at their option funds could provide a maternity benefit
to non-employed wives of covered workers. German health insurance also included a funeral benefit. The features of the German
program favored by American health insurance experts included
the use of local mutual funds, their administration of both medical and cash benefits, the system of wage-related contributions
and cash benefits, and provision for hospital and funeral benefits.

Americans endorsed the British principle of state financial
participation, but objected to the multiplicity of carriers, separation of cash and medical benefits, flat-rate contributions and cash
benefits, the absence of hospital and specialist services, and omission of a funeral benefit. The British National Insurance Act of
1911, establishing compulsory unemployment as well as health
insurance, climaxed the era of social legislation which followed
the return of the Liberal Party to power in 1906.[8] Health insurance was identified with Lloyd George, who had visited Germany
in 1908 and returned greatly impressed with its system of state
insurance.[9]

Unlike the German plan, English legislation provided for the
administration of cash benefits by "approved societies" (mostly
fraternals and nonprofit divisions of commercial insurance companies). Medical benefits were administered by newly formed
local committees which included representatives of approved
societies, the medical profession, and county or borough councils.
Compulsory upon all wage-earners and others earning up to £160
($800) a year, the law covered some 14,000,000 persons. Em-
ployees contributed 4d. a week; employers, 3d.; the state, 2d.[10]
Medical benefits included physician services, drugs, appliances,
and sanatorium care for consumptives.[11] Cash benefits (totaling
10s a week for men, 7s 6d. for women) continued for thirteen

weeks. If illness persisted, the cash benefit for the next thirteen weeks dropped to 5s; thereafter, it became an invalidity benefit of 5s a week until the patient was eligible for an old-age pension. Insured women received medical and cash benefits for maternity; non-employed wives of insured persons received a cash maternity benefit. Funeral benefits were excluded at the insistence of the insurance companies.

Concessions to the fraternals and medical profession, as well as the insurance companies, made National Health Insurance possible. The authorization of approved societies to serve as carriers primarily benefited the fraternals and insurance companies, who would have opposed the measure if they had been excluded. Requirements for approved society status included non-profit operation, and membership or democratic control (which was not achieved).[12]

The medical profession was responsible for the second distinctive feature of English health insurance — separation of the cash and medical benefit. Health insurance emerged as an issue in the "period of transition from the folk medicine of the nineteenth century to rational medicine in the twentieth century." In the course of this transition, there erupted a "widespread revolt among the doctors against the developing system of contract practice. Culminating in the legislation of 1911, this period can be seen as one which the doctors were engaged in a Hobbesian struggle for independence from the power and authority exercised over their lives, their work and their professional values by voluntary associations and private enterprise."[13] A British Medical Association report, published in 1905, revealed that medical practice under fraternal contract agreements combined low earnings for the physician and poor service for patients. Paid on a per capita basis, doctors rarely received more than 5s per member and from this sum they were obliged to supply medicines and drugs.[14] The competitive conditions of contract practice, combined with insecurity of tenure, left the physician at the mercy of the "organisation men of the times; the administrators, lay committees and bureaucrats of the voluntary associations and insurance companies."[15]

While the insurance bill was under consideration, the medical profession submitted a number of demands to the Chancellor of the Exchequer. Designed to protect the profession against the reappearance of contract and club practices under health insurance, the conditions included income limits for the medical benefit; free choice of physician; higher capitation fees; separation of the medical and cash benefit; and representation of the medical profession on all insurance committees. The physicians had hoped, originally, to control the medical benefit entirely, but agreed to the establishment of local insurance committees. The final arrangements proved disappointing to them, for the committees consisted of forty to eighty members, with physicians in the minority. General supervision of National Health Insurance was entrusted to four groups of insurance commissioners (England, Scotland, Wales, and Ireland) and a National Health Insurance Joint Committee composed of representatives from each.[16]

The American health insurance program departed from European models in its emphasis upon use of the insurance mechanism to prevent illness. Sponsors believed that administration by local mutual funds (as in Germany) which combined medical and cash benefits, and included representatives of employers and employees, would stimulate interest in prevention by assigning a cash value to sickness.

The AALL prepared a list of standards for health insurance legislation. It had to be compulsory, and financed by contributions from employer, employee, and the government. All wage-earners below a stipulated yearly income, including casual and home workers if possible, should be included; others could enroll under a parallel voluntary program. Benefits should continue for a specified period, probably twenty-six weeks, but provision for invalidity could be made under a separate administrative arrangement. The favored mechanism should be local mutual funds managed by employers and employees; other nonprofit carriers could be allowed if not detrimental to the local funds and subject to strict government supervision. The insurance should provide both medical and cash benefits. It was "highly desirable that prevention be emphasized so that the introduction of a compulsory health and invalidity insurance system shall lead to a campaign of health conservation similar to the safety movement resulting from workmen's compensation." [17]

The AALL's Committee on Social Insurance published a tentative bill in November 1915 (subsequently revised), incorporating these standards.[18] It covered all manual workers and others earning less than $1200 a year. Local mutual funds were proposed which might provide the medical benefit through a panel arrangement, salaried physicians, or some other system. Funds were encouraged to employ a supervising medical officer so that the same physician would not be responsible for treating patients and determining eligibility for the cash benefit. The latter would amount to 66⅔ percent of wages for twenty-six weeks. The medical benefit included general medical and surgical care, nursing, and appliances; its most advanced features provided for dependents of the insured and a hospital benefit in lieu of a proportion of the cash benefit. Maternity and funeral benefits were also included. Employees and employers each contributed two-fifths and the state one-fifth of a sum equal to 4 percent of wages. This amount was "about what the German experience shows would be necessary."

The case for compulsory health insurance rested upon six propositions.[19] The first concerned the "high sickness and death rates . . . prevalent among American wage-earners." It was charged, next, that low-income groups received inadequate care. The poor often lacked the "advice of physicians and the most elementary nursing — even in maternity cases." [20] Medical service was a function of ability to pay rather than of need. Third, illness produced widespread poverty. Unless the wage-earner could be relieved of the entire economic burden attributable to illness, it "must be expected to produce in the future as in the past its yearly harvest of destitution and demoralization." [21] Fourth, "energetic efforts for the prevention of sickness" were as essential as economic relief. But prevention depended upon health insurance which would "directly stimulate both workman and employer to reduce the risk of occupational illness to the minimum." [22] The most crucial, controversial proposition, was the fifth, that "existing agencies cannot meet these needs." Medical charities were criticized on several grounds. They lacked adequate budgets, their distribution and services depended as much upon the whim of givers as objective need, they failed to encourage preventive measures, and the average worker possessed a "wholesome distaste for charity." [23] Establishment funds, a second voluntary resource, depended too much upon the initiative and financial backing of employers. Organized labor objected to them as obstructions to the mobility and independence of workers. Social insurance experts viewed industrial medicine as an American precedent for better schemes of prepaid care; and it provided a clue to the plan of organization under health insurance — the "group handling of the sickness problem." [24] Through health insurance the principles of prepayment and group practice could be extended, the quality of service improved, and the system removed from the employer's control.

The collective approach to financing and organizing medical care had a second root in the early twentieth century. Some advocates of health insurance cited the emergence of prepaid health clinics at universities, notably the University of California. In 1906 California established an infirmary staffed with salaried physicians where students were treated for a small fee per semester. The University proceeded despite the objections of the medical profession, which condemned the plan as "being unethical — a form of socialized medicine involving contract practice." [25] Boston and New York physicians similarly criticized proposals for pay clinics because they would "be an unnecessary pauperization of individuals and an injury to the medical profession." [26]

Another voluntary resource, commercial health insurance, was underdeveloped, costly, devoid of medical benefits, and infrequently purchased by workers. Insurance companies, recognizing their neglect of this field and fearful of compulsory health insurance, began promoting the idea of group disability policies. The Metropolitan Life Insurance Company established a disability insurance department around 1914.[27] This protection also depended upon the initiative of employers, and reached only a small percentage of the working force.

Trade unions could not supply the medical needs of the low-income population. Most workers were unorganized, and the unions which provided disability benefits rarely included medical services. The sponsors of health insurance and the medical profession joined in criticism of fraternal organizations. Although the proportion of wage-earners among Catholic and immigrant orders was "probably fairly high," according to the AALL, a substantial proportion of fraternal membership consisted of skilled mechanics, businessmen, and professional men. Fraternal organizations were more likely to provide a cash rather than a medical benefit; among those which did provide medical benefits, the members "do not receive proper attention nor the physician adequate pay." Most often, the capitation fee was set at a dollar a year. Consequently, lodge medicine was "largely in the hands of inexperienced or second-rate doctors," and club practice had become a "by-word among the profession." [28]

Several state commissions collected detailed information confirming the insufficiency of voluntary arrangements for medical care. The California Social Insurance Commission examined the local branches of more than twenty fraternal orders.[29] The "great majority" were composed of "better paid wage earners." It estimated that 300,000 persons were entitled to a sick benefit, or about 35 percent of the state's fraternal membership. Only a minority of lodges provided a medical benefit, and only one included hospital care. The cash benefit usually amounted to $7 to $10 a week for thirteen weeks. An extensive survey of union disability programs revealed that 41 percent of union membership in California was eligible for benefits, but that few unions made "provision for medical service in addition to the cash benefits." Two types of commercial health insurance were available. A few commercial hospital associations had been established. Much of the premium was consumed in overhead costs, and the diseases compensated were "so limited that the protection which they furnish the member is most inadequate." A small number of workers purchased health and accident policies from commercial

insurance companies. Premiums collected totaled less than $2,000,-
000 in 1915. Establishment funds had limited coverage. Of 602
manufacturing firms which supplied data, only 26 made "systematic" provision for disability.

The Illinois Health Insurance Commission's survey of fraternals
revealed that some 350,000–400,000 members out of over 1,000-
000 had disability protection.[30] No more than 75 percent were
wage-earners. Less than one-fifth of the lodges provided medical
care through a physician who received a capitation fee of a
dollar or two a year. About one-third of the union membership — 135,000–145,000 — were elegible for disability benefits.
Except for four locals, there was a "complete absence of medical and hospital care." At the end of 1917, about 250,000 commercial health and accident policies were in force in Illinois,
purchased by "business men, professional men, farmers, and
others of the non-wage-earning classes." They usually provided cash benefits for total disability for fifty-two weeks. These
commercial health policies were supplemented by mutual assessment associations which claimed approximately 230,000 policies
in force. Establishment funds included some 200,000 workers,
mostly concentrated in large industrial plants and utilities in the
Chicago, Moline, and East St. Louis areas. They ordinarily provided only cash benefits. The Commission estimated that voluntary health insurance covered 30 percent of the state's wage-
earners who bore almost the entire cost.

The Ohio Commission estimated that a comparable 35 percent
of that state's wage-earners had some form of sickness insurance.[31] Under all auspices, cash benefits were more common than
medical benefits, and the insurance covered only 10 to 15 percent
of the total economic loss. Some 540,000 persons acquired insurance protection through fraternals. They received cash benefits
of $5 to $7 a week, but provision for medical attendance was
infrequent. Union disability funds provided cash benefits for
85,000 workers. Commercial health premiums for the year ending
June 1917 totaled less than $3,500,000, and approximately 80 per-
cent was purchased by non-wage-earners. The Commission found
150 establishment funds in Ohio in 1917; these provided cash
benefits of $5 to $7 a week for 100,000 persons.

According to the findings of the Pennsylvania Health Insurance Commission, which were similar to those to California, Illinois, and Ohio,[32] the "facilities for medical care among wage earners are not satisfactory, whether considered from the standpoint of extent, cost, or proportion of persons receiving care in time of sickness." Insurance, as in Illinois and Ohio, again was estimated to cover some 30 percent of the workers, but "seemingly least often among those who need it most." Existing insurance arrangements seldom provided "good medical care and cash benefits," whether fraternals, unions, commercial policies, or establishment funds. An intensive survey covering 743 families (3198 individuals) was made in the Kensington area. Compared to the 77 percent protected by industrial (funeral) policies, only 34 percent of the workers carried sickness insurance. Fraternals provided most of this insurance; less than 3 percent carried commercial policies.[33]

The Pennsylvania Commission also revealed that a serious shortage of medical facilities existed. Sixteen of the sixty-seven Pennsylvania counties lacked any hospital beds, and nine other counties had less than 1 per 1000 persons. In the nineteen counties of the bituminous coal region, which contained 34.38 percent of the population, there were less than 9000 hospital beds, or 3.1 per 1000 persons. More than two-thirds were concentrated in Allegheny County. Exclusive of Allegheny, the figure dropped to 0.14 beds per 1000 persons.

The investigations of the state commissions and other groups led to the sixth proposition of the AALL — that compulsory health insurance was the only effective solution to the medical problems of the wage-earner. It had four specific advantages over voluntary efforts. The compulsory feature substituted universal for partial coverage, and eliminated the need for expensive reserve requirements. Second, compulsory insurance supplied most medical needs of the eligible population, including maternity and funeral benefits, in addition to larger cash allowances. Third, these superior benefits at less cost to the wage-earner were possible because the employer and the state assumed most of the economic burden. It became a truism in health insurance propaganda that this redistributive feature was equitable as well as socially expedient. All three groups — worker, employer, and state — presumably were responsible for illness. The employer's responsibility arose from the "conditions in his establishment which make for ill health." An analogy was drawn with workmen's compensation; sickness, like accidents, should be viewed as a legitimate overhead cost. The state was responsible for sickness to the degree it failed to control the environmental conditions which produced disease. Health insurance experts argued, in the fourth place, that compulsory insurance stimulated preventive efforts. The cash benefit equal to two-thirds of wages would "call attention forcibly to the cumulative financial loss involved in sickness, a loss which to-day is not brought home to the public because it is borne in silence by scattered individuals." Prevention would be encouraged by the opportunities provided for early and thorough medical care. Public health efforts would intensify because of the "increase in the state contribution to the sick funds with an increase in the amount of illnesss." [34]

Compulsory health insurance alone could guarantee universal coverage, a uniform, minimum range of medical and cash benefits, an equitable distribution of cost, and, not least important, prevention. Achievement of these ends was contingent upon substantial augmentation of the welfare functions and powers of government at the expense of various voluntary institutions. The medical profession would have to make the most drastic adjustments. Health insurance challenged the profession's corporate autonomy and power. The objectives of compulsory insurance conflicted with the tradition of entrepreneurial, solo practice which the profession equated with its status, economic interests, and standards of medical care.

Health insurance, physicians feared, would revolutionize the "organization of medical aid." If the organizational status quo were preserved, Rubinow argued, it would "utterly fail to make health insurance a powerful fulcrum for lifting general health conditions." There had to be "some change in the customary conditions of private practice." [35] Rubinow and others were critical of the British scheme which made no provision for specialist or hospital services. It was, in this respect, an anachronism whose norm was the family generalist of the nineteenth century rather than the specialization, organization, and medical technology of the twentieth. Health insurance, Rubinow insisted, should exploit scientific progress. The poor currently received substandard care because private practice was too expensive, or they persisted in a "harmful tendency to self-medication," and the use of "injurious nostra." At best, they relied almost exclusively upon "so-called 'general practitioners'" whose "persistence is out of all harmony with the recent phenomenal development of scientific medicine." [36]

Ideally, Rubinow maintained, medical organization under health insurance should result in a "state of affairs in which all the medical work to be done for the members of a health-insurance fund would be done by physicians and surgeons . . . who are specially employed for the purpose." Precedents included the German local funds, the "famous system of Russian village medicine," some industrial corporations, the military, and the "brilliant results achieved by thorough organization of medical service in the building of the Panama Canal." Much was said about the exercise of free choice, but this had little reality for those millions who could not afford medical care; it was not found in hospitals or clinics, nor did it have any scientific foundation. It may have had some psychological significance when the "function of a physician was exercised largely by moral suasion." In an era of scientific medicine, diagnosis and treatment could not "depend for their success upon such whimsical considerations." Nowadays, in the modern industrial community, the "poetic 'country doctor,' who took care of several generations, has long since given way to the modern commercialized practitioner. It is preposterous to imagine that the average working-man or woman . . . is able to pass intelligent judgment upon the professional accomplishment of his physicians." The only justification for retaining free choice or solo practice was expediency: physicians and patients insisted on it. Still, it was "quite certain that there will be a gradual development of group practice and a gradual increase of institutional medical work . . . and that the principle of salaried work will probably continue to make inroads." [37]

The hospital and dispensary served as the models for medical reorganization along group lines. Michael M. Davis, Jr., director of the Boston Dispensary, described them as the embodiment of the "specialist system *plus* organization." These two "essential developing elements in modern medical service" had to constitute the foundation of the coming health insurance system. Health insurance in Germany and England had effected a revolution by extending professional medical service to the entire working population, but it was defective from the "standpoint of medical efficiency." Medicine had not, under health insurance, been organized "beyond the stage of individualistic private practice." Health insurance had to be related to existing or new hospital and clinic facilities because "only by utilizing a joint diagnostic and therapeutic equipment, and the teamwork of a group of physicians, can the maximum service of modern medical science in the cure and prevention of diseases, be made financially accessible to the mass of the community." Davis noted that only 23 percent of the physicians of Boston were on hospital or dispensary staffs, and that 15 percent of them did most of the work. Hospital care was available mainly to patients who could afford their "relatively high rates," and there existed a "separation between the rank and file of medical men and those who have access to the best diagnostic resources." [38] Health insurance should correct both faults.

The noted Boston physician Richard C. Cabot agreed that English and German health insurance were defective in their failure to *center their medical service around organized groups of physicians — that is, around hospitals.* The medical concept was primitive — "the doctor working alone, like a cobbler or a peddler, not in organized groups." Cabot paid tribute to the clinical arrangements made at the universities of California, Michigan, and Wisconsin. In these group settings, the interests of the salaried physician and patient were identical. There was no "financial temptation" to overmedicate as in private practice where the "more visits the patient makes, the better it is for the doctor." More important, private practice lacked comprehensiveness and quality controls, and was, therefore, "unnecessarily productive of wrong diagnoses and wrong treatments." Organized medical institutions, like the university clinics, hospitals, and Mayo Clinic, made good medicine possible through "group work, with proper division of labor and utilization of the resources of modern science." [39]

The medical profession remained adamantly opposed to health insurance proposals which would extend the principle of collective, prepaid service and lead to salaried arrangements, closed panels, or group practice. One difficulty, Rubinow suggested, was that the "psychology of the medical man has been adjusted to a speculative hope of exceptional success, a factor wholly absent in most other liberal and scientific professions, and one which frequently has an injurious effect upon the entire psychology of the profession and [the] attitude of the average physician to social problems." [40] His individualistic orientation made him hostile to any suggestion of cooperative medicine, despite its advantages in terms of cost and efficiency in an era of specialized, scientific medicine. [41]

The entrepreneurial mentality of the American medical profession presented one problem; a second was the abhorrence of contract practice under industrial or fraternal auspices. British physicians had seized upon health insurance, given certain safeguards, as an opportunity to liberate themselves from the oppressions of contract practice. American physicians viewed compulsory insurance as a scheme to universalize a contract system which had made only limited progress. The experience with workmen's compensation had shaped their attitude. It had crystallized and intensified their resistance to any deviation from solo, fee-for-service practice, and especially to any further extension of state insurance affecting the physician's status.

Most states authorized the agencies which administered workmen's compensation to fix or approve fees charged for medical work, and usually required the worker to accept the physician supplied by the employer or, more likely, the insurance company.[42] Physicians complained bitterly about the absence of free choice and exploitation by the insurance companies. In New York the Academy of Medicine noted that the minimum fee schedule prepared by the compensation authorities had been adopted as a maximum by the insurance companies, and that the "controversies arising from this difference of opinion caused so much trouble that the State Medical Society . . . since repudiated the fee schedule." The relation of the compensation law in Massachusetts to "medical men and medical problems" proved to be the "cause of most apparent friction in its administration." A Massachusetts Commission on Social Insurance reported that "some of the physicians frankly admitted that one of the reasons for their opposition to sickness insurance was that they had suffered a serious economic loss as a result of the passage of the Workmen's Compensation Act, and it was their belief that a similar loss would result from the passage of a health insurance bill." The Chicago and Illinois medical societies wanted "no new health insurance legislation . . . before we rectify the unfairness of the present compensation law." The social insurance committee of the American Medical Association observed that there was "no question but that the intense reaction in many states against sickness insurance or any further expansion of the social insurance laws in this country is due to the injustice and cold-blooded unfairness by which physicians and their patients have been treated under the workmen's compensation laws." Dr. Alexander Lambert, a president of the AMA who supported health insurance, agreed that much of the opposition of his colleagues was rooted in the compensation experience. And Rubinow observed that the fear of the consequences of health insurance legislation "upon the economic and social status of the medical profession," was based "to a very large extent upon the experience of medical practice under workmen's compensation." [43]

The Committee on Medical Economics of the New York State Medical Society prepared a detailed critique of compensation arrangements. It cited the lack of supervision, placing a "premium . . . on incompetent work." When injured workers used their own physician, fees were uncollectible if insurance companies refused to provide the money. The insurance companies' contract arrangements enabled physicians in some communities to monopolize the work, and farm out some of it. Generally, "it seems to be agreed that in the matter of handling their fee bills, physicians are subject to both indignity and injustice." [44]

Awareness of the medical profession's dissatisfaction with compensation medicine helped dictate the strategy of health insurance. "If the principle of free choice is guaranteed," Rubinow reflected, "and if insurance capital is definitely kept out of health insurance I think that a great deal will have been accomplished in gaining the enthusiastic support of the medical profession." [45] The strategy proved disastrous. Although willing to compromise with every other voluntary group, the sponsors of health insurance made no concession to the insurance companies; they would not be allowed to participate as carriers, and health insurance had to include a funeral benefit. The medical profession was not mollified, but the insurance companies became implacable foes. Powerful opposition from physicians and insurance companies was reinforced by employers, fraternals, influential segments of organized labor, and Christian Scientists (who played a prominent role in California). In retrospect, Rubinow conceded that American advocates of health insurance should have adopted Lloyd George's tactics and compromised with the insurance companies, at least on the funeral benefit. Their refusal to "make a similar deal" was "perhaps more than any other single cause responsible for the failure of the movement." In insisting upon a funeral benefit, the health insurance movement "signed its own death warrant." [46]

The support of a minority of the medical profession did little to modify the balance of power. It was composed of physicians less identified with entrepreneurial, solo practice: "public health officers, hospital officials, and the teaching force of the larger medical schools" as well as "physicians connected with industrial plants and in touch with conditions affecting the wage-worker." Salaried physicians, medical administrators, and health officials, however, held low status in the medical hierarchy. Their interests allegedly ran contrary to those of practicing physicians, who condemned health insurance as a scheme which would degrade their own status.[47]

As another effort "to exploit the profession by the community," health insurance was sure to "convert the practice of medicine into a vast kind of lodge practice (with all its evils), and is bound to result in incompetent medical service." The American disciples of Bismarck and Lloyd George were determined to make the medical profession an "adjunct of the State under political control instead of an independent vocation such as it has been up to the present time."[48] The economic and status fears of the physician were translated into a concern for high standards of service, and particularly the need to protect the physician — patient relationship. No legislation should be allowed to disturb the feeling of "confidence, trust and personal relationship between doctor and patient." Compulsory health insurance, which "carried with it some form of contract practice," would allow nonmedical agencies to "dictate the terms of . . . services, thus placing them on a purely commercial or business basis." The personal element, a "most important factor in the treatment of the sick," would be destroyed.[49] This line of reasoning ignored certain questions raised by advocates of health insurance. Could the poorer population afford a physician with whom to establish a personal relationship? Did such stress on the personal relationship make sense in an era of specialization, hospitals, and advancing medical science? Were high standards of medical practice so uniquely dependent upon one financing mechanism (fee-for-service) and one method of organization (entrepreneurial, solo practice)?

The health insurance campaigns in California and New York State, where the legislative prospects seemed most promising, provide a case study in the mobilization of political resources by voluntary institutions in a crisis situation. The California Social Insurance Commission, which in 1917 reported in favor of compulsory health insurance, proposed, as the first step, a constitutional amendment, which was placed before the electorate in November 1918.[50] A powerful alliance of Christian Scientists, insurance companies, and physicians launched a well-organized campaign which included a house-to-house canvass. The health insurance movement had the misfortune to coincide with America's involvement in World War I, and its opponents did not fail to emphasize the Germanic origins of the idea. They even charged that Berlin was financing the health insurance movement.[51]

The Christian Scientists operated through a California Research Society of Social Economics, which cooperated closely with insurance interests. (For example, the Society imported Frederick Hoffman of Prudential, an uncompromising foe of health insurance, to lecture.) Its secretary was C. D. Babcock, secretary of the Insurance Economics Society of America, a Detroit organization created to discredit health insurance. Both Babcock and the Society were later active in the New York League for Americanism.[52] Members of the Social Insurance Commission described the involvement of Christian Scientists as akin to a religious crusade.[53] According to the AALL, they were responsible for a "statewide campaign of misrepresentation, hardly ever equalled in legislative campaigns in this country." [54]

The opposition was strengthened by the indifference of Governor Stephens, who had succeeded Hiram Johnson.[55] The endorsement given by the State Board of Health failed to compensate for the frenzied attack launched by the physicians of California, organized in a League for the Conservation of Public Health.[56] The State Medical Society had advised them to make their viewpoint "as politically effective as possible," necessitating an expedient alliance with Christian Scientists and insurance companies.[57] The latter had not wasted any time. A special California bulletin had been published by the Insurance Economics Society. It carried the Kaiser's picture on the front cover, with the words: " 'Made in Germany,' Do you want it in California?" [58] But the doctors were cautioned that the insurance companies would remain "faithful friends and allies — most of you know how long. Just so long as the Legislature agrees to keep them out of the health insurance field. That was their attitude with industrial accident insurance." [59]

After the decisive defeat of the amendment in the California elections of November 1918, the struggle shifted to New York State. In 1916 and 1917 State Senator Ogden L. Mills had introduced a bill sponsored by the AALL. His successor, Courtlandt Nicoll, introduced another AALL-State Federation of Labor bill in 1918. Senator Davenport, a Republican, and Representative Donohue, Assembly Democratic leader, sponsored the legislation of 1919.[60] Supported by Governor Alfred E. Smith, the Davenport-Donohue bill of 1919 passed the Senate by a thirty to twenty vote based on a coalition of Democrats and progressive Republicans. It was then strangled in the Republican-controlled House Rules Committee, the graveyard of social legislation and domain of Speaker Sweet, a conservative upstate manufacturer.[61] Health insurance failed although its sponsors had made major concessions to every interested group except the insurance companies. It allowed for the establishment of panels to which every qualified physician could belong, thus preserving the right of free choice. At the behest of employers and the medical profession, farm and domestic workers, businesses with less than eight employees, and dependents of the insured were omitted. For the benefit of fraternals, the measure authorized the use of nonprofit carriers other than local mutuals.[62]

Around the medical–insurance axis, where opposition centered, hovered other groups such as druggists, fraternals, and employers. The druggist attacked health insurance as a scheme devised by a coalition of "teachers, socialists, sociologists, and reform workers," and a threat to his survival. It would deprive him of three-fourths of his business, compel him to contribute to the insurance of his employees, and increase his taxation. Those druggists who entered into contracts with local funds would find "prices screwed down to the limit." The whole idea was "European paternalism run mad," an expression of unadulterated socialism. It would "build up a political machine" and catapult the "State into the field now occupied by private enterprise." [63] Fraternal organizations were politically more potent than the druggists.

Local lodges disseminated literature to educate members about "the evils of the proposed law." Alice B. Locke of the Women's Benefit Association of the Macabees, dispatched as a lobbyist to New York State, proved "indefatigable in her efforts in opposition to this Bill." [64]

Employers condemned health insurance as un-American and inequitable, a further imposition on businessmen already over-laden with taxes. The unfair burden it imposed on employers would drive industry from the state. Health insurance, further-more, was opposed by "conservative leaders of organized labor"; the agitation had been created "artificially . . . by a skillful prop-aganda." Health progress should be achieved by prevention, and by the adoption of voluntary insurance programs in industry.[65]

Labor leaders critical of health insurance were influenced by the compensation experience and the development of industrial health examinations. Grant Hamilton, a member of the A.F. of L.'s Legislative Committee, maintained that "simultaneously with the advent of compensation laws came the introduction of systems of physical examinations." Businessmen, anxious to lower liability costs, were "insisting upon ever-increasing rigidity in physical examinations and excluding from employment those who show even nonessential defects." By a curious coincidence, "able-bodied, skilled workmen have been dismissed from employment at the recommendation of the company physicians who found in them the disease of unionism." This subterfuge would be per-fected through health insurance, and other controls probably im-posed by administrative agencies empowered to "approve socie-ties and also to withdraw approval at any time." [66]

Employers, insurance companies, and physicians frequently alluded to Gompers' opposition to health insurance, but they conveniently ignored the favorable attitude of the New York State Federation of Labor and other labor organizations.[67] Em-phasizing that few unions provided medical benefits, the Federa-tion attempted to convince workers of the advantages of the AALL-Federation bill. The worker would not have to use a physician supplied by the insurance company or employer, as in compensation. A cash and medical maternity benefit was included, as urged by the Women's Trade Union League and other labor organizations with female members. Private insurance companies would be excluded, and unable to "gain their profits at the expense of the workers." Industry, which had previously "escaped from its responsibility in the matter of sickness, will be made to pay its share." [68] To insure that merit rating would not lead, as in compensation, to medical examinations which deprived individuals of employment, any differentials would be based upon plant physical schedules. Most important, the worker, through health insurance, would be relieved of an enormous financial drain which sapped his income and morale. According to a member of the Federation's Executive Council, workers often saw no point in trying to accumulate savings: "Why should I save money? The moment I get about a hundred dollars together, the wife gets sick, the baby gets sick, or somebody else, and it's all wiped out." The physician was an incubus on the backs of the worker, most of whose savings went "in payment of fees to the medical profession." [69]

Labor's legislative influence paled in comparison to that of the physicians and insurance companies. From the introduction of the first health insurance bill in 1916, insurance agents were alerted to the menace. The Great Eastern Casualty Company distributed a circular warning its agents that the Mills bill was the entering wedge which would lead to "attempts to have such State Insurance of all kinds including Fire." It would mean "the end of all Insurance Companies and Agents and to you personally the complete wrecking of the business and connections you have spent a lifetime in building and the loss of your bread and butter." [70] C. D. Babcock of the Insurance Economics Society moved from California to New York in 1919, operating through the New York League for Americanism.[71] Around 1916 insurance companies began organizing state federations to oppose health insurance; these were linked through a national council.

John B. Andrews condemned Prudential and Metropolitan as the instigators of an "unprincipled campaign" and opportunists who presumably would reverse their position if allowed to participate as carriers and if the legislation would not interfere with their costly burial insurance.[72] Sponsors of health insurance criticized the companies for adopting a calculated policy of "playing upon the seemingly inherent prejudice of doctors against health insurance practice so that the doctors will fight the battle for them." [73] The tactics included the publication of tracts written by physicians. One of the bulletins of the New York League for Americanism contained an address by a Chicago physician. He explained that contract medicine established through health insurance would lead to the deterioration of public morals and the status of the profession: if "you are going to make the average medical man a mere drudge, robbing him of his independence, then overwork and underpay him, you are going to have a less and less efficient class of medical men." [74] The New York League for Americanism worked directly with medical groups in developing propaganda and political tactics. Andrews charged that an agent of the Aetna Life Insurance Company was "busy among the county medical societies" in an effort to organize medical guilds which included nurses, dentists, and pharmacists as well as physicians.[75]

Dr. James F. Rooney, an Albany physician and chairman of the Committee on Legislation of the New York State Medical Society, emerged as the chief political strategist for the medical profession. According to Andrews, "he was tricky, eloquent, and possessed of an undying ambition to ride into the office of President of the State Medical Society on his opposition to health insurance." [76] Rooney himself boasted that from the beginning of the agitation for health insurance, he had "set his face straightly against it, and . . . opposed it in season and out of season." [77]

Rooney represented the conservative medical and social opinion of upstate New York, where much of the opposition to health insurance centered.[78] Throughout the upstate area, medical groups organized and registered their opinion. The medical societies of Monroe, Schenectady, Albany, Erie, and Rensselaer counties, among others, opposed any compulsory health insurance. A Physicians' Protective Association in Buffalo fought the measure, and the agitation spread throughout the state.[79] By the end of 1919 the sponsors of health insurance had abandoned their earlier conviction that the medical profession would ultimately cooperate in the preparation of satisfactory legislation. After the AMA officially denounced health insurance in 1920, Dr. Alexander Lambert suggested that Andrews proceed without further consideration of the medical profession's opinion. Andrews agreed that it was "hopeless to try to bring the medical profession around to a reasonable consideration of the health insurance legislation. They, as a whole, are now opposed even to the study of the subject." [80]

Physicians of the Buffalo area, led by Dr. John H. Pryor, were exceptionally violent in their denunciations.[81] Frederic Almy, secretary of the Buffalo Charity Organization Society, dared not assist in the campaign because the issue was too controversial; his trustees and the new Catholic Bishop, among others, were opposed.[82] A congress of physicians from western New York threatened to refuse to practice medicine under compulsory health insurance. The doctors were addressed by Frederick Hoffman of Prudential, who cited the "ruinous state" of the doctors in England, and by Mark Daly, secretary of the New York State Manufacturers' Association, who emphasized the enormous cost and dangers of a political machine.[83]

A pamphlet published by the Professional Guild of Kings County, after the defeat of the Davenport-Donohue bill in the spring of 1919 warned that the legislation would be reintroduced in 1920, and advised physicians to make their will known. Health insurance was denounced as class legislation, which would harm its intended beneficiaries because it denied the "wage-earner the freedom of choice of who shall stand between him and his family and death when disease enters the home." It was also confiscatory because it penalized businessmen "for the benefit of political office-holders and paid professional philanthropists." Physicians and other health personnel would become "underpaid, discontented piece-workers in a trade with a 'MEDICAL OFFICER' as foreman in charge of each gang to minister to the health needs of 5,000 persons."

Health insurance would "break open the door of the home to the busy-body sociological investigators whose Benefactor-Foundations are part of the force which jammed the bill through the

Senate last March." The prime offender was the American Association for Labor Legislation, which was "MADE IN GERMANY" as part of the "Infamous Kultur and imported to this Country by a Russian disciple of Bolshevism and I WONT WORKISM." The Association's board of directors was composed of hysterical, "vicious," men and women who lacked sympathy and understanding of the workers. They were joined by "some groups of long-haired men and short-haired women with an 'URGE.' " These "PRO-GERMAN," "PRO-BOLSHEVIK," "PRO I.W.W." sponsors of health insurance were responsible "IN GREAT MEASURE FOR THE NEGRO RACE RIOTS AND THE INSOLENT ACTIVITY OF THE 'REDS' WHO THREATEN THE STABILITY OF AMERICAN INSTITUTIONS." If they had their way, the patient's trust in the physician — the foundation of good medical practice — would be undermined. "You are familiar," the Guild explained, "with the sense of security which the visit of the Doctor brings into the home. You are sick and fearsome of complications and results; your anxiety may have had your pulse racing and your fever exaggerated; the Doctor feels that pulse become steady and he knows and you know that it is the faith of a child in the dependability of the Doctor which is at work." [84]

The health insurance campaign of 1915–1920 was a complete disaster. It had one lasting, though wholly unintended, result. The medical profession emerged from the struggle with an awareness of its political power and a determination to use it to protect its corporate self-interest. This was equated with resistance to proposals for change in the financing and organization of medical services.

The medical profession viewed the issue as an apocalyptic struggle to preserve its autonomy and status. Health insurance meant the universalization of contract practice, and a loss of freedom (including the absolute right to determine fees and therefore the level of clientele served). American medicine thereafter would be an island of individualism tempered by charity. Even voluntary, prepaid insurance was resisted as an entering wedge for contract practice and more extreme collective programs. It was not until the 1930's, when confronted by the Depression, the economic plight of the private hospitals, and a new threat of a compulsory health program, that the medical profession officially endorsed voluntary health insurance.[85] It continued to resist compulsory insurance, even in the modified Medicare version limited to the aged and enacted in 1965.[86] Despite twentieth-century medical realities — specialization, hospital organization, higher levels of expectation, and costliness — the medical profession espoused a pre-twentieth-century attitude toward financing, organization, and the role of government. Consequently, successive waves of reformers would discover that progress was contingent, not upon the cooperation of the medical profession, but upon the power to overcome its obstructions. In medicine, as elsewhere, the prerogatives of voluntarism did not always prove compatible with the public interest.

# V  Mothers' Pensions and the Renaissance of Public Welfare

The social insurances were work-related, contributory programs. Labor-force participation was a condition of elegibility; benefits, as a result of the contributory feature, were considered a contractual right. Public assistance involved neither contributions nor labor-force participation; aid was contingent upon need as determined by a means test. The crucial difference between the two techniques of income-maintenance concerned the degree of administrative discretion which governed eligibility and benefits — minimal in social insurance, but paramount in public assistance.[1]

The social insurance movement, nonetheless, was identified with efforts to establish categorical assistance (pension) programs for dependent mothers and the aged. Both programs were committed to a transfer of welfare functions from the private to the public sector; and both challenged the prerogatives of voluntarism. Rubinow cited mothers' pensions as perhaps the best illustration of the "irresistible development of social insurance principles in the United States." It mattered little, he explained, that mothers' pensions had nothing to do with insurance and were influenced by "moral considerations" as much as "economic ones." Dependent motherhood was "distinctly recognized" as a problem of mass poverty which could not be relegated to "voluntary charity." [2]

The reaction of the insurance companies to monopoly state

funds in workmen's compensation, of physicians to compulsory health insurance, and of employers to unemployment insurance had a counterpart in the stand taken by private social work agencies against mothers' pensions. The new concept of public welfare and the role of government clashed with inherited ideology and institutions.

Public assistance in the United States had long been an object of contempt. As early as the 1820's, the Yates (New York) and Quincy (Massachusetts) reports criticized public outdoor relief as a source of dependency and pauperization. Like the famous English Poor Law Commission of 1834, American reformers demanded a punitive, limited public welfare system. Its major resource was the institution, and it concentrated upon two categories of dependency: the non-able-bodied poor, who required long-term custodial supervision, and the able-bodied who found work distasteful. The workhouse test would insure that the condition of able-bodied dependents would be inferior to that of the lowest-paid, but independent, laborer. Outdoor relief would be the responsibility of voluntary agencies, whose character-building influences would prevent it from degenerating into a dole. Thus safeguarded, charitable relief would not undermine the incentives and sanctions which sustained the economic order.

In England and the United States, the charity organization movement of the late nineteenth century reaffirmed the "principles of 1834." American charity organization achieved considerable success in discrediting public welfare and inducing counties or municipalities to abolish outdoor relief.[3] Its leaders condemned public assistance as incompatible with biological and economic law as well as social stability. Only voluntary philanthropy, which combined relief with careful investigation and diagnosis of each case, could prevent widespread pauperization of the working population.

Public relief was condemned as superfluous. Private agencies could satisfy all relief needs if the state withdrew, and ceased to levy taxes which competed with fund-raising efforts. Public relief was not only unnecessary, it was inordinately expensive and a source of graft and corruption. Government officials could afford to be generous with other people's money! Public relief was expensive, too, because it created more poverty than it relieved. Tax money, withdrawn from productive capital and the nation's wage-fund, was transferred to those who, "working by the side of unsubsidized labor, can and will take work at lower rates, and compel the entire class to accept the lower rates." [4]

Public relief fostered political and social instability. Implicit in the poor law was the collectivist dogma, "To every man according to his needs," which nurtured "communistic doctrines and sentiments and impulses." Ultimately, the state aroused bitterness and hostility through its thoughtless generosity. Those accustomed to relief degenerated into permanent paupers, and, because the state could never satisfy all the expectations it aroused, the frustrated pauper became a "public enemy" and foe of order.[5] Public relief exaggerated the difference between rich and poor by making "the only bond between the prosperous and the broken that of the officials who dole relief from a treasury." The private charity visitor who visited the poor in their homes, created a "personal tie of humanity." [6] It was better to deal with poverty directly than through the intermediary of a public bureaucracy. Voluntarism served as an important liaison between individuals and classes, and this contribution was more important than any money dole.

Perhaps the most ominous connotation of public relief was the prospect of racial decay. Individual ambition and independance were "born only of energy and effort . . . and whosoever and whatsoever remove these working and invigorating factors of daily life from the man enervate him and injure him." The greatest incentive to labor was animal necessity, but the pauper, "learning that there is a fund for his support, basks in the sunshine of constant expectation, neither toiling nor spinning." Although improvement of the human race depended upon breeding from the higher to the lower classes, public relief sustained the degenerate types who brought into the world a "race of dependents, physically, morally, and mentally deficient." [7]

From the viewpoint of the private charities, there was a "clear and easy division of the field — the public authorities to maintain the public institutions and the private societies to give the family relief." [8] Their self-confidence and assertiveness in the early twentieth century were reinforced by a quest for professional skills and status.[9] In contrast to the mechanical dole provided by public officials, the trained social workers of the voluntary agencies presumably were developing scientific casework skills to help in the permanent rehabilitation of dependent individuals or families.

In the mothers' pensions movement private social workers confronted a dramatic, crusading effort to upgrade the status of public welfare. The clash between the voluntary agencies and the advocates of mothers' pensions was among the bitterest ever to arise in American philanthropy. The pension crusade had roots in the broader reform movement of the progressive era, with its awareness of the environmental origins of poverty and the necessity for state intervention to insure social and economic justice. Mothers' pensions also had roots in the organized social insurance movement, which embodied the principle of public income guarantees. Child welfare experts by the early twentieth century stressed the superiority of home life rather than institutional commitment for the normal child. And mothers' pensions emerged simultaneously with the Board of Public Welfare (BPW) idea, which attempted to discredit the philanthropic division of labor proposed by voluntary agencies and redefine the governmental welfare function in an industrial-urban society.

The BPW originated in Kansas City, whose common council in 1908 established a Board of Pardons and Parole on behalf of workhouse inmates. The next year it assumed responsibility for administering the workhouse. In 1910 its functions were vastly enlarged to include the "duties of the city toward all the poor, the delinquent, the unemployed, the deserted and unfortunate classes in the community, and to supervise the private agencies which solicited money from the public for these purposes." [10] Within a few years other cities, including Chicago,

Cleveland, Cincinnati, Dayton, Grand Rapids, St. Joseph, St. Louis, Dallas, and Omaha, established similar agencies. The BPW idea was identified with L. A. Halbert, who became general superintendent of the Kansas City Board, and with Rev. Theodore Hanson of Kansas City. Hanson was instrumental in the formation of the National Public Welfare League in 1916.[11]

The BPW was an effort to unify "all of those municipal activities which attempt to ameliorate distress, prevent injustice, improve the environment, or administer treatment to deliquent persons."[12] The departments established under the pioneer Kansas City Board included a Municipal Farm, for delinquent males; Women's Reformatory; Paroles; Legal Aid; Factory Inspection and Labor Statistics; Research; Censorship and Recreation; Loans; Homes and Unemployed; and a School of Social Service.[13] To its advocates the BPW was a revolt against a limited, negative conception of public welfare. Through centralization, efficiency attained through scientific research and use of trained personnel, and efforts to prevent dependency, the BPW would redress the balance of power and prestige between the public and private sectors.

The BPW innovations grew out of the widespread realization that poverty was often attributable to social inequities rather than personal defects. If the causes of poverty were "largely social, society or the community should assume the function and bear the burden of cure and prevention." Relief became an "expression of public justice rather than of private charity." The assumption that only voluntary agencies could dispense relief ignored the possibility that standards of public administration could be raised. In their sectarian exclusiveness, private agencies failed to understand that it was "more consistent with democratic principles that the poor should seek assistance from the city government than from philanthropy supported by the rich." An era sensitive to the "inequalities and iniquities" which produced dependency demanded that "public social needs should be met by the democracy, that is, by the people in their corporate capacity." City government was the only agency through which the "collective will . . . can find its full expression."[14]

Practically speaking, voluntary agencies lacked the resources to cope with mass dependency; they could not compete with the municipality in its capacity to mobilize the "tremendous financial, intellectual and organizing strength of the entire community." They strained unsuccessfully to cope with the entire range of dependency, while a "few charitably disposed people in any given community bear the entire cost." [15] Those seeking a redefinition of the public welfare function recognized that many charges of past incompetence and prodigality were valid. The BPW idea was associated with efforts to professionalize the public welfare sector. By means of the "new type of trained professional social workers, by means of sociological research, and by using the books which set forth the findings of social science, the Board of Public Welfare aims to achieve scientific social action." [16] Professionalization (combined with the expansion and centralization of welfare functions) would enable public agencies to engage in preventive social work, and "effectively control the conditions of living and remove the causes of misery." Instead of the traditional custodial, deterrent role, the public agency would help create the "reasonably good environment in which to . . . live and . . . work and . . . play." [17]

Both the BPW and mothers' pension movements were committed to expanded governmental welfare functions. In the case of mothers' pensions, however, the conflict between the voluntary inheritance and the new conception of the public welfare role was much fiercer and widely publicized for it introduced an emotional dimension centering on the image of the dependent mother and child.

Beginning in the 1860's and 1870's, states launched vigorous efforts to remove children from mixed almshouses. Four general systems of public child care developed. Michigan, Minnesota, Wisconsin, and several other states adopted a "state school" and placing-out program. Ohio, Connecticut, and Indiana favored the establishment of county children's homes. New York, California, Maryland, and other states provided for the support of children in private institutions. Massachusetts and New Jersey developed a public placing- or boarding-out program which in Pennsylvania operated through a private agency — the Children's Aid Society. By 1900 the maintenance of children in mixed institutions had been discredited, and progress had been made under public and private auspices in substituting foster-care for asylums.

The revolt against institutions was identified with the Children's Aid societies. They had long stressed the superiority of foster care, believing that the best institution was inferior to a home or family environment for the rearing of normal children. Institutional life was artificial; it did not equip the child to assume his adult responsibilities, and was incompatible with differential child care. The ideal of differential child care, which helped discredit the institutional commitment of normal children, was nurtured in the early twentieth century by two other developments. One was the juvenile court which, as established in Chicago in 1899, combined probation, separate hearings, and the use of special judges in dealing with youthful offenders. The second was the emergence of child guidance. Here again Chicago pioneered through the establishment in 1909 of the Juvenile Psychopathic Institute, headed by Dr. William Healy. Linked to the Juvenile Court, the Institute provided expert diagnosis of the mental and physical condition of delinquents.[18]

The mothers' pensions movement combined the two nuclear, closely related principles of progressive child care: individualization, and the superiority of the home to the institution. An important stimulus to the pension campaign came from the 1909 Conference on the Care of Dependent Children, called by President Theodore Roosevelt. This Conference was the outgrowth of a "child rescue" crusade launched by the *Delineator*, a magazine edited by Theodore Dreiser from 1907-1909, in which case histories of dependent children offered for adoption by social agencies were published each month.[19] James E. West, a lawyer who later became executive director of the Boy Scouts, joined Dreiser in 1908, and brought the work of the newly organized Child Rescue League to the attention of President Roosevelt.[20]

The Conference recommendations, embodying the most advanced child welfare principles of the time, became the commandments of the mothers' pensions movement. The pivotal, first recommendation was also one of the most famous policy declarations in the history of American social welfare:

"Home life is the highest and finest product of civilization. It is the great molding force of mind and of character. Children should not be deprived of it except for urgent and compelling reasons. Children of parents of worthy character, suffering from temporary misfortune and children of reasonably efficient and deserving mothers who are without the support of the normal breadwinner, should, as a rule, be kept with their parents, such aid being given as may be necessary to maintain suitable homes for the rearing of the children. . . . Except in unusual circumstances, the home should not be broken up for reasons of poverty, but only for considerations of inefficiency or immorality." [21]

President Roosevelt agreed that "poverty alone should not disrupt the home." [22] Significantly, the Conference suggested that aid should preferably take the form of private charity. As of 1909 the voluntary agencies still retained sufficient power to commit the Conference to a limited public role. [23]

The Conference urged that normal children who had no homes, or had to be removed from them, "should be cared for in families whenever practicable. The carefully selected foster home is for the normal child the best substitute for the natural home." Placement had to be on an individualized basis, the homes "selected by a most careful process of investigation." If children had to be temporarily or permanently placed in institutions, then "these institutions should be conducted on the cottage plan, in order that routine and impersonal care may not unduly suppress individuality and initiative." In order to permit "effective personal relations between the adult caretaker or caretakers of each cottage and each child therein," a limit of twenty-five children was suggested for each cottage unit. [24]

Favored by the recommendations of the White House Conference, the emergence of the organized social insurance and BPW movements, and the emphasis upon the social origins of poverty in the early twentieth century, mothers' pensions legislation swept across the nation after 1911. There had been some earlier experiments. Following the San Francisco earthquake of 1906, the juvenile courts of a few California counties authorized assistance for the care of children in their own homes. An Oklahoma measure of 1908 permitted counties to provide "school scholarships" (upon recommendation of school authorities) to children of widows. Michigan enacted similar legislation in 1911. The first unambiguous mothers' aid legislation was enacted by Missouri in 1911, but it applied only to Jackson County (Kansas City) and, later in the year, to St. Louis. The juvenile court administered the law. Milwaukee County in 1912 also adopted a resolution authorizing mothers' aid through the juvenile court.[25] Under voluntary auspices a Widowed Mothers' Fund Association, established in New York City in 1908, provided regular allotments to dependent mothers who might otherwise have been forced to commit children for reasons of poverty. The organizers of the Fund believed that voluntary agencies, despite lip-service to the ideal of family integrity, were breaking up families because they lacked the financial resources to provide long-term, adequate assistance.[26]

In 1911, Illinois enacted the first statewide measure; it was followed by Colorado and Iowa in 1912, and sixteen more states in 1913. Widowed mothers were eligible for assistance in all these states, but in some eligibility was extended to dependent mothers whose husbands had deserted, or were divorced, imprisoned, confined to a mental institution, or permanently disabled. With few exceptions, assistance was limited to children up to fourteen or sixteen years of age. The maximum allowance for the first child was from $6.25 to $15; it usually was reduced for additional children. Thirty-nine states had enacted mothers' pensions legislation by 1919, but it represented no significant departure from the old poor-law tradition of local administration and financing. In the majority of states the juvenile court (or its county equivalent) or the county commissioners administered the measure. Financial aid in some form was provided by approximately 25 percent of the states. State supervision was minimal.[27]

The mothers' pensions movement was strengthened by the support of the juvenile courts and women's organizations. Juvenile court judges had been dismayed because they were forced to remove children from homes when mothers could not earn a living or because the working mother could not supervise children who subsequently embarked upon delinquent careers.[28] E. E. Porterfield, judge of the Kansas City Juvenile Court, was in great part responsible for the Missouri legislation of 1911.[29] Disturbed by the frequency with which children of working, widowed mothers were hauled into court charged with criminal offences, Porterfield went before the Missouri legislature to plead for help from the state. A child, he argued, "should never be taken away from a good mother. If the poverty of the mother forces her to neglect her child the poverty should be removed and not the child. A good mother can rear her children better than the best institution. A mediocre home is better than any institution." [30]

The pioneer Illinois law was closely identified with Merritt W. Pinckney, judge of the Chicago Juvenile Court. Like Porterfield, Pinckney interpreted the problem of dependent mothers in terms of preservation of the home. Always, he observed, "my chief endeavor has been to keep the home intact and when this was impossible . . . I have sought to substitute another family fireside and the maternal love and care of some other good woman." [31] In Colorado, the Denver Juvenile Court, headed by Judge Lindsey, played a leading role in the enactment of pension legislation.[32]

Women active in charitable and club work were outstanding publicists of mothers' pensions. In Tennessee an alliance of the "W.C.T.U., the women's clubs and the Parent-Teachers' Association" was responsible for the 1915 legislation.[33] A prime mover in Massachusetts was Clara Cahill Park, who served as secretary of the State investigating commission appointed in 1912.[34] She had developed a personal interest in the problems of women who "have to try to be both father and mother," and discovered that others shared her concern when she attended the National Congress of Mothers in 1911. Missouri recently had set "an example of active and practical legislation," and she urged the Congress of Mothers to unite on one principle: "that families should not be separated for poverty alone." Mrs. Park exhibited the romantic,

if not fanatic, idealization of motherhood and home which pervaded the mothers' pensions movement. To remove children from
a mother, "is like taking away her life, for the connection is so
close and subtle." [35]

The Mothers' Pension League of Allegheny County (Pennsylvania) was organized in 1913, through the "advocacy of this
movement by an excellent group of young women." [36] And in
New York State the most vocal, uncompromising apostles of
mothers' pensions included Sophie Irene Loeb and Hannah Einstein. Both were vituperative critics of New York City's private
social agencies such as the New York Charity Organization Society (COS) and Russell Sage Foundation, among the most
powerful and influential in the nation.[37] Their defeat in 1915, by
the enactment of the New York State Child Welfare Law, was a
watershed in the history of American social welfare. The doctrine
that voluntary welfare institutions should serve as the community's chief relief resource was successfully challenged.


Attempts before 1915 to institute a system of state aid to
dependent mothers had been thwarted by the COS and other
private agencies. As early as 1897 a bill authorizing the New
York City Commissioner of Charities to place children in the cus-
tody of their mothers and provide an allowance equal to the
amount otherwise allowed for institutional care had passed the
legislature; but it was vetoed by the Mayor at the urging of the
private charities.[38] The general secretary of the COS spoke out
against a similar bill before the Senate Cities Committee in 1899.
This effort to reestablish public outdoor relief in New York City
under the guise of a pension for widows differed only in name
from ordinary public assistance, which was "mechanical and arbi-
trary," and a source of "demoralization." Charity which originated
in the public treasury seemed to multiply the number of those
"who think they have a claim on it which they will urge more
strongly than if it comes from private sources." Homer Folks of
the State Charities Aid Association agreed that "out-door relief
to families at their homes . . . is harmful to the poor." Children

would "grow up accustomed to the idea that they are depending upon it. It takes the life of independence out of them." [39] The Committee failed to report the measure.

Beginning in 1911, mothers' assistance bills were introduced into every session of the legislature, where they were consistently opposed by private agencies. The vanguard of the opposition centered in New York City. Mary Richmond, director of the Charity Organization Department of the Russell Sage Foundation and the leading casework theorist of the time, directed attention to one major source of controversy—whether mothers' pensions differed in nature from public outdoor relief. Their advocates defended them as an obligation of the state and a mother's right. The family was the "*fundamental* social institution" and the mother who reared healthy, responsible citizens was a benefactor of the state who performed a public service. Miss Richmond's interpretation differed. Along with Edward T. Devine, secretary of the COS, she insisted that the "mixture and confusion of the two ideas of service pensions and relief grants will make nothing but trouble. It is a confusion that has cost our country dear already." Despite the fact that "three-fourths of the soldiers of the Civil War are in their graves," soldiers' pensions were costing more than they ever had.[40] Mothers' pensions, soldiers' pensions, and public outdoor relief created special interest groups which worked tirelessly to exploit the public treasury.

In the final analysis it made little difference whether mothers' pensions were defended as a right in return for a service or condemned as a dole. The practical issue concerned community relief policy, and who would control it. Would voluntary agencies retain their hegemony or would mothers' pensions become the instrument through which the public welfare sector transcended the limited and negative function it had been assigned in the nineteenth century? Were public agencies capable of anything more than a mechanical dole which acted as a stimulus to pauperization? Referring to the plight of dependent mothers, Miss Richmond argued that "if individualized care is not necessary at this point, if 'casework' has no place, then we are confronted here with the solitary exception in the whole range of social endeavor." [41]

The COS asserted that the "administration of relief within the homes of the poor is the peculiar function of private philanthropy." This "delicate" ministry required "deep, abiding, personal and sympathetic interest" in sharp contrast to the "mechanical, indiscriminate, wasteful, unconstructive and harmful" procedures of public agencies; the latter, taking account simply of material needs, "fostered that degradation of character manifested in pauperism." [42] Private social work, having emerged in the nineteenth century to reinforce rather than challenge the imperatives of the American work culture, seemed to view money as the commodity least needed by the poor.[43] The services provided by voluntary social agencies were more important than money; they reduced class barriers and uplifted character. "If the duty of helping their less fortunate neighbors were taken off the shoulders of those who are able to help by having the city or State assume that burden, much of the neighborly intercourse between the poorer and the richer would cease. Public outdoor relief makes for a class separation and the enmity of classes. Private charity makes for the brotherhood of men." [44]

Mothers' pensions were the most dangerous proposals affecting the philanthropic division of labor. They possessed a powerful "sentimental appeal" which threatened to become an "entering wedge towards State socialism." As interpreted by Otto T. Bannard, vice-president of the COS, the "battle cry" of the widowed mothers was "not alms, but their right to share. The subsequent steps are old age pensions, free food, clothing and coal to the unemployed and the right to be given work." Such an attitude breeds "candidates for alms, multiplies upon itself, represses the desire for self-help, self-respect and independence and inflicts upon its beneficiaries what is termed in England the government stroke of paralysis. It is not American; it is not virile." [45]

Defenders of the philanthropic status quo were vulnerable on two crucial points. Few defended the past performance of public relief agencies, but leaders of private agencies could convince no one but themselves that the public welfare sector was incapable of being improved. Their position was even less defensible because mothers' pensions advocates had committed themselves to a constructive casework program similar to that of the private agencies. The attitude of the private agencies seemed negative, selfish, and rooted in the absurd proposition that the public sector had no capacity for change.

Private social agencies were equally vulnerable to the charge of ineffectuality. They agreed, no less than the sponsors of mothers' pensions, that children should not be separated from their mothers for reasons of poverty alone; yet their ideological rigidities forced them into the position of opposing public assistance, even though they themselves lacked the resources to prevent such separations.

The opposition of the private charities to mothers' pensions proved costly. Rarely before had the prestigious voluntary societies been subjected to such condemnation and humiliation. "I think," Lee K. Frankel reported, "no more serious situation has confronted us in the last few years than the attack upon private charitable institutions in New York City during the time the passage of the Child Welfare Law was being considered. It has hurt many of them immeasurably; it has made it impossible for many of them to continue their standards of efficiency." [46] A Buffalo social worker complained that the mothers' pension controversy was inciting violent criticism everywhere of all private charities.[47] Hannah Einstein described the treatment of the widowed mother by private charities as "one of the blackest pages in the history of philanthropic endeavor." She declared her astonishment over the "nature of the objections raised by various representatives of private charity societies, who stand in awe of the bugbear of public outdoor relief." Founder of the Widowed Mothers' Fund Association, she lashed out at the "bureaucrats of philanthropy" who dared defend asylum care for a child in preference to the "care and love of its own mother." Breaking up families because of poverty was not only a tragedy but a crime," a *gross criminal act* perpetrated by private organizations every *working day* in the year." Lacking sufficient funds themselves, but opposing mothers' pensions, they created a *"monstrous"* impasse leading to the institutional commitment of children "because the mother cannot pay the rent or doctor's bill." [48]

The sponsors of mothers' pensions persuaded the legislature to appoint a Commission on Relief for Widowed Mothers in 1913.[49] It reported favorably on a pension bill, prepared a merciless indictment of the private charities, and offered five "fundamentally true" propositions: (1) the mother was the "best guardian of her children"; (2) no mother could be both "home-maker and the bread-winner of her family"; (3) preventive social work had to deal with the child and the home; (4) since "normal family life" was the "foundation of the state . . . its conservation is an inherent duty of government"; (5) poverty was "too big a problem for private philanthropy." [50]

The Commission hammered relentlessly on the two points where the private charities were most vulnerable. The experience of other states had demonstrated that "public officials can be found who can administer such assistance as wisely and as sympathetically as can private social workers." Social work executives like Edward T. Devine of the COS had long preached the doctrine of constructive family casework; now he and others "should give the public credit for understanding and appreciating it and being willing to adapt it to their own work." The COS and Brooklyn Bureau of Charities were singled out as prime offenders against the interests of dependent mothers and, therefore, the community itself. These agencies had "refused to cooperate with this Commission in the course of this investigation, and preferred, apparently, to confuse the issue with personal bickerings and evasions than to join in a fair and impartial examination of the facts." The social workers who "dominate the New York School of Philanthropy and the Russell Sage Foundation" were no less culpable.[51]

By the pragmatic test, the private charities had failed in their responsibility to the dependent mother and child. The Commission claimed that 2716 children were institutionalized in New York State because of destitution alone; another 933 children had been committed because of the mother's illness, "resulting often from overwork and overworry that might easily have been prevented." [52] Richard Neustadt, secretary of the Commission and assistant headworker of University Settlement, dealt at length with the broad issue of the relation between the public and voluntary welfare sectors raised by the pension controversy. He suggested that private charities performed their most useful service in developing "newer and better standards and methods for the government to undertake." It was not, and should never have been, the "function of private charity to supplant that of the government." The voluntary sector lacked the funds and could not, "in the future, raise the funds to give adequate relief in the home, nor to administer such funds in the efficient, wise and sympathetic manner which it has itself set up as the ideal." [53]

When private agencies presumed to usurp responsibilities which properly belonged to government, as in the case of dependent mothers, the results were disastrous. The break-up of families because of poverty was a "crime." Such an outrage was possible because the public had been "blind — blinded even by some of those very individuals who have undertaken its philanthropic work." If private agencies lacked sufficient funds, the general public was partially to blame, but, "where the societies or their executives have maintained that their funds are adequate, and have defeated any attempt to have the government step in to perform this work, they and they alone are guilty of this social crime." Private agencies which espoused ideals of adequate relief but could not provide it themselves had no right to "oppose further the adoption of a properly protected and wisely drawn system of public aid." [54]

The mothers' pensions movement was a liberating, innovating force in American social welfare. It questioned the conventional wisdom which delegated to voluntary institutions the main responsibility for social action. Whatever the validity of this public-private dichotomy in the past, changes in the economic and family system by the twentieth century required greater government intervention. The individual's survival was contingent upon uninterrupted earnings. Yet because of sickness, forced unemployment, and other hazards he could not always participate in the labor force. His vulnerability required the establishment of mechanisms which assured income flow in the event of a decline in his earning capacity. Income maintenance was especially necessary because industrialization and urbanization had undermined the capacity of the family to act as a buffer. The economic and familial structure of the twentieth century left the mother with dependent children uniquely helpless, and required state intervention to keep the family intact.

The advocates of social insurance and mothers' pensions challenged the assumption that economic assistance was a marginal social work function. The New York State Commission charged that, until recently, the private charities "held as a fundamental principle that financial aid was a very minor, if not a negligible, element of family rehabilitation." Geared to problems of character and personality defect, the American social work system did not "appreciate the economic basis of poverty," implausible as this sounded. Fearing economic assistance, or unable to provide it, voluntary agencies made excessive demands upon the family itself, upon neighbors or relatives, or the individual visitor assigned to the applicant by the agency.[55]

Although advocates of mothers' pensions emphasized high standards of economic assistance, they did not question the claim of voluntary agencies that family "rehabilitation" was the real objective. They did not seek to discredit this principle, but rather the corollary that public agencies could not perform the task. They favored enlarging the government welfare function, but did not defend economic assistance in a wage-centered economy as an end in itself and the prime responsibility of the public welfare sector. On the contrary, they equated the prestige and respectability of public assistance with the socialization and casework functions idealized by the voluntary sector.

The public agency "caring for the poor in their own homes" had to "secure for its applicants whatever treatment is needed for their disabilities and for the conservation and development of their own powers of self-maintenance." Economic assistance had to be dispensed as one element in a broader plan of "social treatment." Dependency frequently arose from "the unwise use of resources," originating in "ignorance, from a wrong set of values, from shiftlessness or from a broken spirit. Whatever the cause, successful treatment of such families must include the "re-education of habit and emphasis upon right standards — through personal influence." [56]

The explicit model was the private casework agency. Helen G. Tyson, supervisor of the Mothers' Assistance Fund of Pennsylvania, maintained that "in many ways the fatherless family offers the ideal group for a demonstration of the value of social case treatment." Hopefully, the mothers' pension experiment would ultimately produce a "superior piece of public relief machinery . . . embodying all the principles of case diagnosis and treatment that have been worked out so carefully by the private agencies in the past." [57] Gertrude Vaile, of the Denver Department of Social Welfare, conceded that private charities in the past had "been justified in their distrust of public relief." But with mothers' pensions an effort was being made to "do real social service, seeking to understand and permanently improve the conditions of people in want." Denver was striving to transform the "old archaic county agent office for doles of coal and groceries into a real department of social service along the lines of the charity organization society." [58]

The failure to defend economic assistance as an end in itself had unfortunate consequences. It compromised any claim that the pension was a right, and substituted behavioral for economic criteria in determining eligibility. Behavioral supervision of the dependent family was justified if economic assistance was incidental to social treatment. Yet sponsors of mothers' pensions originally had argued that the problems of the dependent mother originated in poverty arising from the loss of the breadwinner. An uneasy balance of economic and vague moral criteria complicated the administration of this legislation.

The New York City Board of Child Welfare, to take one example, placed great emphasis upon its advisory and counseling services.[59] The law required the visit of a Board representative to each pension recipient at least once every three months. Although the visits were presumably "not made in the spirit of detection," the condition of the home was "always noted." As far as the Board was concerned, its work brought a sense of security to troubled clients, who could depend not only upon regular financial assistance but help and advice "at all times in matters relating to the welfare of the home and the children." [60]

The Board's regulations for the guidance of field investigators left ample scope for refusal or termination of an allowance in the event of misconduct. The sense of security was questionable when vague moralistic imperatives competed with objective economic needs. Under the guise of "social treatment," an effort was made to impose community behavioral norms as interpreted by the agency. Acquiescence in these, as much as objective economic need, might determine the right to a pension. Thus, the New York Board would not grant or continue a pension if the mother was "mentally, morally and physically" unable to care for the children; if she exhibited a "record of intemperance, wastefulness, or of misconduct"; if the "presence and behavior of lodgers are such as to bring the widow into disrepute"; if the "home and the children are not kept clean and orderly, or are otherwise neglected, or where the children are unnecessarily kept from school or from work." [61] On occasion a mothers' pension agency led clients to understand that church attendance and activity were viewed with favor.[62]

The effort to combine relief and "social treatment" in a single public agency intensified the defects arising from local administration of the laws. Frustration and disappointment resulted when skimpy local appropriations made neither adequate assistance nor casework services possible. After nearly two decades of experience, mothers' pensions laws offered the "most obvious evidence of the seriousness of placing laws on the statute books but failing to make them practically effective through adequate appropriation and proper administration." [63]

The evolution of mothers' pensions in Illinois exposed the "evils . . . inseparable from irresponsible local administration. That a great public relief experiment could be safely left to 102 different local authorities . . . without any centralized supervision or control was inconceivable." Mothers' pensions, because of this fatal blunder, marked an administrative retrogression; the legislation copied the "old pauper law with its principle of local responsibility rather than the new principle of State control, which has been adopted for the care of the insane and of other special groups." [64] The spirit of the poor laws exerted a controlling influence under the guise of "social treatment." Application for a pension was presumptive evidence of an inadequacy which differentiated the family from the community mainstream and justified intervention in the client's personal life. Mothers' pensions eliminated neither the means test nor the wide administrative discretion characteristic of ordinary poor relief.

In Illinois, after a decade of operation, there was "marked unevenness of administration, few qualified officers . . . available for supervision, and inequality in the amounts of the pensions." Not one of the 102 counties provided "adequate funds for pensions or for the necessary investigations and supervision." [65] The law in some downstate counties was nullified by county court judges who refused to grant pensions, or by county supervisors who failed to appropriate funds. Even in Cook County hundreds of mothers suffered because the county refused to authorize larger appropriations. In New York the amount of economic assistance was described as "one of the darkest aspects of pension administration." [66] And in Pennsylvania the state supervisor complained that because of insufficient funds less than 50 percent of eligible mothers were being assisted. Only a few Pennsylvania county boards employed trained social workers.[67]


The mothers' pension movement had successfully challenged the philanthropic division of labor which attributed to public agencies a marginal, negative function, and removed some of the stigma attached to public outdoor assistance. But it failed in the opportunity presented to modernize the public welfare system. Local administration perpetuated the Elizabeth poor-law tradition which had been imported to the colonies in the seventeenth century; the willingness and ability of local jurisdictions to pay, rather than need, determined the substance of the program. Equally important, the sponsors of mothers' pensions adopted the private charity organization society as the model for a public assistance program. This meant, essentially, adoption of casework goals aimed at family rehabilitation. The first major categorical assistance program in the United States proved apologetic about its economic responsibilities. The legacy of mothers' pensions was the evolution of a public welfare sector which failed to defend economic assistance as a legitimate, constructive end in itself. The nuclear social insurance principle — predictable, semi-automatic income guarantees in the event of exposure to a specified risk — was compromised and the public sector burdened with the dual functions of economic assistance and socialization.

A major source of conflict and tension in the subsequent evolution of the American public assistance system has been this tendency for behavioral considerations to compete with problems of objective economic need. The result (especially in the Aid to Dependent Children program) is frequently a combination of inadequate assistance and harassment of the recipient. The fact of dependency is sufficient justification for such policies; it is evidence of personal inadequacy if not pathology. Latter-day resentments against public welfare recipients crystallized in the summer of 1961 when City Manager Joseph McD. Mitchell of Newburgh, New York launched his memorable crusade against "welfare chiselers." The thirteen-point program adopted by the city council had a single objective — to make relief as unpalatable as possible. The whole episode testified to the viability of the classic nineteenth-century principle of "less eligibility" in contemporary welfare programs. If sufficient indignities could be associated with relief, then potential applicants might adopt any expedient (even work) in preference to public assistance.[68] It is clearer now than it was in the early twentieth century, or the 1930's, that any effort to combine economic and behavioral objectives in a single welfare program is hazardous. Abuses are inevitable when eligibility and benefits are dependent upon administrative discretion in the context of local community mores and pressures.

# VI  The Aged and the State

After a decade of strenuous activity, the American social insurance movement faltered. Workmen's compensation and mothers' pensions had proven disappointing. Economic benefits were low; state and local control produced an administrative diversity at odds with ideals of rationalization. Little had been accomplished in the prevention or insurance of unemployment, and health insurance had been a frustrating, devastating failure. John B. Andrews lost interest in social insurance. The period was "too reactionary . . . and energies are naturally turned in other directions for the present." [1] Leifur Magnusson of the International Labor Office described the social insurance field in the United States as "practically untouched, irrelevant and meaningless; a mirage in a sunlight sea of prosperity." [2]

There was a sharp contrast between European progress in the postwar period and American inertness, but the social insurance movement was not so defunct as Magnusson feared.[3] Throughout the 1920's, it persisted as an issue in American social politics, generating conflict as it challenged voluntary institutions. The older leadership — Andrews, Rubinow, and the AALL — was reinforced (if not superseded) by new individuals and organizations: Abraham Epstein, Paul Douglas, Eveline Burns, the American Association for Old Age Security, and the Fraternal Order of Eagles. The bitter health insurance campaign had convinced Commons and Andrews that the less identification with Europe, the better the prospects for social insurance. "I think it is a mistake," Andrews explained, "for us in this country to spend an undue amount of time discussing the British or any other system of European unemployment insurance. I think we can much more wisely build out of our own American experiences with accident insurance a practical unemployment compensation system with much better prospects of enactment here." [4] As formulated in the 1920's, the American plan of Commons and Andrews implied a social insurance mechanism geared to prevention rather than income maintenance; it implied limited economic and social objectives. By the early 1930's an internal conflict, centering on unemployment compensation policy, erupted between the advocates of the American plan and those who believed with Rubinow and Epstein that income maintenance and redistribution were the primary goals.

Along with changes in leadership and the self-conscious declaration of independence from Europe, the 1920's witnessed the emergence of the aged as a key issue in social politics. The drive for old-age pensions was a connecting link between the first social insurance movement and that launched after the onset of the Great Depression.

Stimulating awareness of the special problems of the aged, and their elevation from a marginal to a central status in the social insurance movement, were demographic realities. The aged, as a percentage of the total population, had been increasing since the mid-nineteenth century. It is estimated that the aged (65 or over) constituted 2.1 percent of the population in 1850, rising to 4.07 by 1900, 4.30 by 1910, and 5.67 by 1920. This rate of increase was greater for each decade between 1900 and 1930 than the national increase, or the population under 65 (with the sharpest rate of increase, 3.01, registered between 1920 and 1930). Life expectancy at birth in the United States had been 47.88 (males) and 50.70 (females) in 1900; by 1929 the figures had risen to 57.71 and 60.99.[5]

At the same time the capacity of the aged for self-support was being undermined. Changes in economic organization and family structure had relegated them to a marginal status in the modern industrial society. The key to the plight of the aged, Rubinow explained, was the increasing dependence of the "majority of mankind . . . upon a wage-contract for their means of existence." The wage-system led to economic superannuation in advance of "physiologic old age." It made no difference if the aged worker remained "fit for productive activity"; he experienced an abrupt and total economic disability if he fell "below the minimum level of productivity set by the employer." Modern industrial techniques, including scientific management, hastened economic superannuation by using up "human energy, at greater speed, within a shorter time." There had always been old men and women, but in the "primitive agricultural community . . . where the patriarchal family prevails, there can be no acute old-age problem. The authority of the patriarch is paramount and lasts longer than his productive powers. . . . The family is one large consumption unit, its members all prosper or starve together." [6] Lacking both authority and a significant economic function, the aged were also affected by the spatial mobility of the modern nucleated family. The economic system depended upon this mobility, but it "loosened home ties and family solidarity." [7]

The aged could no longer rely upon the institutional buffers which had protected them against dependency in preindustrial societies.[8] Yet, protection through voluntary thrift or insurance was more impractical than in the case of any other risk. Aging, Rubinow observed, differed from accidents or sickness in that it was not "an abnormal occurrence, but a normal stage of human life." In contrast to other areas, where preventive efforts lessened risk, "improvement in hygiene seems to aggravate it rather than relieve it." Since preventive medicine aggravated the problem, and since old age was a long-term rather than a transitory condition, the amount of saving required was greater than most workers could afford. There was no way of knowing the amount of savings required because of the uncertain duration of old age. Aging, the final emergency, was "preceded by all other emergencies of a workingman's existence," thus depleting any savings. The remoteness of the risk tended to discourage saving and, most important perhaps, "special saving for old age would only be possible through a persistent, systematic, and obstinate disregard of the needs of the workingman's family, which would make the preaching of such special savings a decidedly immoral force." [9] To argue that old-age assistance threatened family solidarity because, in the last resort, children would support their aged parents was equally immoral and absurd. Many workers could barely support their own families, and the argument had no relevance to the aged without children.

The challenge to voluntarism posed by the social insurance movement was not a conflict between collectivist ideals and ideals of atomistic individualism. Social insurance, as a source of social politics, can best be understood as a clash between two kinds of collectivism. Defenders of the voluntary tradition rarely maintained that economic security was exclusively an individual responsibility. They conceded the need for and urged the development of collective security mechanisms under voluntary auspices. They viewed the issue in terms of the relative balance of power between public and private institutions and the social function of government as opposed to voluntary groups. Collective security attained through voluntary institutions was compatible with American traditions of individual responsibility and liberty, with maintenance of the incentives and deterrents which sustained the work culture, and with American democratic values. Just as a New Freedom and New Nationalism were expounded in the early twentieth century, one might speak of the emergence of a "New Individualism." In the case of the aged this was closely identified with welfare capitalism; it idealized voluntary association to achieve collective ends and was embodied, ultimately, in the social philosophy of Herbert Hoover.[10]

The hero of the New Individualism was reminiscent of Charles Graham Sumner's idealized middle-class citizen — the "Forgotten Man," who, among other things, was perfectly capable of supporting himself in old age. Frederick L. Hoffman of Prudential Life Insurance agreed with Sumner that it was not "sympathy with suffering that is needed, but sympathy with hard struggling"; regrettably, the "kindly thought of the world" was often "wasted upon those who least deserve it." The "backbone of the nation" was the independent citizen who managed "in some way or another, by self-help . . . to avoid the more or less humiliating reliance upon public support." He had most to lose if the state were to provide pensions, not only because of the tax burden but because of the threat to his self-reliance. Noncontributory pensions would neither dispose of the problem of dependency nor prevent poverty; they would merely corrupt a class of citizenry hitherto outside the "scope of poor law administration or private charitable aid." They would "undermine . . . the self-respecting character of our people as citizens in a democracy where economic independence, achieved by individual effort, self-sacrifice, and self-denial, is, after all, the only aim and end worth while." [11]

At stake was the future of the nation and race. The fearsome prospect of old-age dependency was the "most powerful incentive which makes for character and growth in a democracy." Abolish it for the "vast majority of the thrifty and industrious members of society," and an irreparable blow would be struck against the "root of national life and character." Progress was synonymous with struggle, but the national "capacity for suffering, self-sacrifice, and self-denial" was already on the decline, and pensions would hasten the deterioration. We were "too near to our barbarian ancestors" to trifle "in so reckless and ill-advised a manner as this." [12]

For all Hoffman's tributes to proud, independent citizenship, he stressed the attainment of economic security through collective means. It was a voluntary collectivism, a "mutual aid of the right kind" which operated through "voluntary thrift agencies in the form of savings banks, fraternal relief societies, insurance." The soundest contribution the state could make to old-age security was education, especially of the young, in "ideals of right living." Such education might include the teaching of thrift in the public schools along with "household economy" and the "industrial arts." Those who had acquired the technique of "rational expenditure" could reduce waste and increase the "margin available for voluntary savings, investments, and insurance." [13]

If state old-age pensions would frustrate the ability of the individual to compete in the struggle for survival, they were equally unsound by the criteria of political economy and family cohesion. These latter considerations were stressed by the Massachusetts Commission on Old Age Pensions, whose appointment in 1907 marked the first significant entry of the aged into American social politics. According to the Commission, the population of Massachusetts sixty-five years or over in 1910 was 177,000, 135,788 of whom were nondependent. Of the dependent aged, 3,480 resided in almshouses, and more than 5,000 received public or private relief.[14] Conditions did not justify radical pension or insurance schemes which, in the long run, operated against the worker's best interests by reducing wages. The labor market would become glutted as persons from other parts of the country rushed into the Commonwealth to exploit its generosity. Aged pensioners, willing to accept substandard wages, would exert an additional downward pressure. A so-called "reflex competition" would have the same effect; workers would accept lower wages in anticipation of a state pension. The industries of the state, burdened by additional taxes, would shift the costs to the consumer or to the worker through lower wages. The family, as well as the economic system, would suffer from the effects of state pensions. "Impairment of family integrity" was among the "most serious dangers." Family cohesion was rooted in "filial obligation for the support of aged parents." [15]

Essentially a "counsel of despair," old-age pensions would testify to the failure of American economic and social institutions. Compulsory, contributory insurance would be preferable, but the very idea was "essentially distasteful to Americans" and of dubious constitutionality. Exercising an "enervating influence on wage-earners," compulsion was "not favorable to the highest development of individual initiative, independence, responsibility, and self-reliance." [16]

Old-age dependency could be prevented through nurture of the New Individualism. The proper line of action consisted of the "development and extension of various agencies of voluntary saving." The Commission proposed, in order to "strengthen voluntary thrift agencies," that the public schools include thrift as a compulsory subject of instruction.[17] Such instruction, already provided in Germany and France, would deal with the individual and social ethics of saving, and illustrate principles of investment and insurance. Additional legislation was proposed to encourage the growth of voluntary pension plans under business, fraternal, and insurance auspices.

The Commission's recognition that voluntary, contributory insurance had an inherently limited appeal, coupled with its advice that the state refrain from action in light of the establishment in 1907 of the Massachusetts Savings Bank Insurance System, was altogether inconsistent. Aware that similar institutions in Europe had made little progress, the Commission nonetheless urged that the Massachusetts system be "allowed ample opportunity to demonstrate its full effects." [18] Savings Bank Insurance was the handiwork of Louis Brandeis, who was motivated by the high cost of private insurance and objections to discretionary industrial pension programs. These he condemned as a "form of *strike insurance*," a device to rob the worker of "his little remaining industrial liberty." [19] The leading precedent for voluntary, contributory insurance had been the British Postal Savings Bank Act of 1864, which authorized postal savings banks to underwrite life and old-age insurance. Elimination of profit and loading expenses made cheap insurance possible, but the amount was limited to £100 pounds for life, and a £50 annuity. The British scheme had averaged only a few hundred policyholders a year.[20]

The Massachusetts Act of 1907 authorized savings banks to establish insurance departments, which could sell life policies up to $500 or annuities up to $200 per annum.[21] In 1911, Wisconsin established a state life insurance fund along similar lines.[22] These two experiments had little practical significance. They represented, along with state compensation funds and the War Risk Insurance of World War I, the few examples of government-sponsored, contributory insurance in the United States.[23]

The French National Old-Age Insurance Institution, established in 1850, and similar organizations created by Bel-

gium, Italy (1898), and Spain (1908) differed from the British
Postal Savings and Massachusetts Savings Bank systems in providing, at the inception of the program or later, a small subsidy.[24] Still another model, exemplified by the German program
launched in 1889, was compulsory old-age insurance. Germany
was followed by Luxembourg, Austria (1906), France (1910),
Roumania (1912), and Sweden (1913).[25] The two most important
systems — the German and French — were similar in their effort
to cover the working-class population, to combine old-age and
invalidity insurance, and to subsidize premiums through employer
contributions and a state supplement to each matured pension.
They differed in their methods of computing premiums, the
amount of pensions, and administrative arrangements.[26]

There was never, prior to the 1930's, any serious consideration
of compulsory, contributory old-age insurance in the United
States. The pension approach was more expedient; it avoided the
onus of compulsion, was simpler to administer, and bypassed
the problem of workers already retired or nearing old age. As an
assistance rather than an insurance program, pensions could be
made conditional and work incentives protected. Consequently,
European old-age pension legislation proved most relevant to
American debate over economic security for the aged.

Denmark, in 1891, was the first nation to institute a national
old-age pension system.[27] In 1897, France adopted an optional
system of state subsidies to departments or communes which
provided pensions; it was made obligatory in 1905 (and was
followed in 1910 by the compulsory act). New Zealand established a pension system in 1898, and those of New South Wales
(1900) and Victoria (1901) were superseded by the national
Australian legislation of 1908.[28] England established its national
pension system the same year, climaxing three decades of discussion and agitation.

The emergence of the aged as an issue in English social politics
is usually dated from 1878, when Rev. William L. Blackley presented his scheme for a national society or club. Membership in
the club would be compulsory, and the post office would administer it. In return for the contributions, the worker would be

insured against sickness and old age.[29] A National Providence League was established to publicize Blackley's plan, which was adamantly opposed by the friendly societies. They feared the effects of compulsory insurance upon the thrift habit, and especially the direct competition of government in the area of health insurance. The societies voiced their opposition before a Select Committee of the House of Commons, appointed in 1885 to investigate the problem of aged dependency. In its report of 1887 the Committee advised against the adoption of old-age insurance, and recommended instead that schools include thrift education in the curriculum.[30]

The issue of old-age dependency became prominent in the 1890's, when Charles Booth and Joseph Chamberlain enlisted in the cause and Parliament appointed a series of investigating committees. Like Blackley, whom he lauded as the "father of the movement" in England, Booth sought a relief formula which would cope with the economic problem of old-age pauperism without undermining the thrift habit or work discipline. Any proposal which "disturbed the basis of work and wages, discouraged thrift, or undermined even in the slightest degree self-respect, or the forces of individuality upon which morality as well as industry depends" stood condemned. Booth maintained that the "endowment of old age," or the "provision whether much or little, granted to all old people from a common purse" was compatible with morals and economic principle. A subsistence pension, far from pauperizing the worker, would "surely encourage self-supporting effort both before and after old age." [31] The removal of a large number of aged from poor-law jurisdiction would establish a sound basis for handling other dependent groups more efficiently.

Joseph Chamberlain favored contributory old-age insurance,[32] but voluntary rather than compulsory, and including a government subsidy. In addition to individual contributions totaling £5 before age twenty-five, and thereafter premiums of £1 a year up to age sixty-five, the state would contribute £15 and guarantee an annuity of £13 a year.[33] (Blackley, by the 1890's, had decided that state subsidy would be necessary, but he argued that

Chamberlain's scheme would only go a "little way" because it lacked compulsion.)[34]

Several parliamentary committees explored the pension issue in the 1890's.[35] Although the Boer War precluded further legislative consideration of old-age pensions for a few years, a number of developments around the turn of the century insured their enactment once the budgetary strain had eased. Old-age pensions received the endorsement of several powerful voluntary interests whose support enabled the Liberal Government to ignore charity organization leaders and others who voiced the classic objections to public assistance and bitterly resisted its extension.

Charles S. Loch, secretary of the London COS, argued that the best way to deal with old-age pauperism was to return to the principles of 1834: make outdoor relief the exception, and "above all . . . give no outdoor relief to the able-bodied, whether men or women."[36] If lax administration of the poor laws ended and the original deterrent objectives were reaffirmed, individuals would quickly provide for support in old age. Loch was a member of the Royal Commission of 1895, which condemned any categorical assistance programs interfering with the power of poor law authorities to deal with individual cases on their merits. As far as the Commission was concerned, the friendly societies, post office savings banks, and similar agencies demonstrated the "great development of habits of thrift and providence among the working classes, and has satisfied us of the general ability of those who are in any regular employment to make direct or indirect provision for old age as well as for sickness and other contingencies."[37]

Octavia Hill, famed pioneer in the development of volunteer friendly visiting and paternal housing management, agreed that the "more thrifty and respectable of the poor have done already many things for themselves, and it seems to me it would be far better to leave the provision for old age on the same sort of footing to be done by voluntary associations." Already people were "looking more and more to what can be done for them, and less and less to what they can do themselves, and in my talk with all the poorer people, that is the great tendency that I find among them." [38] Old-age pensions would accelerate this visible deterioration of character. William Lecky related old-age pensions to broader issues of industrial efficiency and voluntarism. The prosperity of the English masses was attributable to "their increased sobriety, and . . . habits of thrift and providence that have followed the spread of education." Legislation touching on poverty should not "impair these industrial qualities, or weaken these vast voluntary organizations of self-help which are their result." [39]

The two great constraints of voluntarism and the work culture existed in England as in the United States. Yet, by 1911, England had established an economic security system no less comprehensive than the German. Following the return of the Liberal Party to power in 1906, Lloyd George and Winston Churchill became committed to social insurance as a means of advancing their political fortunes while coping with the social problems of the time.[40] They were unencumbered by the federal and constitutional obstacles which existed in the United States. High in the pantheon of American mythology was the belief that the federal system of government encouraged experimentation, and enabled the states to function as laboratories in social legislation. The federal system, at the same time, presumably insured that legislation was adapted to local needs and circumstances. The experience of social insurance and pension programs demonstrated otherwise. Individual states feared to initiate legislation or depart from established standards. Local considerations seem to have been less important in determining the content of legislation than a desire to keep expenditures to a minimum. Federal initiative in 1935 produced more concrete results in one year than the state-centered social insurance movement had in the preceding thirty.

The roles of voluntary institutions in Britain and the United States also differed. Old-age pension legislation was enacted in England following the decision of powerful voluntary groups around 1900 to lend their support. The friendly societies, burdened with financial difficulties, reversed their position. Their rate of growth had slowed, "owing partly to secessions from membership and partly to the failure of young men to join. Friendly societies were generally suffering from increases in demands for sick pay from members, particularly the aged." [41] Although the Manchester Unity and the Foresters were hesitant to seek government assistance, the Hearts of Oak benefit society resolved at its annual meeting in 1901 that the state should provide pensions up to 5s to every person over sixty-five who claimed membership in a friendly society for at least twenty years. The National Conference of Friendly Societies endorsed the proposal in 1902, as did a special conference the following year.

Labor groups, in combination with private individuals, established a National Committee of Organized Labour for Promoting Old Age Pensions in 1898–99.[42] W. C. Steadman of the Barge Workers' Union was instrumental in the Trades Union Congress' 1899 endorsement of old-age pensions. Further support came in 1901 when the Cooperative Congress voted in favor of pensions. Union and cooperative society representatives jointly endorsed pensions at a conference a year later. In the elections of January 1906, labor organizations included pensions among the demands made upon candidates. The National Council of Labour, prior to the opening of the 1908 parliamentary session, sent letters to all members of Parliament, requesting pension legislation; that spring Prime Minister Asquith included a pension proposal in his budget.[43] Citing the precedents of Denmark, New Zealand, New South Wales, and Victoria, the government rejected both contributory schemes and the expensive endowment of old age favored by Booth. Legislation provided for pensions up to 5s a week, conditional upon property, residence, and moral requirements.[44]

The comparative simplicity and expediency of the pension approach shaped the character of the debate in the United States. And, as its advocates emphasized, pension precedents were ample. Mothers' assistance after 1911 provided one; old-age pensions were described as an extension of this idea.[45] Pension legislation for the blind, which began in the early twentieth century, was less controversial but spread more slowly. By 1929,

*The Aged and the State*  125

assistance for this group, authorized by some twenty states, ranged from $150 to $600 a year.[46] Even in the case of the blind charity organization views remained consistent. Referring to an Illinois law of 1915 which required counties to aid the dependent blind, the general secretary of the United Charities of Chicago complained that the measure unfortunately passed "when not many socially thoughtful persons were looking." In an era of "enlightened" social work, committed to prevention and rehabilitation, there was absolutely no "sound reason for picking out a special class of disabled persons for special relief." To presume by state fiat that the blind constituted a dependent class was "vicious" and an invitation to "scandal." [47]

Expenditures for dependent mothers and the blind were trivial compared to the sums devoted to military pensions. Federal disbursements, which rose from $21,000,000 in 1867 to $153,000,-000 in 1912, led Rubinow to exclaim that it was "idle to speak of a popular system of old-age pensions as a radical departure from American traditions, when our pension roll numbers several hundred thousand more names than that of Great Britain." To defend military pensions as a sentimental or patriotic gesture was "childish"; we were "clearly dealing here with an economic measure which aims to solve the problem of dependent old age and widowhood." [48] In addition to federal expenditures, Southern states maintained their own programs, costing $4,000,000 annually for 85,000 pensioners by the early twentieth century. In Rubinow's estimation the most scandalous feature of the military pension system was that for the most part it benefited a native American white population *"least in need of old-age pensions."* [49]

The evolution of programs for federal, state, and municipal employees offered additional evidence that old-age pensions did not depart radically from American tradition. The unanimous support for government employee pensions provided an important impetus to the broader movement. Government administrators found the absence of pensions a frustrating obstacle to efficiency. It is "high time and most important," remarked the Secretary of the Treasury back in 1911, "that a retiring allowance should be established for the civil service of the Federal Government." Like everybody else, the Secretary was "tied up . . . in any effort really to produce economy and efficiency." [50] Pensions would hasten the departure of those whose productive efficiency had declined as a result of old age or invalidity. They would increase morale by creating a sense of security and new opportunities for promotion. Government could better recruit and hold a "higher grade of men." [51] The old-age pension movement reached a "high-water mark in the law" when the Sterling–Lehlbach Act of 1920 established a retirement system for the 300,000 federal employees in the classified civil service.[52] Andrews anticipated that the measure would "quicken the growing movement for old-age pension legislation by the states" in a manner comparable to the federal workmen's compensation act of 1908.[53]

Early state and municipal pension programs were sporadic, limited to police, firemen, and teachers, noncontributory, and rather informally financed.[54] The Massachusetts Commission of 1910, surveying fifty-six cities outside the state with a population of 25,000 or more, found that twenty-five had no pension arrangements; of the remaining thirty-one only nine included all three groups in their pension program.[55] The major growth occurred after 1910. By the late 1920's municipal retirement systems for firemen and policemen were practically universal, and teachers' pensions were common. Nine cities with populations of 400,000 or more had established comprehensive retirement systems covering other groups as well.[56] Massachusetts, in 1911, was the first to establish a comprehensive retirement program for state employees. The number of states increased to half a dozen by the early 1920's, but many others established teachers' retirement programs.[57]

The 1920's witnessed the emergence of comprehensive state and municipal retirement systems as well as a federal retirement program. There was an increasing preference for contributory plans, and more concern with actuarial soundness. The noncontributory plans had long been under attack, as unduly expensive and "likely to be somewhat demoralizing." They threatened to "encourage agitation for the introduction of general state pension schemes for the aged." [58]


The spread of industrial pensions was often cited as evidence that voluntary institutions were sufficient. "It is a fact of striking interest," reported the Massachusetts Commission on Old Age Pensions in 1910, "that, at a time when European governments are instituting systems of State insurance and pensions . . . the American railroad and industrial corporations are attempting to solve this problem on their own initiative, through private systems supported by the revenues of the pensioning company." [59] (The Commission exaggerated since the most rapid growth of industrial pensions occurred after 1910.) A comprehensive survey by the Industrial Relations Counselors covered 397 formal industrial programs existing in 1929; of these, only 60 had been established by 1910. The largest number, 280, were created between 1911 and 1925, with 211 emerging between 1911 and 1920. The remaining 57 came into existence between 1926 and 1929. [60]

Railroads, public utilities, metal trades, oil, banking, and insurance, along with electrical apparatus and supply industries, accounted for more than 80 percent of employees covered. Only one-eighth of all manufacturing employees were potential pensioners; formal pension programs had barely "touched the construction, motion picture, or automobile repair industries, and the coverage of mine and quarry workers and employees of chain stores, department stores, and hotels and restaurants" was negligible. The 4 largest companies providing pensions employed nearly 25 percent of those covered; the 125 smallest, only 1.4 percent. [61]

A second tabulation by the Industrial Relations Counselors in 1932 uncovered 21 additional plans established prior to 1929, all but one in the period 1911–1925. Despite the Depression, 69 new plans were established between 1929 and 1932. The same period, however, witnessed the most rapid rate of discontinuance, affecting almost 10 percent of all the plans operating in 1929. A total of 434 pension systems was reported in existence in 1932; the 391 providing information on coverage employed some 3,-722,000 workers. It was estimated that in 1932 about 140,000 persons were receiving industrial pensions, and that less than 15 percent of all wage and salaried employees were covered.[62]

Many studies of industrial pensions criticized the lax, surprisingly unbusinesslike funding. It was "amazing," according to the Merchants Association of New York, "that ordinarily there is no definite provision made by the employer providing for adequate financing of his pension system." Pension programs usually "operated on a cash basis with no limitations to the possible demand upon the company's funds and no provision for accrued liabilities. . . . In fact, some pension plans state definitely that pension rates will be reduced in case of insufficient funds available." [63] A study of industrial pensions in the middle 1920's, prepared by Abraham Epstein for the Pennsylvania Commission, was highly critical of this financial instability and other administrative faults.

Epstein found 370 pension programs in operation; another 224 firms paid pensions on an informal basis. Total coverage by the formal plans, he estimated, was about 4,000,000 employees; some 90,000 persons, 5 percent of the needy aged, were receiving pensions under formal and informal plans combined. Railroads, public utilities, and metal industries accounted for nearly 80 percent of the workers covered. Epstein dismissed the informal pension systems as "morally repugnant to sensitive wage-earners"; the method carried "all the odium and stigma of charity" and weakened the "efforts of workers' organizations." [64]

The overwhelming majority of established pension plans — 282 out of 370 — were formal-discretionary, implying a moral rather than a legal obligation on the part of the employer. Another 43 were formal-limited-contractual; the employer relinquished the right to terminate pensions once granted. Another 28 were compulsory-contributory, but not necessarily funded or reinsured. Only a handful of plans took the form of single-premium-deferred annuities. Both vested and funded, they were satisfactory in terms of labor mobility and financial solvency. Urged by some large

insurance companies in the 1920's, these plans involved the payment by employers of fixed sums each year for each employee,
resulting in a guaranteed pension whose size depended upon the
cumulative premium. Epstein was pessimistic about their growth
potential: "Our present investigations indicate that, by and large,
American employers will hesitate a long time before they will
recognize advantages in a system which permits the employe
to leave his employment without the loss of his pension rights." [65]
As an alternative, insurance companies began promoting the mod-
ified-deferred-annuity plan. Employees, under this arrangement,
did not possess vested rights to the pension until they had com-
pleted a stipulated term of service.

Hardly a dozen of the industrial pension plans claimed any
scientific funding. They had been established "without actuarial
calculations and no legal guarantees"; thus "their contractual
provisions, even if entered into in the best of faith," were meaningless." [66] The fact that 10 percent of the plans failed after 1929
substantiated this criticism, as did the failure of the Morris and
Company pension fund in the 1920's. This meat-packing firm
had established a contributory plan in 1909. Upon its merger with
Armour and Company, the latter refused to assume the pension
liabilities (affecting 600 pensioners and a sum of $7,000,000).
Armour and Company was sustained by the Illinois Circuit Court.
It was not until the late 1920's that business firms acknowledged
the irresponsible, inequitable practices of the past. Many of the
plans established after 1926 were reinsured.[67]

The New Individualism, if measured by the success of business
firms in providing for old-age dependency, was a colossal failure.
By 1932 only 15 percent of American workers were covered, and
they were concentrated in a few industries. No less important,
"the great majority of pension plans in American industry have
been established with no accurate calculation of their future
costs and with no adequate provision for financing them." [68]

The industrial pension was, first and foremost, a technique of
labor control. This helps explain the indifference to funding and
especially to vesting employees with legal rights. Industrial pensions raised a fundamental conflict of interest between capital

and labor. Trade unions aimed at "commanding the undivided loyalty of the workers . . . for the sake of controlling the labor supply in the trade. . . . To the extent that a pension scheme will enable the employer to attach his working force permanently to himself, it renders him independent of the uncertainties of the labor market, on the one hand, and of union domination, on the other. This is the crux of the conflict so far as union policy is concerned." [69] From this perspective, industrial pensions were objectionable to labor whether justified as benevolence — a reward for long and faithful service — or as a deferred wage. The deferred wage theory interpreted the pension as a wage paid not in money but in the "foregoing of an increase in wages" the worker would have obtained in the absence of a pension program.[70] In reality, the pension represented a conditional rather than a deferred wage, or even a kind of tontine. It would be paid only if the worker remained in service for a certain length of time (usually twenty years) and if he met other company terms. Labor, as always, preferred that any surplus be distributed in the form of a "wage increase by which all the employees gain on some equitable basis." [71] This would not handicap labor in its struggle with capital to control the employment market. If pensions were legitimately to be interpreted as a deferred wage, then they should be vested and left to collective bargaining rather than to the employer's discretion.

By the 1920's any interpretation of pensions as a deferred wage or a benevolence had waned in popularity. Increasingly, emphasis fell upon pensions as a "legitimate business expenditure for which the employer expects to receive definite results in efficiency and economy of operation." [72] Pensions presumably would reduce labor turnover, particularly among older employees. By retaining experienced men, they would reduce accident rates and costs. Superior workers would be attracted to the company. Pensions relieved the employer of any obligation to "keep people on the payroll beyond a period of real productivity." All these results depended, of course, "on the employee's realization that the pension may be withheld in the event of his service falling short of expectation." Needless to say, "strike action" was not compatible with company expectations.[73]

Industrial pensions were among the most dubious contributions of the New Individualism to the problem of economic security. Welfare capitalism, applied to old-age dependency, was riddled with defects in theory and practice. First, only a small percentage of the labor force was covered by the 1930's; and, since pension activity on the part of other voluntary institutions was trivial, the failure of voluntarism was virtually complete. Second, the financing of the pensions was irresponsible; business firms promised a concrete reward for long and faithful service, but assumed no real responsibility for security of the fund. Third, potential beneficiaries proved ungrateful, and employers knew it. Trade unions were "apathetic and even hostile," and workers generally resented the "autocratic and paternalistic" manner in which pension schemes were conducted. Discretionary pensions were especially objectionable to unions as a "subtle attempt to undermine the morale of their movement." [74] Fourth, businessmen lauded economic mobility, opportunity, and freedom of contract, but pensions were a countervailing force to all those attributes of the American economic system.

The ultimate irony was the continued commitment to industrial pensions despite failure to attain most of the managerial objectives. The consensus of employer opinion, according to the Merchants Association of New York, was that pension programs had little "appreciable effect in bringing about increased loyalty, continuance of employment, efficiency or industrial peace." [75] The companies involved in two of the most important strikes of the 1920's — the steel strike in 1919 and the railway shopmen in 1922 — maintained pension programs. Since they were "able to exercise but little influence in keeping on the payroll those already employed, it is hardly to be expected that they would serve as a magnet for attracting desirable employees to the service." [76] If the "framers of the early pension plans" had possessed "extravagant notions" of their value, why did the plans remain a staple of welfare capitalism? Apparently, they possessed at least one "principal potential financial benefit" — per capita pensions averaged less than 50 percent of the final pay of superannuated employees. By the late 1920's payroll relief had become the "tangible economy . . . emphasized almost to the exclusion of others." [77]

A second inducement was the prospect of government action if voluntary institutions proved unwilling or unable to assume the burden. American businessmen, as a rule, favored "voluntary assumption by private industry itself of such responsibility for the welfare of its personnel and the improvement of industrial relations as it is capable of discharging efficiently." State pensions would result in "waste, extravagance and corruption," and would "undermine individual thrift on the part of workers and . . . place a premium upon inefficiency and improvidence." [78] They marked a step in the direction of socialism.

Welfare capitalism was one expression of the broader ideal of voluntarism as the form of collective action best suited to American ideals and institutions. As Rubinow and critics of welfare capitalism in the 1920's like John Lapp and Leo Wolman emphasized, this approach embodied a central fallacy: that voluntary institutions were a bona fide substitute for social legislation.[79] The choice lay, Wolman believed, "between public and private paternalism; between the grudging, limited distribution of small favors by established private interests, on the one hand, and, on the other, the winning by a free people of permanent, constitutional rights." [80]


Whatever their limitations, industrial pensions and welfare capitalism testified to the need for a collective solution to problems of old-age dependency. They acknowledged implicitly that the aged confronted economic difficulties, that charitable provision was inadequate, and that wages were too low to permit the savings required for self-support in old age. One of the few investigations of the aged by social workers before the 1920's was conducted by Mabel Nassau and was based upon a sample of one hundred aged individuals residing in Greenwich Village. She found them living in a state of chronic "economic fear," especially the "fear of being forced into some institution," and of the effects of illness. With few exceptions they worked as long as possible, and tried to avoid charity. Children assisted when parents could no longer work, but at great sacrifice; the "families' struggles were often too great, and . . . the whole economic standard of the families was thereby lowered." Consider the dilemma "of the middle generation trying to decide whether to support the aged parents and thus have less to eat for themselves and for their children . . . or to put the old people in an institution!" A visit to Blackwell's Island explained why the prospect of institutionalization was abhorrent, particularly to aged women. "We were guided around faithfully until in spite of long years of tenement visiting I could stand no longer the sight of such depressed, hopeless, sad, vacant, wretched faces. All seemed to live such a hopelessly monotonous life with no individuality or scope for personal effort." [81] Miss Nassau concluded that no solution to old-age dependency could be anticipated through individual saving. Incomes were simply insufficient. It was impossible to accumulate a reserve when a large proportion of working class families was "forever hovering on the brink of destitution, always making an effort to have enough to eat and a decent place in which to sleep, and yet seldom achieving even that, being forever underfed, usually badly housed, and often in overcrowded quarters." [82]

A Wisconsin study of the aged confirmed that institutionalization was "gall and wormwood to the self-respecting poor"; yet the almshouse served as the major public relief measure for the aged in that state. Pensions, the Commission suggested, were not only more dignified but cheaper.[83] The old-age pension movement was a revolt against institutions as a welfare resource. Resentment against the confinement and segregation of the aged, whose only crime was poverty, was an important stimulus to the pension idea. A survey by the Bureau of Labor Statistics in the middle 1920's covering 2183 almshouses — 90 percent of the number in the United States — suggests why they were so repulsive to the aged and the source of extreme indignation on the part of pension advocates. "[D]ilapidation, inadequacy, and even indecency"

were their "outstanding physical features . . . Ignorance, unfit-
ness, and a complete lack of comprehension of the social element
involved in the conduct of a public institution [were] characteristic of a large part of their managing personnel. Among the inmates themselves insanity, feeble-mindedness, depravity, and
respectable old age [were] mingled in haphazard unconcern." [84]
There was, perhaps, "no sadder chapter in American social history
than the callous neglect in dehumanized poorhouses for the care
of aged dependents." [85]

Some insight into the general economic status of the aged in
the 1920's is provided by investigations conducted by the Commonwealth of Massachusetts and by the National Civic Federation (NCF). The Massachusetts study covered 19,000 aged. Those
who owned property worth $5000 or more, or had incomes of
$1000 or more a year, comprised 55 percent of the aged. On the
other hand, 16.8 percent had no incomes at all, and another 6.4
percent had less than $100 a year. The majority of aged with less
than $5000 worth of property or $1000 income were partially or
entirely supported by others, mostly children.[86]

The NCF investigated 14,000 aged, 65 or over, in eleven cities
and two towns in four states — New York, New Jersey, Pennsylvania, and Connecticut. Its findings were similar to those of the
Massachusetts Commission. Approximately 42 percent owned
property worth $5000 or more, and 56.8 percent owned $5000
worth of property or had incomes of $1000 or more. An identical
16.8 percent had no income or property.[87] The NCF was greatly
impressed by the fact that nearly six out of ten were worth $5000
or more in property or $1000 or more in income — thus discredit-
ing the "propagandist ammunition of reckless radicals." There
was no need for state intervention in a field "traditionally reserved
in our country for personal liberty, private effort and self-
providence." Pension advocates, particularly those enthralled by
European legislation, minimized the high wages and the "opportunities for self-providence which this country has offered to its
people." [88] These included land investment, railroad and industrial
securities, savings banks, building and loan associations, and life
insurance.

The NCF and Massachusetts Commission percentages of aged with substantial property or income seem extraordinarily high. Conceivably, business and professional classes were overrepresented in the sample, or the sampling procedures were otherwise faulty.[89] Even assuming the validity of the figures, it is possible to arrive at conclusions different from those of the NCF. One could argue that nearly 50 percent of the aged owned property or received income which totaled less than $5000 and $1000, respectively. According to the Massachusetts Commission, 65 percent of this group was dependent on outside assistance. There is no way of determining the sacrifices made by those who received no assistance, or the burden imposed on children who supported aged parents on limited incomes. Unlike the NCF, the Massachusetts Commission concluded that old-age dependency was sufficiently widespread to justify a state pension program.

Old-age pension legislation had been introduced in some states and Congress earlier than 1920. Representative William B. Wilson of Pennsylvania (later United States Secretary of Labor) prepared a bill in 1909 providing for pensions of $120 a year to those aged who satisfied the property or income qualifications. It established a Corps in the War Department called the Old Age Home Guard of the United States Army. As privates in the Guard, the aged would report annually to the Secretary of War on military and patriotic sentiment in their communities. These peculiar arrangements were designed to avoid any constitutional objections to federal pensions. The bill was never reported out of the Committee on Military Affairs.[90] In 1911 Congressman Victor L. Berger of Wisconsin, a Socialist, introduced a bill which provided pensions up to $4 a week for those aged whose income was less than $10 a week. It too failed, but "attracted great attention and brought the problem of old-age pensions before the public at that time as never before." [91]

A bill introduced into the Massachusetts legislature in 1903 was probably the first on the state level; it was followed by others in almost every Massachusetts legislative session.[92] Before the

1920's, however, Arizona was the only state to enact an old-age pension measure, and, since it was declared unconstitutional, an Alaska pension law of 1915 was the only one in operation until 1923.

Although marginal to the social insurance movement which flourished in the decade after 1911, old-age pensions became the leading issue in the 1920's. The pension drive reached a climax after the onset of the Depression in 1929, when it was reinforced by demands for unemployment insurance. Between 1923 and 1933 the majority of states enacted old-age pension legislation. Pennsylvania, Montana, and Nevada took the initiative in 1923. Pennsylvania's law was declared unconstitutional in 1924, and the Nevada measure was converted from a compulsory to an optional status in 1925. In 1925 Wisconsin passed a pension law, but a similar measure in California was vetoed by the governor. In 1926, the Kentucky and Washington legislatures acted, but the Washington measure was vetoed. Maryland and Colorado passed pension bills in 1927, and a Wyoming law was vetoed that year.[93] Progress was swifter beginning in 1929, and a number of bills were passed: California, Minnesota, Utah, and Wyoming (1929); New York and Massachusetts (1930); Delaware, New Hampshire, Idaho, New Jersey, West Virginia, and Indiana, declared unconstitutional (1931); Arkansas, Maine, North Dakota, Oregon, Indiana, Colorado, Arizona, and Washington (1933). Through 1928, in summary, eleven states had enacted pension laws; two (Pennsylvania and the Arizona Law of 1914) had been declared unconstitutional, and another three (California, Washington, and Wyoming) vetoed. Between 1929 and 1933, nineteen states were added. Except for Minnesota, all these laws were compulsory; and the California legislation was not only compulsory but provided for state contributions.[94]

The six measures in effect up to 1929 were optional and locally financed. Like similar mothers' pension legislation, they were either inoperative or defective. Nevada had never granted pensions, only one Kentucky county did, and little more was accomplished in Maryland or Colorado. Montana, a handful of Wisconsin counties, and Alaska accounted for the 1,200-odd aged receiving pensions totaling around $222,000. The increase in the number of pension states after 1929, plus the tendency toward compulsory laws and state financial assistance, raised the total by 1932 to 102,000 pensioners and $22,000,000.[95]

A shift in the content of proposed federal legislation also occurred in the late 1920's and early 1930's. The measure introduced in 1927 by Representative William I. Sirovich of New York, which had been prepared by the American Association for Old Age Security, substituted the federal grant-in-aid technique for direct federal pensions. A similar bill was introduced in 1932 by Senator Clarence Dill and Representative William Connery, Jr. Reported favorably by the House Labor and Senate Pensions Committees, it failed to come to a vote before the Congressional sessions ended in March 1933.[96] These proposals, along with the precedents established in vocational rehabilitation and maternal and child care during the 1920's, helped pave the way for the federal categorical assistance programs later included in the Social Security Act.

To understand the emergence of the aged as a major source of social politics in the 1920's it is not enough to cite long-term demographic, economic, and familial trends, or figures demonstrating the scope of old-age dependency. The appearance of a new social insurance leadership, which adopted old-age pensions as the primary objective, was equally important; in this respect, the campaigns launched by the Fraternal Order of Eagles (FOE) and the work of Abraham Epstein were significant.

The Indiana State Aerie of the FOE, in May 1921, adopted a resolution favoring government old-age pensions. Endorsed by other Eagle conventions, the resolution was passed by the Grand Aerie in August.[97] The prime mover in the campaign was Frank E. Hering, "Past Grand Worthy President," and author of the original Indiana resolution. Hering became president of the Old Age Pension Commission established by the Eagles. Explaining the purpose of the drive, Hering emphasized that the "Fraternity is built basically upon the home and is dedicated to promoting the welfare and integrity of that institution." In the name of home, it was time to stop sending "our unfortunate aged to pauper institutions, humiliated, humbled, degraded, and, not infrequently, mistreated." [98]

The Eagles collaborated with Andrews and the AALL in the preparation of a Standard Bill in 1922. Subsequently, under Hering's leadership, the Eagle's Old Age Pension Commission developed a systematic legislative and publicity campaign. It included the organization of pension committees by subordinate Aeries, and a great deal of grass-roots legislative pressure. The introduction of a pension bill in Minnesota in 1923, for example, was attributable to the "movement inaugurated and carried on . . . by the Fraternal Order of Eagles," particularly Duluth Aerie No. 79. The Commission cooperated with state federations of labor — Indiana, Wisconsin, Texas, Ohio, Pennsylvania, Michigan, and California — as well as the National Old Age Pension Committee of the United Mine Workers. The FOE organized an old-age pension club in every Indiana community with an Aerie, and awakened legislators "to the fact that they will have the voting strengths of these clubs to contend with." In Illinois, Ohio, and elsewhere Aeries sponsored city-wide public meetings to discuss the issue. The old-age pension legislation introduced in Rhode Island, Ohio, and other states was prepared by the Eagles.[99]

Abraham Epstein helped direct the Eagle campaign in 1922–23, when he was employed as Hering's assistant. Born in Russia in 1892, Epstein had emigrated to the United States in 1910, and, after a year and a half in New York City, moved to Pittsburgh. His fanatic thirst for education overcame economic hardships, and he was awarded a B.S. degree from the University of Pittsburgh in 1917. Epstein devoted another year to graduate study in the School of Economics under Dr. Francis Tyson, an economist who became his lifelong friend and adviser. Epstein's thesis, *The Negro Migrant in Pittsburgh,* was published in 1918. Tyson helped him secure an appointment as research director of the Pennsylvania Commission on Old Age Pensions, which had been established in 1917; except for his brief (and unhappy) interlude with the FOE, he remained with the Commission until 1927. Its chairman, James Maurer, also president of the Pennsylvania State

Federation of Labor, helped stimulate his interest in labor problems. Epstein participated in the Interchurch Investigation of the 1919 steel strike, and was instrumental in organizing the Workers' Education Bureau. Upon the demise of the Pennsylvania Commission in 1927, he established the American Association for Old Age Security, which broadened its program in 1933 and became the American Association for Social Security.

As research director and executive secretary of the Pennsylvania Commission, Epstein played the major role in its extensive investigations of old-age dependency and legislative activities. The Commission made no concrete recommendation in an exhaustive report of 1919, but drafted a bill two years later which was introduced into the legislature by Senator Max G. Leslie. It failed, and was reintroduced with minor changes in 1923 by Senator William S. Vare.[100] The amended bill provided for the establishment of county old-age assistance boards financed by the state. Although the measure passed, the legislature failed to authorize the necessary appropriations. Nonetheless, Epstein began organizing the county assistance boards. The Dauphin County Court ruled it unconstitutional in 1924 on the grounds that the Pennsylvania constitution prohibited state assistance to private individuals.[101] The 1925 legislature adopted a joint resolution to amend the constitution, but two successive legislatures had to approve and the resolution failed in 1927.

The Pennsylvania experience illustrates the conflict which arose between the pension ideal and business institutions. Commercial and industrial organizations, notably the Pennsylvania State Chamber of Commerce and Pennsylvania Manufacturers Association, worked tirelessly to defeat pension proposals throughout the 1920's. The former, referring to efforts to amend the state constitution after 1924, condemned any such action as "un-American and socialistic and unmistakably ear-marked as an entering wedge of communistic propaganda in Pennsylvania." Old-age pensions, legalized doles in reality, marked an "insidious experiment in paternalistic government which would sap the self-respect and destroy the moral fibre of thousands of people, besides costing the taxpayers millions of dollars." Members were urged to interview their legislative representatives and "bring all possible pressure of influence." [102]

The Pennsylvania Manufacturers Association similarly objected to expensive doles disguised as pensions. They had "ruined other countries. . . . They incite pauperism and kill ambition and self-respect." The Association congratulated itself on its role in defeating the proposed amendment in 1927, thus saving the state from a "costly and vicious scheme" which would "make necessary a Manufacturers' Tax, or an Income Tax, or both." [103] Earlier, in 1924, the State Chamber of Commerce apparently assumed the initiative in the proceedings leading to the unfavorable court decision.[104]

The National Civic Federation was also active in opposing pension legislation. Andrews singled out the Federation for its "pernicious and underhanded activities . . . in this field." [105] The NCF launched a fund-raising campaign in 1923 to assist its Welfare Department in waging war "against non-contributory old-age state pensions." Its tactics included the distribution of literature to key men in states where pension bills were introduced.[106]

To concede the need for a pension program was to concede that welfare capitalism, voluntarism, had failed. If government assumed the responsibility, then business would lose any advantages, real or imagined, attributed to company pension programs. Thus, Owen D. Young of General Electric refused to admit a need for government old-age pensions. Government could not be trusted to keep the costs within reasonable limits, such pensions would exert a pauperizing influence, and industrial pensions formed part of a broader effort to achieve collective security through voluntary means which deserved encouragement.[107]

The legislative achievement before 1929 was nowhere commensurate with the intensive drive led by the Eagles and Epstein. The main reason for the failure was the effective opposition inspired by business organizations. Nor did a bitter controversy which erupted between Epstein, on the one hand, the Eagles and Andrews, on the other, help the situation. Epstein's break with Hering and the Eagles, whom he had joined in September 1922, occurred sometime in April 1923. Early in the month Hering had lauded Epstein for his great contributions to the Eagle campaign.[108] By the end of the month Epstein was accusing his superior of nastiness, lack of principle, and pettiness; Hering allegedly was less interested in the aged than in promoting his own power and acquiring members for the Eagles. He had even, Epstein charged, fired a stenographer in the Indianapolis office who continued to talk to him.[109] James Maurer, who believed that Epstein was better informed on the subject of the aged than any Eagle, agreed that he was treated in a manner beneath his dignity and capacity.[110] Hering dismissed Epstein as of July 1, 1923, and informed him that he had alienated old-age pension leaders in every state he had visited by his egotism, unwillingness to cooperate, and inordinate personal ambitions.[111] Subsequently, the old-age pension movement was subjected to the spectacle of mutual recrimination and competition for credit between Epstein and the Eagles.[112]

The personality clash should not obscure more important policy differences. The Eagles, in Epstein's estimation, were too prone to accept bad legislation. As Rubinow later explained, the Eagles "certainly were successful in putting the legislation through," but they also "came very near destroying the entire value of the old-age pension movement" by their willingness to compromise on optional legislation.[113] Even Andrews was disturbed by their indifference to the content of pension legislation, and recommended a firmer stand against "county option with its obviously unsatisfactory results." [114]

Epstein's views on the economic and social function of old-age pensions also differed from those of the Eagles. He favored a sharp break with the poor-law tradition; the Eagles confused issues of objective economic need with morality and behavioral norms. The pensioner, Hering reassuringly explained, would have to be an "exceedingly good citizen" and demonstrate a "history of habitual industriousness, habitual loyalty to family obligations, and freedom from all crimes involving more than four months imprisonment." [115]

Epstein's controversy with Andrews was rooted, initially, in his belief that the AALL had lost interest in social insurance and could no longer claim leadership. When the AALL became active again, after 1929, serious doctrinal differences arose over the substance of unemployment insurance. Following a trip to Europe in 1925, Epstein, impressed with the progress and acceptance of social insurance abroad, consulted with Rubinow on the desirability of reviving the American movement. Rubinow agreed and informed Andrews that it had been dormant too long, that an awakening was in order, and that old-age assistance might preferably be established on an insurance rather than a pension basis.[116] Apparently this and subsequent attempts to enlist Andrews' cooperation proved unsuccessful; thus Epstein, in 1926, initiated action leading in 1927 to the organization of the American Association for Old Age Security (AAOAS).[117]

Andrews never admitted a need for the new organization which, he insisted, would sabotage the fund-raising and membership drives of the AALL.[118] He suggested that Epstein head an old-age pension department within the AALL.[119] Paul Douglas made no headway in his efforts to mediate the dispute.[120] Epstein refused to disband his organization and become a salaried employee of the AALL; in any case, Andrews had decided by the spring of 1927 that he would be more of a liability than an asset. Close association with Epstein, "some little harmonizer," would cause misunderstanding in light of the AALL's "pleasantly" cooperative relationship with the Eagles.[121] Andrews was critical of the shift from old-age pensions to insurance which Epstein and Rubinow were beginning to urge. The AALL had adopted a pension policy in 1922, and Andrews remained firm in its support.[122]

Despite Andrews' resentment, Rubinow and others felt that Epstein's actions were fully justified by the leadership vacuum in the social insurance field. Rubinow now supported Epstein's organization because Andrews had not responded to pleas for a social insurance revival.[123] Paul Douglas agreed that the failure of the AALL to exercise leadership was responsible for the AAOAS, though he appreciated the reasons for Andrews' hesitation — the grueling, frustrating campaign for health insurance and the ostensible failure of social insurance by 1921. Epstein was a difficult person, but he had contributed more to the old-age pension movement than any single individual.[124] Relations between Andrews and Epstein deteriorated further in 1928 when the AAOAS prepared an old-age pension bill for New York State; the AALL countered with a proposal for an investigating commission. Thereupon, Andrews charged, Epstein "after all our years of activity . . . promptly writes letters to members of our Executive Committee and others insinuating that our Association is trying to kill old age pension legislation!" [125]

These personal and organizational rivalries were overshadowed after 1929 by disagreement over the function of social insurance. The clash between the Wisconsin (Commons-Andrews) and Ohio (Rubinow) approach to unemployment compensation raised larger issues of the underlying purpose of the social insurances. Epstein went beyond Rubinow in his interpretation of social insurance as a means to economic redistribution. Most strikingly, Epstein urged the need for the government's financial participation to achieve this redistributive purpose. Otherwise, the burden of cost would fall most heavily on those least able to afford it, and benefits would be too low.

# VII  *Unemployment — Prevention or Insurance?*

Plans for the relief and prevention of unemployment were coupled with industrial pensions as examples of progressive welfare capitalism, and an alternative to state economic security programs. The unemployed, no less than the aged, were beneficiaries of a New Individualism which provided security under collective but voluntary auspices. Unlike other social insurance or pension movements unemployment relief had emerged as an issue in American social politics during the nineteenth century. Agrarian-labor radicalism from the 1870's to the 1890's was associated with numerous proposals for government public works programs. These were significant in their emphasis upon federal responsibility, and in their implication that society owed citizens the right to work.

Peter Cooper, Independent Party candidate for President of the United States in 1876, advocated the settlement of idle workers on unoccupied Western lands and their employment on internal improvement projects. He called upon the federal government to issue legal-tender currency which states and cities could exchange for bonds and use for their own public works programs. William A. Carsey, a Greenback-Labor Party official, suggested to a House Committee in 1878 that the federal government aid the jobless with Western lands, public works, and loans.[1] The "industrial army" petitions during the depression of the 1890's invariably demanded government expenditures for public works and internal improvements. Jacob Coxey's "Commonweal of Christ" petitioned

Congress for a good roads bill involving an expenditure of $500,-
000,000, and a bill which authorized states and localities to issue
non-interest-bearing bonds as security for legal tender loans issued by the Secretary of the Treasury.[2] Middle-class radicals
joined in the demand for work relief. A Massachusetts Board, appointed to examine the unemployment issue, heard Edward
Bellamy propose a system of state workshops which would guarantee employment and a minimum income.[3]

Demands for work guarantees during the 1890's were stimulated by widespread fear of imminent catastrophe. The workers,
John Graham Brooks contended, were fed up with the indignities
and paternalism associated with charity, and with "every assumption that individuals were to blame for being poor or out of
work." [4] Benjamin O. Flower, editor of the *Arena*, warned that "if
a crisis is precipitated, fed by blind hate and a bitterness born of
a consciousness of injustice long endured, it will assume the form
of an uncontrollable storm, a blind, passionate outburst, in which
the guiding influences of reason, judgment, and conscience will
be absent." In the name of "human brotherhood" as well as self-
preservation, we should follow the precedent of the ancient
Romans and Peruvians and give "every person productive work." [5]

Relief agencies and charity organization societies endorsed no
such principle as the right to work. Even in a depression relief
had to be restricted and controlled, not extended through vast
public expenditures. The 1890's, like previous depression eras,
witnessed a proliferation of public and private, regular and emergency, relief programs. The period was distinctive for its experiments in work relief, as a supplement to relief in money or com-
modities.[6] Charity organization leaders emphasized that preference should be given to the private and regular channels of assistance; even these should be viewed as a last resort after appeal
to employers, friends, and relatives. It was imperative at all times
to maintain the standards and practices of "scientific" philanthropy. Relief had to be safeguarded by the use of visitors, "who
would influence for good all who apply to them, and as far as
possible help them permanently." Work relief if offered should
not be allowed to compete with the private market. Most im-

portant, it had to be *"continuous, hard,* and *underpaid"* in order to prevent pauperization.[7]

Josephine Shaw Lowell sharply criticized relief practices in New York City during the winter of 1893–94. The worst was the free food, clothing, and coal campaign launched by New York's *World, Herald,* and *Tribune.*[8] This extravagant relief carnival fostered the "socialistic teaching that such gifts were not a favor received, but only a small part of what was due from the rich to the poor." The main purpose of relief was to "protect the character on every side, and not to weaken it either economically or morally." Indiscriminate depression relief encouraged those "who are naturally disinclined to provide for their future wants . . . to continue in that course by the assurance that some one else will provide for them." [9]

Fear of the pauperizing effects of relief was intensified by an increase in the army of tramps, vagrants, and beggars — groups which had long challenged the ingenuity of relief societies. Their numbers were swelled during the 1890's by an influx from the ranks of "strikers and of sick persons who, during enforced idleness, have made the fatal discovery of the others that living and labor are not interchangeable terms." [10] The depression experience, combined with the rise of hereditarian and eugenic thought after the turn of the century, produced a substantial literature dealing with these deviant groups. It was discovered that feeblemindedness constituted a major source of poverty, pauperism, and crime.[11]

For all its pseudo-scientific and racist overtones, hereditarianism contributed to one useful advance in social work thought. It focused attention upon the need for discrimination between three categories of unemployed: the temporarily misfortunate worker, the industrially unfit or handicapped, and the professional pauper. Awareness of the need for discrimination, joined with the emphasis upon the environmental and social origins of poverty in the early twentieth century, encouraged the adoption of new policies toward unemployment. European experiments in labor and reformatory colonies suggested the need for similar institutions to train the incompetent and discipline those who refused to "maintain a position in the competitive industries." [12] It became clearer, on the other hand, that the involuntarily unemployed had to be treated differently from the unfit and incorrigible, and that treatment had to be adapted to the fact that unemployment was rooted in social rather than individual maladjustment. The objective was the prevention of unemployment. If society rather than the individual was responsible for mass unemployment, it was society's responsibility to help prevent it; by the same token, if society failed, then the worker had a right to protection against income losses caused by defective economic organization.

The American Association for Labor Legislation sponsored two national conferences on unemployment in 1914, from which its "Practical Program" of 1914–15 evolved. [13] The methods suggested for preventing (and to a lesser extent, relieving) unemployment were representative of American thought on the subject for nearly two decades. "The time is past," John Andrews explained, "when the problem of unemployment could be disposed of either by ignoring it, as was the practice until recent years in America, or by attributing it to mere laziness and inefficiency. We are beginning to recognize that unemployment is not so much due to individual causes and to the shiftlessness of 'won't-works,' as social and inherent in our present method of industrial organization." If personal incompetence was only a small part of the problem, and if society was mainly responsible for large-scale unemployment, it followed that government had to assume broader responsibilities for its prevention and relief.

First, the establishment of public employment exchanges was proposed as a method of prevention of unemployment through labor market rationalization. Although the need for market organization was "recognized in every other field of economic activity," little progress had been made in the labor field. The nucleus of a comprehensive employment exchange system would be the local offices, subdivided into special departments and services for men, women, children, and various industrial groups. In line with a growing interest in the United States and England in vocational guidance as a means of prevention, the local exchanges would include a department to place the young "where they will have an opportunity for industrial training and for real advancement, instead of leaving them to drift into blind-alley occupations." While discharging their general responsibility for labor market organization, the exchanges would devote particular attention to the "decasualization of casual labor." Supplementing the local exchanges would be state and national offices which could compile statistics and operate in a cooperating and supervising capacity.

The AALL's practical program included, secondly, a plea for regular and emergency public works programs in periods of economic decline. These would benefit the individual and community more than public or private charity. But public works should not be confused with artificial work relief. In distinguishing between public works and work relief the AALL adhered to the policy recommendations of English authorities like William H. Beveridge and the Webbs.

The third element of the AALL program, and the dominant one by the 1920's, was regularization of industry. Public employment exchanges could insure a broad adjustment of supply-demand relations in the labor market, but employers had to strive "within the limits of each business to make every job a steady job." Employment departments, headed by trained managers, would "study the problems of unemployment in the individual shop and . . . devise ways of meeting them." Techniques to regularize employment and reduce labor turnover included departmental transfers, part-time employment spread over the labor force, production planning, development of a slack season trade, maintenance of a stock department, the quest for steady rather than speculative business, and careful market analysis.

Social insurance was recommended as a fourth technique to control unemployment. Although, Andrews explained, prevention could be "accomplished through the voluntary efforts of enlightened employers, there is also needed that powerful element of social compulsion which can be exerted through the constant financial pressure of a carefully adjusted system of insurance."

By the 1920's Andrews and Commons, generalizing from the workmen's compensation experience and stung by the failure of health insurance, would depict unemployment insurance as little more than a stimulus to prevention and regularization.

The AALL proposed a number of supplementary measures to assist in preventing unemployment. They included industrial training for adults as well as children; an "agricultural revival" designed to make rural life more alluring; a "constructive immigration policy" which aimed at the "proper distribution of America's enormous immigration"; legislation prohibiting or restricting child labor; and measures on behalf of the inefficient and unemployable such as health insurance, old-age pensions, agricultural and industrial training, segregation of the feebleminded, and penal farm colonies for professional paupers and semi-criminals.

American thought on unemployment was greatly influenced by Beveridge. As Sub-Warden of Toynbee Hall (the first English social settlement), he became immersed in problems of unemployment relief caused by the trade recession of 1903. Before leaving the settlement in 1905 to join the *Morning Post*, he had become convinced that something "had gone wrong with economic laws in East London," and that "casual charity was an evil of the same type as casual employment." As administrator of the Mansion House Fund of 1903–04, he had assisted in providing men with work at the Salvation Army colony at Hadleigh, and at Osea Island (Essex). Follow-up investigations disclosed that nothing had changed; most of them "were as before — dropping into and out of jobs, scratching along somehow — just as they had done for years." [14] Further reflection on the failure of contemporary relief policy led to the critique, theory, and constructive program expounded in *Unemployment: A Problem of Industry*, published in 1909.

Efforts had been made in England between 1886 and 1905 to remove the unemployed from the jurisdiction of the Poor Laws. Joseph Chamberlain, president of the Local Government Board in 1886, had issued a circular urging special work relief programs for the temporarily unemployed. In 1904–05 a semi-official scheme known as the London Unemployed Fund (LUF) was launched through the initiative of Walter Long, another president of the Local Government Board. Attempts to liberate the unemployed from Poor Law control were climaxed by the Unemployed Workmen Act of 1905, an extension of the LUF, which "reversed the principles of 1834 and enshrined in the statute book the policy of relieving the unemployed without the disqualifications of the Poor law." [15] Beveridge's primary interest in the LUF and its successor, the Central Unemployed Body (CUB), lay in the opportunity to promote the labor exchange idea. He became chairman of the CUB's Employment Exchanges Committee, and established its system of exchanges. His work was supported by Nathaniel Cohen, representative to the CUB from the London County Council, and founder of the first English employment exchange at Egham in 1885.

Beveridge visited Germany in August 1907 to "supplement the argument for labour exchanges" and to examine the contributory insurance programs. Although he had declined previous offers, he accepted an invitation from Winston Churchill, then its president, to join the Board of Trade; the decisive consideration was the opportunity offered to "organise the labour market by labour exchanges." [16] Following the Act of 1909, which established the national exchange system, he became Director of Labor Exchanges.

Beveridge maintained that, except for the labor exchanges, the work of the CUB was a dismal failure. The Unemployed Workmen Act of 1905 required the establishment of Distress Committees (composed of councilors, guardians, and relief experts) in municipal boroughs or urban districts with a population of 50,000 or more. The Committees were responsible for accumulating data on unemployment, processing applications for relief, and assisting the unemployed through aided emigration, internal migration, or provision of temporary work relief. Beveridge argued that the Unemployed Workmen Act broke down at every point. It had been anticipated that voluntary contributions would provide most of the financing; but this did not happen. The Local Government Board expected that "assistance should be less eligible than independence," but this principle was abandoned in practice. Instead of benefiting regularly employed workers who were temporarily distressed, the machinery of the Unemployed Workmen Act was clogged by an influx of hard-pressed casual laborers. Most important, the Act never achieved its main purpose — the restoration to regular employment of applicants. Experience demonstrated "beyond question . . . the inadequacy of all measures which, like itself [the Act], leave industrial disorganisation untouched and deal only with the resultant human suffering." [17] Work relief of the type provided since the Chamberlain Circular of 1886 was doomed to failure because it was based upon a false theory of unemployment; it led inevitably to superficial remedies.

"The problem of unemployment," Beveridge explained, "lies . . . at the root of most other social problems." Employment security "for the bread-winner is the basis of all private duties and all sound social action." Employment security had to be understood as a problem of industrial organization. It required a labor market adjustment which correlated supply and demand, and reduced unemployment to a minimum. Unemployment was rooted in "specific imperfections of adjustment." [18]

Seasonal and cyclical fluctuation comprised one source of maladjustment. Beveridge dismissed seasonal unemployment as a problem of wages rather than labor market organization. No industry was self-supporting if it failed to maintain men "not only while they are at work, but also while they must stand idle and in reserve." Cyclical fluctuation, on the other hand, could be controlled neither by employers nor workers. No available theory of causation was fully acceptable, and "within the range of practical politics no cure . . . can be hoped for." The object, at best, was "palliation." In "changes of industrial structure," a second source of unemployment, he included technological innovation and other circumstances which changed the nature of the demand for labor.[19] Here again the possibilities of control were limited.

The most important cause of unemployment, yet the one least understood and readily subject to control, was the "requirement in each trade of reserves of labour to meet the fluctuations of work incidental even to years of prosperity. The men forming these reserves are constantly passing into and out of employment." These reserves explained the paradox of unemployment. The supply of labor always seemed to exceed the demand simply because "there is no one labour market but only an infinite number of separate labour markets." The docks and building trades best illustrated this dissipation of demand "between many different centres and different employers each subject to fluctuation." The problem of unemployment was essentially one of casual employment or underemployment produced by the dissipation of demand and the accumulation of separate reserves for each employer. Underemployment could be reduced through "deliberate organisation of the labour market" or the establishment of labor exchanges whose primary objective would be "de-casualization." If all employees for each trade were hired through exchanges, it would be possible to "concentrate employment upon the smallest number that will suffice for the work of the group as a whole." Successive jobs for different employers would go to the same individual rather than "being spread over several men each idle half or more than half his time." [20]

The theory of underemployment and labor reserves explained the futility of traditional relief policy. Trade depression, Beveridge explained, acted "not to reduce to destitution men formerly in regular employment (though no doubt this also happens to some extent), but to precipitate into distress men who are always on its verge. For poverty of this type the sixteen weeks of relief work is obviously no remedy. To men of this type a reduction of earnings brought about by shortening the hours is no deterrent." [21] Beveridge objected, not to efforts to remove the unemployed from Poor Law jurisdiction, but to charitable measures which failed to eliminate the labor market maladjustments which generated unemployment.

Decasualization was the most important but not the only function of the labor exchange. It could help organize the labor market through the transfer of workers in seasonal industries; assistance and training for those displaced by changes in industrial quality; placement of older workers; and guidance of juveniles. By sifting out unemployables from the labor market, it could more efficiently deal with the other categories. The exchange made possible a more effective and dignified work test than any offered by public or private charity and was a prerequisite to any system of unemployment insurance.

Beveridge had been in close touch with the Royal Commission on the Poor Laws and Relief of Distress (1905–1909). He discussed the unemployment issue with the Webbs at great length, and prepared a memorandum on behalf of the Board of Trade. The Majority and Minority reports, delivered in February 1909, enthusiastically endorsed the labor exchange principle and followed Beveridge's theory of unemployment. Six months earlier Winston Churchill had already committed the Board of Trade to a national labor exchange system.[22] Introduced in May 1909, the Labour Exchanges Bill was passed in September. The first exchanges were organized early in 1910, and by the end of 1912 Beveridge administered some 12 regional divisions, 414 exchanges, and 1000 local offices. Administration was transferred in 1916 from the Board of Trade to the newly established Ministry of Labour.

William M. Leiserson, an American economist and leading advocate of labor exchanges, paid tribute to Beveridge as the one who "turned the whole trend of discussion away from the individual and to 'Unemployment — A Problem of Industry.'" The new doctrine "is one of maladjustment" arising from "defects in industrial organization which may be rectified."[23] The organization of a coordinated system of public employment bureaus was the solution of the unemployment problem. Don D. Lescohier, another American economist and disciple of Beveridge, agreed that his "work is the foundation upon which all subsequent writers have builded."[24]

Beveridge's theory and program appeared at a time when many American social reformers were convinced that environment rather than individual failure was the leading cause of poverty. They were compatible with the emphasis upon prevention which pervaded the social reform and social insurance movements of the early twentieth century. To add to their popularity they presented a feasible alternative to Marxist and other radical solutions. Controlled through labor market organization, the industrial reserves were by "no means a fatal weakness of the capitalist system." [25] And for those Americans who recognized that voluntary and involuntary unemployment had to be treated differently, Beveridge suggested a concrete course of action.

American interest in employment exchanges reached a peak during the depression of 1914–15 and the World War I period. However, labor exchanges had existed since 1890 when Ohio established five offices. By 1907, thirteen states had employment offices or authorized cities to establish them; some California and Washington cities had exchanges despite the absence of statutory provision.[26] City or state exchanges existed in twenty-six states by 1915.[27] Interpretation of their function differed sharply before and after 1910. Originally they had been created to compete with commercial, fee-charging agencies in placing individual workers. The private agencies allegedly took fees whether or not a position was found, sent workers to distant cities for nonexistent jobs, and conspired to split fees with contractors or foremen who fired workers soon after they were hired.[28] The immigrant in particular was "dependent in most cases upon the private employment agent and he becomes, because of his ignorance and necessities, a great temptation to an honest agent and a great opportunity to an unscrupulous one." [29] Before 1910 initiative in the establishment of public offices often was taken by labor groups or state labor officials. The exchanges operated for protection and placement of farm hands and unskilled, transient workers rather than skilled union members.[30]

After 1910 Beveridge's ideal of labor market rationalization dominated thought on the role of the public bureaus. But the bureaus were no more successful in achieving this objective than they had been in achieving the more limited ones of private agency regulation and placement. Employers, some of whom had their own trade employment organization, and labor unions proved indifferent or hostile.[31] They feared the use of public bureaus for partisan purposes.[32] Employers were not committed to any such principle as abolition of the labor reserves which exerted a downward pressure upon wages. Skilled workers preferred the informal or formal placement machinery of their unions, and were reluctant to be identified with the type of worker served by the public bureaus.[33] The public, the director of the New York State Bureau of Employment complained, "generally has rather a low regard for employment offices of all kinds, and too often public employment offices have been regarded merely as places to handle common labor, or else to cater to the unemployable or near-unemployable." [34]

Not even the staunchest advocate of labor market organization denied that in practice most public bureaus were administrative nightmares. The employment offices in several states were little more than mail order or correspondence services conducted through the state bureau of labor.[35] They lacked uniformity of standards and coordination, their statistics were not "worth the trouble of studying," and the "blighting influence of local politics" led to the appointment of incompetent officials.[36] Appropriations for support of the public offices were trivial. Three leading American disciples of Beveridge — William Leiserson, Don Lescohier, and Charles B. Barnes — coupled grandiose aspirations for labor market organization through public exchanges with sharp criticism of their actual performance. "Our public employment bureaus," Leiserson conceded, "have in the main been crude and ineffective. Their work . . . has been quite primitive and their methods unbusinesslike; their main activity is with the lowest grades of unskilled and casual laborers and the statistics they publish are often valueless and unreliable." [37] Lescohier and Barnes charged that the public employment offices had become the "dumping grounds for labor politicians" and were "turned over to men who had had little or no experience and who were not naturally fitted for the work." [38]

With few exceptions the public offices were a "distinct failure" and were not "doing the thing for which they were established." [39] Employers justified refusal to patronize them on the grounds of their inability to provide superior workers, while skilled workers remained aloof because they did not "wish to be classified with the general run of applicants attracted to the public office." [40] Whether in 1910 or 1930, their atmosphere was depressing; with few exceptions they were "generally located on dingy streets and are dirty and unattractive." [41]

During World War I, advocates of labor market organization turned hopefully to the prospect of a national employment exchange system to correct chronic deficiencies. War-induced competition for labor, turnover, and scarcities demonstrated the need for a national program of labor market adjustment.[42] There had been a skeleton federal service since 1907, when a Division of Information in the Bureau of Immigration was created. In 1914–15 the Commissioner of Immigration established eighteen employment zones, each with an employment branch station and sub-stations. After the United States entered the war, this mail-order service was extended to thirty-seven states with offices in forty-one cities and branches in fifty-two others. The Secretary of Labor, in 1917, requested $750,000 to finance a genuine national employment service. Congress authorized only $250,000 in October, but in December President Wilson allocated an additional $825,000 from the national security and defense fund. The employment service was separated from the Bureau of Immigration in January 1918 and became the United States Employment Service (USES) of the Department of Labor.[43]

The federal service was divided into thirteen divisions, each administered by a director. Other federal officials were appointed for each state, and several national sections dealt with specialized population or trade groups.[44] The prestige of the USES was enhanced in June 1918 when President Wilson proclaimed that all unskilled labor had to be recruited through the Service. At its zenith, early in 1919, it operated through 854 offices and more than four thousand employees. Its decline was precipitous; the number of federally financed offices dropped to 56 by March 1919, and field service terminated that fall. Employment exchanges were viewed as ad hoc expedients rather than the basis of a rational plan for labor market organization.

Meanwhile, the establishment of the USES raised hopes that the nation would possess a permanent, national exchange system.

The issue, Lescohier proclaimed, was whether "to revert to the old labor-supply policy; or . . . develop constructive policies which will enable our industries to carry on production with smaller labor-reserves." [45] Several plans were proposed for a peacetime federal service. George Barnett favored a centralized, federally administered system on the grounds of superior efficiency, personnel, and prestige.[46] Henry Seager, on behalf of the AALL, recommended a cooperative national–state–municipal arrangement including federal grants-in-aid; this proposal was embodied in the Robinson-Keating bill, introduced in December 1917.[47] It was also favored by Leiserson, who drew an analogy between the structure and function of a national employment service and the Federal Reserve System.[48] Postwar proposals generally favored the cooperative rather than the national form of organization. The Kenyon-Nolan bill, first introduced in 1919, and legislation introduced by Senator Wagner in 1928 and 1930 adopted the cooperative principle and provided for federal grants-in-aid. In 1933, the Wagner-Peyser Act established the United States Employment Service in the Department of Labor. This provided grants-in-aid to states which created a public employment service (at the time there were 120 offices in twenty-three states). The United States Employment Service was transferred in 1939 from the Department of Labor to the Bureau of Employment Security under the Social Security Board.[49]

The ideal of labor market adjustment through public employment exchanges, launched with such burning enthusiasm in the United States and Britain in the early twentieth century, proved a failure. In both countries employment offices came to function as adjuncts to unemployment insurance (rather than the reverse as was anticipated). Beveridge himself wrote an obituary for the English exchanges in 1930. Their unique mission of decasualization had "gone by the board"; here, in their area of "highest utility," they "achieved just nothing at all." After a "hopeful start," they had "sunk in a flood of war tasks and post-war doles." Employers used them as an occasional rather than a regular source of labor, and casual labor and underemployment persisted.[50] Their failure in the United States could not be explained because they were burdened with the administration of insurance benefits before the 1930's. Administrative defects and inadequate appropriations reflected a more fundamental flaw — the indifference of employers and workers to labor market organization under public auspices. Employers did not want a decasualization which reduced their labor reserves, and workers did not wish to be decasualized.

It became obvious by the 1920's that prevention would not be achieved through a national public exchange system. Wesley Mitchell and other economists now directed attention to the business cycle — to the role of money, credit, investment, technological change, and other variables.[51] The second element of the AALL's practical program of 1914–15 — public works construction — aroused considerable interest as a counter-cyclical device. Public works planning, closely identified with Otto T. Mallery, a Philadelphia manufacturer and chairman of the AALL Committee on Public Works, was endorsed by the President's Conference on Unemployment in 1921.[52]

If those responsible for public works and public utility construction would "systematically put aside financial reserves to be provided in times of prosperity for the deliberate purpose of improvement and expansion in times of depressions, we would not only greatly decrease the depth of depressions but we would at the same time diminish the height of booms."[53] Precedents included the establishment of a Public Works Fund by Pennsylvania in 1917 and similar action by California in 1921.[54] Andrews agreed that "emergency work can be made an important agency in maintaining during slack periods the labor reserves needed when industry is booming." It was crucial that public works planning not be confused with work relief. Construction had to "be done in the ordinary way, the workers being employed at the standard wage and under the usual working conditions and hired on the basis of efficiency, not merely because they happen to be unemployed."[55] Timed correctly, the influence of public works expenditure was "effective out of all proportion to its size."[56] It was estimated that by 1928–29 public works amounted to 35 to 40 percent of all public and private construction and totaled some $3,500,000,000.[57]

Mallery proposed a "prosperity reserve" program to protect the nation "against the worst consequences of industrial depressions."[58] According to this, the federal government, localities, and states would commit themselves to "integrated and synchronized" plans for construction budgets, credit arrangements, and specifications. The prosperity reserve made no more progress than labor market organization through public employment exchanges. Americans were not accustomed to central economic planning, and public authorities preferred to "follow the practice of individual enterprises in constructing works as the occasion arises."[59]

The public employment and public works ideals were significant, in retrospect, for their emphasis upon cooperative federal-state-local arrangements. Like the vocational rehabilitation and maternal and child care programs of the 1920's, they helped familiarize Americans with techniques adopted for the relief and social security programs in the 1930's.


It made little difference, in a sense, whether public exchanges or public works helped prevent unemployment. These approaches were secondary compared to emphasis upon stabilization through the efforts of employers. Employment stabilization emerged as the leading technique of prevention in the 1920's. Other methods were making little progress, and employment stabilization had an advantage over employment exchanges or public works in depending upon the initiative of businessmen rather than government. At the same time it could be justified as a business proposition designed to reduce costs and raise profits. It was compatible with two broad business trends — the emergence of personnel management, and welfare capitalism. The AALL lauded stabilization through employer initiative as a uniquely American, preventive approach to social insurance.

The early twentieth century had witnessed a "phenomenal growth in interest on the part of employers in ideas of personnel and the problems connected with personnel work." The problems of hiring and turnover during World War I stimulated the creation or expansion of employment departments. Employment management was described as a "new profession," and logical evolution in industry from exclusive concentration upon "processes, machines and buildings." [60]

The objective of the employment department was the organization of a work environment which increased efficiency and profits. In the eyes of the manager, it was "obvious beyond argument that every unnecessary dismissal of an employe must mean a definite economic waste to the employer, to the employe, and to society." He measured the efficiency of his department by turnover statistics.[61] The goal of reduced labor turnover was interpreted even more broadly in the 1920's. It implied a positive responsibility on the part of industry to provide job security. Here was an even greater challenge to industrial statesmanship than old-age security.

Job security through efficient industrial management was proclaimed as the outstanding American contribution to the theory and prevention of unemployment. Beveridge had failed to "inquire whether there is a need for the excessive hiring and firing which causes so many dislocations from jobs." He had not looked into "the process of operation inside the plant to question the efficiency or considerateness of management." The report of the Royal Poor Law Commission of 1909 was criticized on similar grounds. With the possible exception of S. Seebohm Rowntree, English thought continued to ignore this "essential phase of a thoroughgoing remedial program." For once the traditional individualism of American businessmen, which had thwarted social legislation, could be adapted to collective ends; it focused "attention on the need for eliminating unemployment, rather than accepting all of it as inevitable and paying for it through relief measures." [62]

Philosophers of welfare capitalism like Sam A. Lewisohn or Ernest Draper and the economist-reformer like John Commons agreed that in dealing with unemployment the primary objective was prevention by means of enlightened business leadership.[63]

Each employer should strive to stabilize employment by adjusting production to demand. This required research, diversification which minimized seasonal fluctuation, in-plant training and transfer, and the cooperation of consumer, dealer, and sale force in timing or spacing orders "in the manner most conducive to continuous production." [64] Throughout the 1920's the same few companies were cited as examples of successful regularization: Dennison Manufacturing, Framingham, Mass.; Hills Brothers, Philadelphia; Procter and Gamble, Cincinnati; and Eastman Kodak, Rochester.

In 1921 the National Industrial Conference Board extolled the emergence of "scientific management" as an "outstanding feature of industrial development," and urged that unemployment insurance "should not be applied until a fair chance has been given management to reduce unemployment to the minimum through stabilization of industry and efficient distribution of the labor supply." [65] This admonition did not apply to insurance plans established voluntarily, which represented self-imposed penalities for failure to regularize. Yet unemployment prevention through voluntary regularization proved an even greater chimera than old-age security through the medium of welfare capitalism. With or without insurance, regularization was the exception rather than the rule in American business. (Indeed, the few firms cited as pioneers in regularization were often the ones which established an insurance plan.)

A survey published by the Industrial Relations Counselors found eleven company plans in existence in 1928, all of which had been "initiated largely by employers interested in scientific management, and for the most part . . . adopted as part of a broad program for regularizing employment." [66] Two others had been terminated, and two more were established in 1930 by General Electric and a group of five firms in Wisconsin. There were, in addition, twenty-two joint employer-union plans, mostly in the clothing industry, while another two had been abandoned. Only four national unions, covering 1,323 workers, paid unemployment benefits in 1928; thirty-seven local union benefit programs affected 33,400 workers (representing 1 percent of A.F. of L. member-

ship). The twenty-two joint plans covered 63,500 employees, and
the eleven company plans another 8,500. Voluntary unemployment insurance plans in 1928–29 thus enrolled some 106,723 workers, and one-third depended upon union rather than company
benefits.

In April 1931, a Bureau of Labor Statistics survey found fifteen
company plans covering 50,000 workers. The number of joint
plans dropped to sixteen (with 65,000 employees). Adding 45,000
workers eligible for trade union benefits, the total covered by
voluntary unemployment insurance increased from 106,000 in
1929 to 116,000 in 1931.[67] The earliest company plan was created
by Dennison in 1916. The latest, and most unique perhaps, was
established in Rochester, New York, early in 1931. It was a joint
arrangement among fourteen firms whose employees totaled one-
third of the city's industrial workers. The first employer-union
plan was established in the wallpaper industry in 1894. The second, adopted in the women's clothing industry in Cleveland, did
not take effect until 1921. Of the 65,000 covered in the sixteen
joint plans in 1931, 43,000 were employed in the men's clothing
industry in Chicago, New York City, and Rochester.[68]

The Cleveland and Chicago joint-agreement plans were frequently cited. Commons served as chairman of the joint trustees
of the Chicago insurance fund, an experience which helped shape
his theory of unemployment compensation. The Cleveland plan
took the form of a work guarantee. Each participating manufacturer guaranteed employees of the International Ladies Garment
Workers Union a minimum of twenty weeks of work each half
year. If he failed, the employee was entitled to two-thirds of
wages for the weeks of unemployment. As later revised, the plan
guaranteed forty weeks of work per year, and half-pay for the
period of unemployment. No manufacturer was liable for more
than 7½ percent of payroll costs under the original agreement, or
10 percent under the revised program. The Chicago agreement
lacked the work-guarantee feature. It was financed by equal contributions from employers and employees, representing seventy-
five manufacturers and the Amalgamated Clothing Workers. Contributions equaled 3 percent of payroll; benefits were fixed at

40 percent of wages (limited to five weeks per calendar year), and a maximum of twenty dollars per week.[69]

Commons, Andrews, and their followers interpreted the few examples of regularization or insurance as evidence that prevention of unemployment through employer initiative was practical. Commons described unemployment as the critical defect of capitalism, the leading source of conflict between capital and labor for a hundred years, and the stimulus to both trade unions and socialism. In order to survive, capitalism had to provide the wage-earner with job security — just as security was provided for the investor. Neither the government nor the wage-earner in a free enterprise system could control the conditions which determined the level of employment. The only "businesslike way" to deal with unemployment was to "place the responsibility on the businessmen, who alone are in a position to prevent it." This was the clue to the "modern idea of social insurance, as we have learned from the accident compensation laws." [70]

Yet, if the prevention of unemployment through managerial innovation was both possible and profitable, why wasn't it a routine practice in the business world? If it was profitable for businessmen to reduce labor turnover and provide job security, why did they need the incentive allegedly provided by unemployment compensation? Perhaps, as Rubinow, Epstein, Douglas, and others suggested, it could not be presumed that individual employers had unlimited control over the situation, or that stabilization was desired by businessmen. Paul Douglas challenged the presumption that American management was capable of "changing the face of the universe." Enthusiastic but unsophisticated advocates of regularization presumed its universal applicability, and ignored variables like product standardization, style factors, level of monopoly or quasi-monopoly, and storage costs. Individual employers could not control the impact of technological change or cyclical fluctuation? In any case, Douglas argued, the "average businessman" believed regularization was "financially impracticable." It would be easier and more effective to stabilize workers' incomes through insurance.[71]

Rubinow challenged the feasibility of an unemployment compensation program geared to regularization. It was the same old story of prevention versus insurance. If the "force of national pride," was added, insurance "characterized as the ineffective European method, and stabilization as the American contribution to the problem of unemployment," an important point could be gained. The fallacy in this argument was that we are "altogether uncertain of the ways of counteracting economic crises, as we are uncertain of their causation." With tiresome regularity the apostle of prevention "mentions . . . some well-known examples — the Dennison Manufacturing Company, and Hills Brothers, packers of Dromedary dates, the Procter and Gamble plan, which made Cincinnati famous, and . . . usually stops there." In all these cases of successful stabilization, "very favorable market conditions" were present.[72]

Ideals of regularization and unemployment compensation designed to provide incentives to employers were inspired by a false analogy with workmen's compensation. Not only was it questionable that compensation had significantly lowered accident rates, but unemployment differed in that "to a very much lesser degree does it depend upon the care exercised by an individual employer." [73] If employment stabilization was to be achieved, it would be through an insurance method which maintained consumer purchasing power. The controversy over the possibilities of prevention, and the purpose of an unemployment compensation program, reached a climax in the early 1930's. It raised broad questions of the economic and social function of government welfare programs which persist to the present.

The original unemployment compensation legislation introduced by the AALL was inspired by England — the only nation to establish a national compulsory program before 1919. Beveridge, the Webbs, and both the Majority and Minority of the Royal Poor Law Commission of 1909 had endorsed labor exchanges, but only Beveridge favored compulsory unemployment insurance. The essential principle of the poor-law reform, suggested by Sidney and Beatrice Webb and embodied in the Minority Report, was the break-up of the poor law and the transfer of all welfare functions to other agencies of local or national government. The kind of service required, rather than the presence or absence of destitution, would be the governing consideration. In large measure this proposal was rooted in the belief that universal availability of health and welfare services afforded superior opportunities for the prevention of sickness, unemployment, and other sources of dependency. The Webbs objected to compulsory unemployment insurance, and social insurance generally, on the grounds of limited preventive possibilities and increased dangers of malingering.[74]

Beveridge, like Rubinow in the United States, never viewed prevention as an alternative to insurance. Insurance was not some inferior substitute for prevention; it had a different function. Designed to deal mainly with chronic underemployment, the labor exchanges could not control unemployment caused by technological change or business fluctuations. The "incalculable changes and irregularities of economic conditions will still make nearly all men insecure. No amount of Labour Exchanges can guarantee that every man falling out of one job shall at once find another job suited to his powers." [75]

Winston Churchill played a key role in the enactment of unemployment insurance.[76] He had been transferred from the Colonial Office to the presidency of the Board of Trade in 1908 as part of Herbert Asquith's cabinet reorganization. Although the Webbs had been his mentors in the field of social legislation, he did not share their objections to compulsory social insurance. He interpreted unemployment insurance, in particular, as an opportunity to dramatize the emergence of a new Liberal Party program, and to cope with a serious social problem in a way that protected the individual's independence and dignity. Lloyd George viewed the issue similarly. Consequently, Britain was committed to the social insurance rather than the Webb or Fabian path to the welfare state.

When Churchill, in the fall of 1908, had initiated action leading to the Labour Exchanges Act of 1909, he requested Board of Trade officials to begin work on a plan for unemployment insurance.[77] This was undertaken by Beveridge and Llewellyn Smith, who recognized the importance of acquiring trade union support. The appointment of Isaac Mitchell as Labour Adviser to the Board of Trade proved "invaluable." [78] Late in 1908 the president of the Trades Union Congress reported that insurance posed no threat to the continued growth of the labor movement.[79] Lloyd George officially announced in his budget address of April 1909 that a plan for unemployment insurance was under consideration. Beveridge insisted that the scheme as introduced and enacted in 1911 "owed little to any model overseas" except for the German practice of recording insurance contributions in stampbooks. The English trade unions served as the primary model, notably their "practice of requiring signature of a vacant book in working hours as proof of unemployment, and their common provision of a waiting period before benefit began." [80] In contrast to their American counterparts, English unions in the early twentieth century had developed an extensive system of unemployment benefits.[81]

One of the ironies of British social legislation is that Beveridge, a chief architect of the labor exchange and unemployment insurance programs, subsequently became their severest critic. The unemployment insurance system underwent drastic revisions in the 1920's and collapsed, in Beveridge's estimation, under the weight of extended and supplementary benefits as well as indiscriminate coverage. The Munition Workers' Insurance Act of 1916 added 1,250,000 workers to the original 2,250,000 in the seven selected trades of 1911. Noncommissioned war veterans from 1918 to 1921 and civilians from November 1918 to November 1919 were awarded benefits irrespective of contributions. In 1920 coverage was extended to virtually all workers outside agriculture and domestic service. Under the original act workers and employers contributed 2½d. per week and the state 1⅔d., and benefits were limited to 7s a week for fifteen weeks (and no more than one week's benefit for five weeks of contributions). In 1920 benefits were raised to 15s a week. Then, in March 1921, as the "country passed into the worst depression recorded in British history," the extended benefit was introduced, and in November the supplementary allowance for dependants. Originally intended to last for a few months, the extended benefit was continued by successive legislative enactments. The Labour Government in 1924 abolished ministerial discretion in its award, and made the extended benefit unlimited in duration. The Conservative government restored ministerial discretion in 1925, but continued the extended benefit.[82]

The liberalization of unemployment insurance, Beveridge complained, had resulted in a "fundamental reconstruction." Only the "ghost of insurance" remained. It had originally implied a dual contractual relationship: the insured person received "legally enforceable rights without ministerial discretion and without regard to his other resources or private character. Second, it gave these rights in consideration of contributions by or in respect of the insured person." During the 1920's, unemployment insurance experienced a transition from "contract" to "status"; it became a "general system of outdoor relief of the ablebodied, administered by a national tax in place of a local authority, and financed mainly by a tax on employment." [83] Need rather than equity determined eligibility for benefit.

Compulsory unemployment insurance was enacted elsewhere between 1919 and 1927: Italy, Luxembourg, Austria, Queensland (Australia), the Irish Free State, Bulgaria, Poland, Germany, and various Swiss cantons. The British experience was usually cited to strengthen the argument of American business and insurance interests that prevention was preferable to relief, and that compulsory unemployment insurance was unworkable. The generous doles provided by the British system, the National Industrial Conference Board charged, actually lessened any "pressure for prevention." They impeded labor mobility, aided union efforts to freeze wage levels, "encouraged idleness . . . and exerted a demoralizing influence on the entire labor force." No compulsory unemployment insurance program could remain solvent for, as in Britain, it was "subject to constant and irresistible pressure to increase the benefits, extend the limits of coverage, relax the safeguards, and thus expand the plan from a limited self-supporting insurance system to a general relief scheme supported by public funds and, in the end, paid for by taxation."[84]

The British experience confirmed to Commons and Andrews the wisdom of stressing preventive goals and disassociating their proposals from Europe. The British program, Andrews asserted, "was always an exceedingly cumbersome affair and did not approach the matter in a businesslike way for the purpose of preventive work." It suffered from the "suicidal imposition of Government 'doles,' which were promptly confused with genuine insurance by all enemies of progressive social insurance legislation." Unemployment compensation as proposed in the United States stimulated the "great captains of industry . . . into something like intelligent action."[85]

Before fully realizing that the purpose of social insurance was prevention rather than economic security, the AALL had prepared an unemployment insurance bill along English lines. Introduced unsuccessfully into the Massachusetts legislature in 1916, it provided for contributions by employer, employee, and state.[86] The break with the Old World occurred in 1921 when the Huber bill, devised by Commons, was introduced in Wisconsin; amended versions were presented at every legislative session there through 1929. Between 1921 and 1929 unemployment compensation bills were also introduced in legislatures in Massachusetts, New York, Pennsylvania, Minnesota, South Carolina, and Connecticut. The Huber bill served as a model and the AALL, in most cases, participated in drafting the legislation.[87] The limitation of contributions to employers was the distinctive feature of the Huber bill. The 1921 version required insurance to be carried through an employers' mutual, but this was amended in 1923 to allow insurance through any authorized carrier. The underlying idea, Commons explained, was that the "modern businessman is the only person who is in the strategic position and has the managerial ability capable of preventing unemployment."[88]

The AALL bill of December 1930 was based upon the Huber principle. Employers alone contributed a small, fixed percentage of payrolls. Administration was delegated to Employment Stabilization boards in each industry, though employers who furnished proof of ability to pay were exempted from contributions as in workmen's compensation.[89]

A bill introduced in the 1931 Wisconsin legislature by Harold Groves, a former student of Commons and professor at the University of Wisconsin, marked the final stage in the evolution from insurance to prevention. Conceived and drafted by another Wisconsin economist, Paul Raushenbush, and his wife, Elizabeth Brandeis, it abandoned insurance altogether in favor of employer reserves. Acclaimed by Commons and Andrews, Groves's "much superior bill" segregated contributions into individual company funds.[90] Employers resisted its enactment and an Interim Committee was created to expore the unemployment issue and report to a special session of the legislature in the fall of 1931. The Committee reported favorably, and passage was urged by Governor La Follette. The Governor, anticipating continued employer resistance, recommended that the measure take effect only if employers had failed within a year-and-a-half to establish voluntary plans covering a stipulated number of workers. A Wisconsin Committee for Unemployment Reserves Legislation was organized to promote the bill, whose passage was virtually assured when farmer organizations endorsed it on the grounds that industry should support its unemployed and that compensation benefits would help maintain purchasing power.[91]

Signed by La Follette in January 1932, the Groves bill did not take effect in the summer of 1933 even though employers had failed to establish enough voluntary plans. The legislature authorized another year's delay, but eventually, in July 1934, the law took effect. The previous year the AALL had revised its model bill to conform to the Wisconsin individual reserve system (though Andrews had once complained to Paul Raushenbush that this arrangement failed to provide sufficient protection for workers).[92] The Groves bill established a state fund which segregated individual employer accounts. Contributions equaled 2 percent of payroll for the first two years, and continued until an employer's reserve averaged fifty-five dollars per employee; the contribution then dropped to 1 percent until the reserve averaged seventy-five dollars per employee; at that point contributions terminated. The measure was limited to businesses with ten or more employees, and did not cover farm workers, loggers, or employees earning more than $1500 a year. Benefits were awarded after a two-week waiting period, and equaled 50 percent of weekly wages (subject to a five dollar minimum and ten dollar maximum). There was a deduction of one dollar a week for each five dollars that the employer reserve fell below an average of fifty dollars per employee. Benefits were limited to ten weeks, and to those who satisfied the requirement of a two-year state residence and forty weeks of employment within that period.[93]

The Wisconsin plan was virtually unchallenged in 1931–32 and was endorsed by the Governors' Interstate Commission in February 1932.[94] Widely publicized by the AALL, Commons, and Raushenbush, its conservative features were carefully stressed. Commons described it as "extraordinarily . . . individualistic and capitalistic." It should appeal to the "individualism of American capitalists who do not want to be burdened with the inefficiencies or misfortunes of other capitalists, and it fits the public policy of a capitalistic nation which uses the profit motive to prevent unemployment." [95] Like the AALL's American Plan, it was inspired by experience with workmen's compensation and the common business practice of setting aside dividend reserves "to pay stockholders during periods when their plants are idle." [96] An "unemployment reserve fund" was established so that "wage-earners may be tided over temporary periods of involuntary idleness." [97] In the final analysis the Wisconsin plan was the contribution of businessmen and was "fashioned avowedly" upon their own experiments.[98]

The "American approach" centered upon "possibilities of stabilization of employment and not merely a program of relief as in most European countries." It contrasted with European legislation in eschewing legislative appropriations to the reserve funds. It should be made clear, Andrews advised, that the employer's liability was "strictly limited" to his own employees and to the sum available in his individual reserve. He should "feel the very direct incentive to stabilize employment and that, of course, is the very important consideration." [99] Because of its incentives to prevention, appeal to the businessman's competitive instinct, and compatibility with the profit motive in a free enterprise system, the Wisconsin plan had a political leverage in comparison to pooled insurance funds.[100] But, for all the effort to devise an American plan adapted to free enterprise principles it was not embraced enthusiastically by employers — either as an expression of their commitment to stabilization or in order to thwart alternative, more radical proposals.

Apart from stimulating public discussion of unemployment insurance in the early 1930's, the most tangible result of the Wisconsin plan was the dramatization of the contrast between the Rubinow and AALL-Wisconsin traditions of social insurance. The November 1932 report of the Ohio Commission on Unemployment, reflecting Rubinow's views, reasserted the classic European principles of social insurance, and terminated the dominance of the Wisconsin plan. As chief actuary and chairman of the Committee on Research, Rubinow coverted Leiserson and the rest of the Commission from reserves to insurance.[101] The Commission's report, or "Ohio Plan," provided a base from which Epstein, Douglas, and others criticized the Wisconsin approach. The Commission asserted (as Rubinow always had) that "insurance is based on the assumption that the risk itself is inevitable, however much it may be reduced." Insurance was "soundest and most economical when it covers the widest spread of people subject to the risk." [102] Individual employer reserves failed to provide adequate economic security, and could not, as large insurance funds, maintain purchasing power in periods of depression. The Commission recommended unemployment insurance legislation requiring a contribution of 2 percent by employer and 1 percent by employee. Rubinow would have preferred 2-percent contributions by both groups to raise benefit levels, but labor always objected to any contribution. Rubinow noted that the 1932 convention of the A.F. of L. had endorsed unemployment insurance for the first time, but without "any real enthusiasm." [103] Although both the Wisconsin and Ohio legislation limited benefits to 50 percent of weekly wages, the Ohio plan proposed a fifteen dollar maximum compared to Wisconsin's ten dollars, and a benefit period of sixteen rather than ten weeks. A merit-rating provision was included in the Ohio proposal, allowing employer contributions to range 1 to 3½ percent. This was an expedient forced by the "popularity of the Wisconsin idea." [104] Rubinow suggested that if there was any validity to the Wisconsin incentive plan, it should be incorporated in this way as part of a pooled fund.

The Ohio plan was bitterly criticized by some employers. The Ohio Chamber of Commerce charged Rubinow with being a Bolshevik and fraud.[105] In place of unemployment insurance it proposed the "American System" (apparently not even the Wisconsin plan was sufficiently "American"). The essence of the System was self-help among family, relatives, and neighbors and, at the highest level of collectivism, community funds and public charities. Instead of "indicting our institutions" as failures, we should "offer up a thanksgiving for the blessings of our country." It was "indefensible and disloyal" during these trying days to "attempt to foist upon the United States foreign ideals and foreign practices." Unemployment insurance was the "most menacing and revolutionary piece of legislation ever proposed in the history of Ohio!"; it threatened the "complete disruption of our American system of individual responsibility." [106]

Abraham Epstein's criticism of the Wisconsin plan was almost as violent. Individual employer reserves marked the "most stupid undertaking that has ever been suggested." No one in the United States who understood social insurance supported the idea, and "no one, in the entire history of European social insurance, ever suggested such a fantasy." If employers wanted to or could stabilize employment, he informed Raushenbush, the profit motive served as a "sufficient inducement and no penalty levied through an unemployment insurance contribution can equal the loss now encountered through inability to keep their factories going." [107] Andrews resented the aggressive campaign launched on behalf of the Ohio plan. "Our friends in Ohio," he complained, "asked us to keep hands off and let them work out their program without interference. . . . Now it appears that our Ohio friends are very vigorously trying to force the Ohio scheme upon the rest of the country." [108]

No state other than Wisconsin enacted compulsory unemployment compensation before 1935, but a great deal of legislation was introduced reflecting a "sudden" change of attitude after the report of the Ohio Commission.[109] Some fifty-two bills had been introduced in seventeen states in 1931 (in addition to investigating commissions in Wisconsin, Ohio, California, Connecticut, Massachusetts, and New York). Bills were introduced in five states during the legislative off-year of 1932. Among the sixty-eight bills in twenty-five states in 1933, the Ohio plan gained an edge over the Wisconsin individual reserve. Unemployment compensation bills passed one of the legislative houses in seven states that year; and four of these bills provided for pooled funds. After the passage of the Social Security Act in 1935, only seven states established the individual employer reserve, and two of these made provision for a partial pooling. The remaining states established pooled funds (with merit-rating provisions in all but eleven). Eventually every state shifted to a pooled fund with merit-rating features.[110]

The theory of social insurance identified with Andrews, Commons, and the AALL had achieved its clearest formulation after 1921 in connection with the unemployment issue. Influenced by workmen's compensation and the Safety-first campaign, ideals of preventive social legislation, the decisive defeat of compulsory health insurance, and voluntary efforts to regularize employment through scientific management and insurance, this tradition emphasized prevention as the objective of social insurance. It illustrated how a movement which emerged in the early twentieth century to challenge the ideology and institutions of voluntarism came to terms with its incongruous environment. First, the businessman rather than the state would assume the initiative in the quest for security; compulsion was merely a means to enlightened, voluntary self-interest. Second, the

American plan of social insurance used capitalist methods — competition and the profit motive — to achieve collective security. It implied dependence upon the same economic processes which had produced insecurity for much of the working population. The crucial consideration is that the AALL-Wisconsin approach to social insurance was an effort to provide economic security with a minimum of income redistribution. If income maintenance is subordinated to prevention and employer incentives, it follows that a social insurance will have little or no redistributive function.

The tradition embodied in Rubinow and Epstein differed sharply. The challenge to voluntarism was more prominent in light of the emphasis upon government leadership, benefit adequacy, and use of the social insurances to redistribute income. By the 1930's these objectives were supplemented by increasing interest in the role of the social insurances in maintaining consumer purchasing power. The Social Security Act of 1935 attempted to reconcile these two traditions. It expressed a greater commitment to the related goals of income maintenance and redistribution than the Wisconsin plan, but did not go as far as Rubinow and, especially, Epstein preferred.

The purpose of the Social Security Act was summed up in this way: "Only to a very minor degree does it modify the distribution of wealth and it does not alter at all the fundamentals of our capitalistic and individualistic economy. Nor does it relieve the individual of primary responsibility for his own support and that of his dependents. . . . Social security does not dampen initiative or render thrift outmoded." [1] Eligibility and benefits in the contributory old-age and unemployment insurance titles were closely work-related, government contributions were omitted, and fiscal conservatism prevailed in the emphasis upon reserves and the equity principles of private insurance.

Abraham Epstein became the most uncompromising critic of the Social Security Act which, he charged, expressed too limited a conception of economic and social function. It did not provide economic security because it did not entail any significant income redistribution. Epstein's views were colored, in part, by personal disappointment. He was bitter over the failure of the Committee on Economic Security to consult him, Rubinow, or Douglas. "From the very inception," he complained, "the Administration has refused to listen to anyone who knew anything about the problem." [2] To a large degree he attributed this neglect, and the limitations of the Act itself, to Frances Perkins.[3] He became an intemperate critic of the old-age and unemployment titles, hoping the courts would nullify them and urging the states to refuse to participate in the tax-offset unemployment system established in 1935.[4]

Rubinow was disappointed with the Social Security Act, but even more disappointed with Epstein. His friend and disciple had been "treated shabbily by Miss Frances Perkins and all her lieutenants. His services to social insurance entitled him to a more influential position in the counsels of the Committee." [5] Yet, if Epstein had "waited so long as I have and seen one disappointment after another, he wouldn't be quite so ready to advocate this theory of either everything or nothing." [6] Rubinow was irked by Epstein's inordinate praise of the categorical assistance programs which, presumably, were genuine social security because they were financed out of general tax revenues and, hence, redistributive. Because of the "pretty name of pensions," he admonished Epstein, "you prefer a system of public relief to the system of public insurance, and you get away from this difficulty by calling the first social security." I have not, Rubinow added, "preached social insurance for thirty-five years in order now, at this late date, to abandon my ideal for the sake of a somewhat glorified system of public relief with half a dozen means tests." [7]

The substance of Rubinow's criticism of the Social Security Act was similar to Epstein's. Neither admired the tax-offset system of unemployment compensation, and both preferred a national or subsidy plan which was less cumbersome administratively, and would have provided a greater measure of federal control over standards. Both men objected to the equity obsession in the contributory titles and the full reserve requirement in old-age insurance which they believed would worsen the depression by reducing purchasing power. Both criticized the omission of health insurance, and felt that government contributions were necessary to make economic security based upon income redistribution a reality. But Rubinow did not allow personal grievances or disgust over the limitations of the Social Security Act to warp his judgment. He did not lavish uncritical praise upon the categorical assistance titles, or urge that the states decline to participate in unemployment insurance. Most important, he recognized that the Social Security Act marked only a beginning, and that it could be amended to provide for government contributions, health insurance, and other improvements. [8]

Epstein's personal disappointments may have influenced the tone and manner of his criticism, but it should be evaluated in its own right. The Wisconsin plan was an attempt to attain economic security with a minimum of income redistribution. It posed no challenge to the primary or functional system of income distribution which hinged upon efficient labor force participation. This remained fully intact, as did the equity principles of private insurance in which eligibility and benefits were closely tied to individual contributions. For Epstein income redistribution was the fundamental consideration. He believed that traditional methods of wealth allocation should be modified by channeling more income through the social insurances, and that equity insurance principles should be subordinated to goals of social adequacy. Social insurance, Epstein argued, "differs basically from private insurance in that it adds to the private insurance principle of risk distribution the social principle of distributing the cost among all elements in the community." This cost distribution was necessary in order to lighten the economic burden imposed upon the poorest classes and increase their benefits. Social insurance, therefore, did not "seek individual protection according to ability to pay but rather a socially adequate arrangement which will protect all the workers as well as society from certain social hazards." Commitment to a full reserve in old-age insurance illustrated the extent to which the "framers of the Social Security Act confused governmental social insurance with private insurance." [9]

The distinguishing feature of social insurance, which made the subordination of equity to adequacy possible, was a government contribution. This led to a vertical redistribution of national wealth or profits through higher insurance benefits. Payroll taxes, Epstein insisted, burdened the worker and consumer. The Social Security Act, "actually decreases the purchasing power of the masses by depriving them of immediate purchases, by relieving the well-to-do from their share of the social burden, and by making the workers pay the expenses of a vast administration." Governmental contributions would "lighten the unbearable load" placed upon the worker and attack the "maldistribution of our national income." They would enable social security benefits to act as a supplement to wages and increase the purchasing power of the masses. The only justification for worker contributions was psychological — a means of "taking away whatever stigma is attached to governmental relief." [10]

The 1939 amendments to the Social Security Act testified to the validity of many of Epstein's criticisms. In old-age insurance a contingent reserve was substituted for the full reserve by holding contributions stationary and increasing expenditures. The benefit formula was changed by substituting average earnings for lifetime cumulative earnings, and weighting it somewhat in favor of lower-income groups. And, as Epstein had urged, provision was made for dependent and survivor allowances. Although these changes pleased Epstein, they did not suffice. Unemployment insurance remained "inadequate and unrealistic," because it suffered from the vestiges of the "same hopeless private-insurance principle which characterized our original old age annuity plan." Lacking any provision for extended or dependent benefits, it operated in a "social vacuum." [11] The American social security system still lacked any provision for health insurance and did not authorize government contributions.

Together with Rubinow, Epstein personified a social insurance tradition which stressed social adequacy as the ultimate test of an insurance or assistance program. They insisted that social adequacy and strict adherence to the equity principles of private insurance were incompatible, favored government contributions to enable the social insurances to insure adequacy, and cautioned against confusing the income maintenance function of social insurance with prevention or other extraneous goals. Far more than Andrews and Commons, both men favored the use of the social insurances to transfer functions from the voluntary to the public sector, and divert wealth into the secondary system of income distribution.

Post-1935 amendments to the Social Security Act have extended coverage, raised benefits, and introduced disability insurance (1956) and Medicare for the aged (1965). For all its imperfections, the Social Security Act was a turning point in American history. It marked a decisive transfer of welfare functions from voluntary to public institutions, and from the local to the federal level, thus paving the way for contemporary anti-poverty programs.

Yet the American welfare state remains underdeveloped by income-maintenance criteria. Our economic security system was designed in the 1930's, and can still be interpreted as an effort to provide some measure of economic security without significantly affecting income distribution. In dollar volume the social insurances overwhelm the tax-supported public assistance programs, implying a determination to keep economic security as contributory and closely work-related as possible. On the other hand, private benefit plans have advanced rapidly in the United States since World War II. These are the most regressive social welfare measures of all because of their links to employment stability, seniority, and upper echelon personnel.[12]

It is the millions dependent upon public assistance who suffer most in a system of economic security so closely tied to labor-force participation. Contemporary critics emphasize that public assistance, despite federal financing, provides inadequate allowances, fails to reach all those eligible, penalizes incentive because of rigid eligibility requirements, and harasses clients through the imposition of behavioral norms (such as the "suitable home" provisions in the Aid to Families with Dependent Children Program). It is clearer now than it was in the 1930's that abuses are inherent in any economic assistance program which hinges on a means test and the wide range of administrative discretion this allows.

Criticism of public assistance in the 1960's has been linked with reform proposals which may, in time, lead to changes as profound as those of the 1930's, when economic security was established as a public and federal responsibility. Such diverse proposals as the guaranteed income, negative income tax, family allowances or insurance, and the national assistance minimum reflect the widespread dissatisfaction with the state of public assistance; they embody a search for alternatives which will eliminate or minimize the conflict between objective economic need, on the one hand, behavioral norms, penurious local administration, and oppressive eligibility requirements, on the other.[13]

The need for public assistance has not, as was anticipated in the 1930's, "withered away." [14] On the contrary, it has become the Achilles' heel of the American welfare state, its most conspicuous failure. Public assistance confronts the welfare system with its most difficult challenge: Must economic security remain so closely tied to stable, long-term labor force participation? Must the unemployable — dependent children, blind, handicapped, aged, able-bodied but unskilled — who compose the overwhelming percentage of the assistance rolls be penalized for their incapacity to compete in the labor market? If the first phase in the evolution of the twentieth-century welfare state was the establishment of insurance programs related to employment, the second will be a system of predictable, nonpunitive income maintenance for those who cannot participate fully in the labor force.

# Notes

## Chapter 1   The Constraints of Voluntarism

1. Alexis de Tocqueville, *Democracy in America* (New York: Vintage Books, 1954), II, 118, 115, 116.

2. Louis D. Brandeis, "Workingmen's Insurance — The Road to Social Efficiency," National Conference of Charities and Correction, *Proceedings* (1911), 157.

3. Roy Lubove, *The Professional Altruist: The Emergence of Social Work as a Career, 1880–1930* (Cambridge, Mass., 1965).

4. Gaston V. Rimlinger, "Social Security, Incentives and Controls in the U.S. and U.S.S.R.," *Comparative Studies in Society and History,* 4 (1961–62), 105.

5. Eveline M. Burns, "Social Insurance in Evolution," *American Economic Review,* 34 (March 1944), supplement, pt. 2, 199.

6. David Starr Jordan, "Governmental Obstacles to Insurance," *Scientific Monthly* 2 (January 1916), 28.

7. Arthur T. Hadley, *Economics: An Account of the Relations Between Private Property and Public Welfare* (New York, 1900), 63; James H. Hamilton, *Savings and Saving Institutions* (New York, 1902), 128.

8. Mary Willcox Brown, *The Development of Thrift* (New York, 1900), 9; Hadley, *Economics,* 63.

9. Brown, *Development of Thrift,* 37, 38, 12.

10. Hamilton, *Savings and Saving Institutions,* 58, 54. Criticism of these conventional attitudes toward thrift appears in, John A. Lapp, "The Insurance of Thrift," American Academy of Political and Social Science, *Annals,* 87 (January 1920), 21–26.

11. P. Tecumseh Sherman, *Dangerous Tendencies in the American Social Insurance Movement: An Address . . . before . . . the Insurance Society of New York on November 21, 1916* (Insurance Society of New York, 1917), 3; Frederick L. Hoffman, "Autocracy and Paternalism vs. Democracy and Liberty" (address, annual meeting of the International Association of Casualty and Surety Underwriters, New York City, December 4, 1918) in F. L. Hoffman, *Compulsory Health Insurance, 1914–20* (bound volume of pamphlets). 1, 23, 11.

12. Frederick L. Hoffman, "Failure of German Compulsory Health Insurance: A War Revelation" (address, Twelfth Annual Meeting of the Association of Life Insurance Presidents, New York City, December 6, 1918), in Hoffman, *Compulsory Health Insurance*, 3, 9; Hoffman, "Health Insurance and the Public" (reprinted from *Pennsylvania Medical Journal*, July 1919), in Hoffman, *Compulsory Health Insurance*, 17–18.

13. Hoffman, "Autocracy and Paternalism vs. Democracy and Liberty," 21. "There are those who are impatient with what has been done," another critic of social insurance complained, "and who insistently demand the introduction of European systems of so-called social insurance, resting upon un-American principles of political and social life." Forrest F. Dryden, "The Government and Wage-Earners' Insurance," *North American Review*, 207 (June 1918), 866.

14. Paul Monroe, "An American System of Labor Pensions and Insurance," *American Journal of Sociology*, 2 (January 1897), 502.

15. A useful summary is, Robert Presthus, *The Organizational Society: An Analysis and a Theory* (New York, 1962).

16. Nicholas Paine Gilman, *A Dividend to Labor: A Study of Employers' Welfare Institutions* (Boston, 1899), 15, 13.

17. E. A. Vanderlip, "Insurance from the Employers' Standpoint," National Conference of Charities and Correction, *Proceedings* (1906), 457.

18. John R. Commons, "Industrial Relations," in Commons, ed., *Trade Unionism and Labor Problems*, 2nd. series, orig. ed. 1905 (Boston, 1921), 9; Vanderlip, "Insurance from the Employers' Standpoint," 458.

19. Louis D. Brandeis, *Business — A Profession*, orig. ed., 1914 (Boston, 1933), 11–12. Brandeis pointed to the career of William H. McElwain of Boston as another example of "success in professionalized business."

20. Vanderlip, "Insurance from the Employers' Standpoint," 463.

21. United States Commissioner of Labor, *Workmen's Insurance and Benefit Funds in the United States,* Twenty-Third Annual Report, 1908 (Washington, D.C., 1909). Other surveys of industrial welfare in the early twentieth century include: Gilman, *Dividend to Labor;* Charles R. Henderson, *Industrial Insurance in the United States* (Chicago, 1909); Elizabeth L. Otey, "Employers' Welfare Work," U.S. Department of Labor, Bureau of Labor Statistics, *Bulletin,* No. 123 (May 15, 1913); Boris Emmet, "Operation of Establishment and Trade-Union Disability Funds," *Monthly Labor Review,* 5 (August 1917), 217–236; "Welfare Work for Employees in Industrial Establishments in the United States," U.S. Department of Labor, Bureau of Labor Statistics, *Bulletin,* No. 250, February 1919; National Industrial Conference Board, *Experience with Mutual Benefit Associations in the United States,* Research Report Number 65 (New York, 1923).

22. The fourteen industries were described as "agricultural implements, cotton goods, express company, furniture, iron and steel rolling mill, etc., machinery, mining coal, paper and pulp, pottery, printing and binding, railroad shops, shoes, street railways, and store employees." U.S. Commissioner of Labor, *Workmen's Insurance,* 390. It was estimated that by the early 1920's at least 700 to 800 benefit associations existed in industrial firms alone. National Industrial Conference Board, *Experience with Mutual Benefit Associations,* 3.

23. Henderson, *Industrial Insurance,* 213, 239.

24. Railroad relief funds are discussed in, Emory R. Johnson, "Railway Departments for the Relief and Insurance of Employes," American Academy of Political and Social Science, *Annals,* 6 (November 1895), 424–468; M. Riebenack, *Railway Provident Institutions in English-Speaking Countries* (Philadelphia, 1905); M. Riebenack, "Pennsylvania Railroad Pension Departments: Systems East and West of Pittsburgh and Erie, Pa., Status to and Including the Year 1907," American Academy of Political and Social Science, *Annals,* 33 (March 1909), 258–264; U.S. Commissioner of Labor, *Workmen's Insurance;* Henderson, *Industrial Insurance.*

25. Pierce Williams, *The Purchase of Medical Care Through Fixed Periodic Payment* (New York, 1932) includes a discussion of railroad hospital associations in the early 1930's.

26. The Company contributed a sum of $25,000 a year to finance the pensions.

27. This theme is developed in David Brody, *Steelworkers in America: The Nonunion Era* (Cambridge, Mass., 1960). Welfare work in

the steel industry is also discussed in, Charles A. Gulick, *Labor Policy of the United States Steel Corporation* (New York, 1924); and Ida M. Tarbell, *The Life of Elbert H. Gary: The Story of Steel* (New York, 1925).

28. Quoted in United States Steel Corporation, Bureau of Safety, Sanitation and Welfare, *Bulletin No.* 9 (December 1922), 3.

29. Temporary disability benefits began fourteen days after an accident. They totaled 75 cents a day for single men, $1.00 for married men with an additional allowance of 10 cents a day for each child under sixteen (up to a maximum of the average daily wage). Benefits continued for 52 weeks, and at half-rate afterwards. The death benefit totaled $500 for a widow, and an additional $100 for each child under sixteen, up to a maximum of $1200. Eligibility for a pension was contingent upon a minimum of ten years of service with any Carnegie Company. It equaled 1 percent of the average monthly pay, multiplied by the number of years of service. The Corporation could withhold or terminate any accident, death, or old-age benefits in the event of "any misconduct on the part of the beneficiary, or for any cause sufficient." See, *Regulations Governing the Andrew Carnegie Relief Fund Created by Andrew Carnegie, and Applicable to Employees of the Carnegie Company. Taking effect January 1st., 1902.*

30. Under the reorganized plan, accident benefits varied according to the length of service. Single men, for example, received 35 percent of wages up to 52 weeks, and an addition of 2 percent for each year of service over five years, with a maximum limit of $1.50 a day. Married men received 50 percent of wages up to 52 weeks, 2 percent more for each year of service over five, 5 percent more for each child under sixteen, with a maximum limit of $2.50 a day. Permanent disability benefits equaled a certain number of months' wages for the loss of a stipulated body member. Permanent total disability benefits equaled at least the sum allotted for death. See, United States Steel Corporation, Bureau of Safety, Relief, Sanitation and Welfare, *Bulletin No.* 3 (August 1912), 4; United States Steel and Carnegie Pension Fund, *Pension Rules Taking Effect January 1, 1911;* Raynal C. Bolling, "Results of Voluntary Relief Plan of United States Steel Corporation," American Academy of Political and Social Science, *Annals,* 38 (July 1911), 35–44.

31. United States Steel Corporation, Committee of Safety, *Bulletin No.* 2 (July 1, 1911), 1, 2. The safety campaign is examined at length in, "Report on Conditions of Employment in the Iron and Steel Industry in the United States," Vol. IV: *Accidents and Accident Prevention,*

U.S. Senate, 62d Cong., 1st session, Document No. 110, 1911 (Washington, D.C., 1913).

32. The stock subscription plan enabled employees to purchase preferred stock on a monthly installment basis. The Committee on Sanitation was established in 1911, and in 1919 a Committee on Housing was added. In 1914 the name was changed to Bureau of Safety, Sanitation and Welfare.

33. Otey, "Employers' Welfare Work," 13. Also, C. W. Price, "Employees' Benefit Association of the International Harvester Company," *American Academy of Political and Social Science, Annals,* 33 (March 1909), 246–257; and John R. Commons, " 'Welfare Work' in a Great Industrial Plant," *Review of Reviews,* 28 (July 1903), 79–81.

34. Alfred Dolge, Dolgeville, New York, manufacturer, received credit as a late nineteenth-century pioneer in industrial welfare. His business failed in 1898. Gilman, *Dividend to Labor,* 24; Henderson, *Industrial Insurance,* 202; Monroe, "An American System of Labor Pensions and Insurance," 506–508.

35. John Mitchell, *The Wage Earner and His Problems* (Washington, D.C., 1913), 131.

36. *Ibid.,* 165.

37. Samuel Gompers, "Advice Welcome — Intrusion Never," *American Federationist,* 22 (November 1915), 974; Samuel Gompers, " 'Intellectuals,' Please Note," *American Federationist,* 23 (March 1916), 198, 199; Samuel Gompers, "Labor vs. Its Barnacles," *American Federationist,* 23 (April 1916), 268.

38. Gompers, " 'Intellectuals,' Please Note," 198.

39. Social insurance was not the only area of disagreement between organized labor and middle-class reformers. Others included minimum wage legislation, arbitration, and the administration of labor laws. Middle-class reformers on the whole tended to emphasize legislative action rather than trade unionism as the key to social melioration. See Irwin Yellowitz, *Labor and the Progressive Movement in New York State, 1897–1916* (Ithaca, N.Y., 1965).

40. Samuel Gompers, "Not Even Compulsory Benevolence Will Do," *American Federationist,* 24 (January 1917), 48.

41. Gompers, "Labor vs. Its Barnacles," 269; testimony, "Commission to Study Social Insurance and Unemployment," *Hearings before the Committee on Labor,* U.S. Cong., House of Representatives, 64th Cong., 1st session, April 6 and 11, 1916 (Washington, D.C., 1916), 135.

42. *Ibid.,* 185.

43. *Ibid.*, 126, 127. Gompers' views on government and labor are discussed in Fred Greenbaum, "The Social Ideas of Samuel Gompers," *Labor History*, 7 (Winter 1966), 35–61.

44. Union officers were a "unit in declaring that the desire to secure the advantages of the benefits does attract members." James B. Kennedy, *Beneficiary Features of American Trade Unions* (Baltimore, 1908), 16.

45. Isaac M. Rubinow, testimony, "Commission to Study Social Insurance and Unemployment," 180. Rubinow was unimpressed, not only by union benefit funds, but by the claim that unions had raised wages. His own economic studies led him to conclude that real wages had increased slightly between 1870 and 1890, but had fallen rapidly after 1900. They were "not much higher" in 1913 than they were in 1870. Any increase in the worker's standard of living was attributable to smaller families and the entry of women into the labor force. I. M. Rubinow, "The Recent Trend of Real Wages," *American Economic Review*, 4 (December 1914), 793–817; and I. M. Rubinow, "The Present Trend of Real Wages," American Academy of Political and Social Science," *Annals*, 69 (January 1917), 28–33.

46. According to Wolman, the 2,116,317 trade union members in 1910 constituted 5.5 percent of the gainfully employed, and 7.7 percent of wage-earners. Leo Wolman, "The Extent of Labor Organization in the United States in 1910," *Quarterly Journal of Economics*, 30 (May 1916), 499,502. Some 56.9 percent of all union members in 1910 was concentrated in three occupational groups — transportation, building and mining. George E. Barnett, "Growth of Labor Organization in the United States, 1897–1914," *Quarterly Journal of Economics*, 30 (August 1916), 793.

47. Information concerning trade union benefit funds in the early twentieth century can be found in, U.S. Commissioner of Labor, *Workmen's Insurance;* Henderson, *Industrial Insurance;* Kennedy, *Beneficiary Features of American Trade Unions;* Emory R. Johnson, "Brotherhood Relief and Insurance of Railway Employees," U.S. Department of Labor, *Bulletin,* No. 17 (July 1898), 552–596; Edward W. Bemis, "Benefit Features of American Trade Unions," U.S. Department of Labor, *Bulletin,* No. 22 (May 1899), 361–400; D. P. Smelser, *Unemployment and American Trade Unions* (Baltimore, 1919). The benefit system of one union is discussed in, Jesse S. Robinson, *The Amalgamated Association of Iron, Steel and Tin Workers* (Baltimore, 1920), 71ff. It was doubtful, according to Robinson, that benefits increased

membership appreciably, but they were "certainly . . . a factor in retaining members, once they join" (p. 85).

48. The railroad unions included the Grand International Brotherhood of Locomotive Engineers; Order of Railway Conductors of America; Brotherhood of Locomotive Firemen; Brotherhood of Railroad Trainmen; Brotherhood of Railway Trackmen; the Switchmen's Union of North America; the Brotherhood of Railway Carmen; and Order of Railroad Telegraphers.

49. P. H. J. H. Gosden, *The Friendly Societies in England, 1815–1875* (Manchester, 1961), 77. The following discussion of English fraternalism is drawn from this excellent study.

50. Besides the preeminent affiliated orders, English friendly societies of the early 1870's included the following types: ordinary large (general) societies which had no social features; county societies managed by philanthropic "honorary" members; local town, village, and country societies; special trade societies; dividing societies, which were local in character and based upon a division of any surplus at regular intervals; deposit friendly societies, akin to savings banks sponsored by clergy and county gentry; collecting or burial societies; annuity societies; and societies of females. *Ibid.*, 14–15.

51. *Ibid.*, 11–12.

52. Albert C. Stevens, "Fraternal Insurance," *Review of Reviews,* 21 (January 1900), 65.

53. *Ibid.*, 60.

54. Walter S. Nichols, "Fraternal Insurance in the United States: Its Origin, Development, Character and Existing Status," American Academy of Political and Social Science, *Annals,* 70 (March 1917), 119.

55. The 85 members of the National Fraternal Congress included numerous religious and ethnic orders, such as the Catholic Knights of America; German Beneficial Union; Maccabees; National Croation Society of the U.S.A.; Polish National Alliance of the U.S.A.; Slovenic National Benefit Society; Sons of Norway.

56. "Annual Report of the Committee on State of the Orders and Statistics," Second Annual Convention of the National Fraternal Congress of America, *Proceedings* (1915), 466.

57. Rufus M. Potts, "Address," *ibid.*, 67. Potts was Insurance Commissioner of Illinois. Also, Abb Landis, "Life Insurance by Fraternal Orders," American Academy of Political and Social Science, *Annals,* 24 (1904), 481.

58. W. S. Diggs, "Address," Second Annual Convention of the National Fraternal Congress of America, *Proceedings*, 55; F. T. McFaden, "The Influence of Fraternalists on Some Phases of American Life," *ibid.*, 448.

59. Peter Roberts, *Anthracite Coal Communities: A Study of the Demography, the Social, Educational and Moral Life of the Anthracite Regions* (New York, 1904), 259. In towns like Olyphant, Minersville, Shenandoah, Hazleton, and Nanticoke, there were 17 to 60 societies, or as many as one to every 250 to 340 inhabitants. They paid sickness and death benefits.

60. Margaret F. Byington, *Homestead: The Households of a Mill Town* (New York, 1910), 113, 114. All the Homestead societies provided a death benefit, and many a sickness benefit of $5.00 for a period of weeks. Of all the Slavic families included in the budget study, only two did not belong to at least one lodge.

61. Frederick L. Hoffman, *History of the Prudential Insurance Company of America* (*Industrial Insurance*), *1875–1900* (Newark, N.J.: Prudential Press, 1900), 18; W. S. Diggs, "Address," Second Annual Convention of the National Fraternal Congress of America, *Proceedings*, 62. Diggs was chairman of the Committee of National Executives of the Insurance Federation, organized in 1913 to oppose state insurance. Also, Haley Fiske, "Industrial Insurance," *Charities Review*, 8 (March 1898), 30, 31. Vice-president of Metropolitan Life, Fiske charged that the "country is overrun" with small fraternals. They were "innumerable, short-lived, collect all they can, pay out only what they are forced to pay, maintain during their brief existence a constant struggle for life, and finally leave each a small, sad membership to mourn their loss."

62. Hoffman, *History of the Prudential Insurance Company*, 1, 39, 60. The origins and development of industrial insurance are also discussed in, John F. Dryden, *Addresses and Papers on Life Insurance and Other Subjects* (Newark, N.J., 1909); John R. Gegeman, "Industrial Insurance," in William A. Fricke, ed., *"Insurance: 'A Text-Book'"* ([Milwaukee:] National Convention of Insurance Commissioners, 1898), 212–277; Marquis James, *The Metropolitan Life: A Study in Business Growth* (New York, 1947).

63. Dryden, *Addresses and Papers*, 73, 91.

64. Hoffman, *History of the Prudential Insurance Company*, 148; Fiske, "Industrial Insurance," 26. Also, Forrest F. Dryden, "Government and Wage-Earners' Insurance," 865.

65. Dryden, *Addresses and Papers*, 122.

*Chapter II   Social Drift and Social Planning*

1. John Graham Brooks, *Compulsory Insurance in Germany* (*Including an Appendix Relating to Compulsory Insurance in Other Countries in Europe*), Fourth Special Report of the Commissioner of Labor (Washington, D.C., 1893, rev. ed., 1895); Adna F. Weber, "Industrial Accidents and Employers' Responsibility for their Compensation," State of New York, *Seventeenth Annual Report of the Bureau of Labor Statistics for the year 1899* (Albany, Feb. 5, 1900), part II; William F. Willoughby, *Workingmen's Insurance* (New York, 1898); U.S. Commissioner of Labor, "Workmen's Insurance and Compensation Systems in Europe," *Twenty-Fourth Annual Report* (1909), 2 vols. (Washington, D.C., 1911).

2. Brooks, *Compulsory Insurance in Germany*, 287, 288.

3. Willoughby, *Workingmen's Insurance*, 23, iii.

4. *Ibid.*, 112.

5. *Ibid.*, 114. By means of the French establishment funds, Willoughby claimed, "a large proportion of the employés of the large industries, such as railway transportation and mining, as well as of a great many other industrial establishments, have been insured without the intervention of the state." Typical, and most important, of the federated insurance associations was the *Caisse Syndicale d'Assurance Mutuelle des forge de France*, created in 1891 by the *Comité des Forge de France* (Iron and Steel Association).

6. The old-age institution (*Caisse Nationale des Retraites pour la Vieillesse*) operated like a savings bank with a separate account for each depositor. The depositor could be an individual or a group. Some 987,000 accounts had been opened by the early 1890's. Fewer than 200,000 pensioners appeared on the rolls. The average pension was less than $30.00. The accident insurance institution (*Caisse Nationale d'assurance en cas d'accidents*) differed from a private insurance company only in waiving requirements for a medical examination and stipulating a maximum amount of coverage. Between 1868 and 1892, only 33,112 policies were sold. The life insurance institution (*Caisse Nationale d'assurance en cas de Décès*) had sold only 2,097 individual and 1,382 collective policies by the 1890's.

Within a decade, Willoughby apparently changed his mind about the potentialities of voluntary insurance, and favored social insurance as a "wonderfully effective . . . device for performing efficiently, directly, and with certainty, a function which society must in some way discharge." William F. Willoughby, "The Problem of Social Insurance: An Analysis," *American Labor Legislation Review*, 3 (June 1913), 158.

7. Surveys of European social insurance programs in the early twentieth century include: U.S. Commissioner of Labor, "Workmen's Insurance and Compensation Systems"; Lee K. Frankel and Miles M. Dawson (with the cooperation of Louis I. Dublin), *Workingmen's Insurance in Europe* (New York, 1910); I. M. Rubinow, *Social Insurance: with Special Reference to American Conditions* (New York, 1913); William H. Dawson, *Social Insurance in Germany, 1883–1911. Its History, Operation, Results (and a Comparison with the National Insurance Act, 1911)* (London, 1912); Percy Alden, *Democratic England* (New York, 1912).

8. The Germans favored a system of wage-related contributions and benefits, and little or no government contributions; the English social insurance programs included government contributions and a flat schedule of contributions and benefits.

9. The Danish legislation of 1891 was the earliest of the pension laws.

10. The industries included were: building, construction, shipbuilding, mechanical engineering, iron-foundries, vehicle manufacture, saw-milling. Two years earlier, in 1909, a national system of unemployment exchanges had been established.

11. Louis Varlez, a "close student" of unemployment problems, is usually credited with originating the Ghent system.

12. Rubinow, *Social Insurance*, 420. The comparison applied to the year 1911.

13. The AALL originated when a group of social scientists, impressed by the success of the International Association, called a conference at Johns Hopkins in December 1905. The AALL was formally organized at a general meeting in New York the following February. Henry W. Farnam, J. W. Jenks, John De Witt Warner, Clinton Rogers Woodruff, and Adna F. Weber, all American correspondents of the International Association for Labor Legislation, signed the circular which called the first conference at Johns Hopkins. They cited the recent establishment of an English branch in support of their effort. Although some favored affiliation of the proposed organization with the American Economic Association, it was decided to establish it independently. *Circular*, December 19, 1905; Adna F. Weber to Henry W. Farnam, October 27, 1905, American Association for Labor Legis-

lation (John B. Andrews) Papers, Cornell (hereafter cited as Andrews Papers); Adna F. Weber to Frank W. Taussig, November 20, 1905, Andrews Papers; John A. Fitch, "The American Association for Labor Legislation," *John B. Andrews Memorial Symposium on Labor Legislation and Social Security* (Madison: University of Wisconsin, November 4 and 5, 1949), 81.

14. Richard T. Ely to John B. Andrews, August 29, 1909, Andrews Papers; John R. Commons to Robert Hunter, April 14, 1908, Andrews Papers.

15. John R. Commons to Henry W. Farnam, January 12, 1909, December 25, 1909, Andrews Papers.

16. Fitch, "The American Association for Labor Legislation," 95. Chamberlain served as president of the AALL in 1930, and from 1935–42. Other presidents were: Richard T. Ely, 1906–07; Henry W. Farnam, 1908–10; Henry R. Seager, 1911–12 and 1914–15; William F. Willoughby, 1913; Irving Fisher, 1916–17; Samuel McCune Lindsay, 1918–19; Thomas L. Chadbourne, 1920–26; Sam A. Lewisohn, 1927–28; Thomas I. Parkinson, 1929; Ernest G. Draper, 1931–33; Leo Wolman, 1934.

17. Andrews (1880–1943) was a native of Wisconsin. He received his B.A. from the University of Wisconsin in 1904, an M.A. from Dartmouth, 1905, and a Ph.D. from Wisconsin, 1908. He taught economics at Dartmouth and Wisconsin before his appointment as secretary of the AALL.

18. John B. Andrews, "Phosphorus Poisoning in the Match Industry in the United States," Department of Commerce and Labor, Bureau of Labor, *Bulletin, No. 86* (January 1910). Prior to the international treaty of 1906, Finland, Denmark, France, Switzerland, and the Netherlands had already banned the use of white phosphorus. Safe, red phosphorus was prepared by baking the white (yellow) phosphorus in a closed container; poisonous phosphorus was prepared from bones. The effects of phosphorus poisoning were described by Andrews as follows: "Phosphorus necrosis, the peculiar local form of the disease, is caused by the absorption of phosphorus through the teeth or gums. The generally accepted theory is that minute particles of the poison enter, usually, through the cavities of decayed teeth, setting up an inflammation which, if not quickly arrested, extends along the jaw, killing the teeth and bones. The gums become swollen and purple, the teeth loosen and drop out, and the jawbones slowly decompose and pass away in the form of nauseating pus, which sometimes breaks through the neck in the form of an abscess or, if not almost continually

washed out, oozes into the mouth where it mixes with the saliva and is swallowed" (p. 40).

19. Andrews threatened the match manufacturers with a "vigorous and prolonged agitation of the public against the use of the poisonous match." The outcome was the trustee agreement and the Esch bills providing a discriminatory tax on white phosphorus matches. Andrews then pressured the House Committee on Ways and Means to favorably report the legislation. John B. Andrews to Joseph H. Gaines, January 13, 1911; John B. Andrews to F. W. Mackenzie, January 9, 1911; John B. Andrews to Samuel Gompers, January 17, 1911; John B. Andrews to John M. Glenn, January 26, 1911; John B. Andrews to William McEwen, February 2, 1912, Andrews Papers. Despite the efforts of the AALL, none of the three Esch bills of 1910–1911 was ever reported out of committee. The measure finally passed in 1912 was introduced by Representative William Hughes. See, R. Alton Lee, "The Eradication of Phossy Jaw: A Unique Development of Federal Police Power," *Historian*, 29 (November 1966), 1–21.

20. At the urging of Charles Henderson of the University of Chicago, the Governor of Illinois appointed a Commission on Industrial Diseases in 1910. It included Dr. Alice Hamilton of Hull House, and concentrated on the problem of occupational poisons. Dr. Hamilton subsequently devoted great effort to control the effects of lead poisoning. During this same period, Frederick Hoffman of the Prudential Life Insurance Company was investigating the relation between occupation and the incidence of tuberculosis. Dr. George Kober and Dr. William Gilman Thompson also rank among the pioneers in industrial hygiene. The evolution of the movement is discussed in, Alice Hamilton, *Exploring the Dangerous Trades* (Boston, 1943); and Don D. Lescohier, "The Campaigns for Health and Safety in Industry," ch. 19 in John R. Commons, *et al., History of Labor in the United States, 1896–1932* (New York, 1935), vol. III.

21. Andrews urged use of the rock-dusting method. By the early 1930's several hundred mine operators had voluntarily rock-dusted their mines, and legislation had been enacted by seven states. Fitch, "The American Association for Labor Legislation," 86; Henry R. Seager, "Progress of Labor Legislation, 1900–1925," *American Labor Legislation Review*, 15 (December 1925), 293.

22. The Vocational Rehabilitation Act of 1918 provided federal grants-in-aid for the training and placement of disabled veterans. Originally, it was administered by the Federal Board for Vocational Education, created by the Smith-Hughes Vocational Education Act

of 1917. In 1921, administration was transferred to the newly established Veteran's Bureau. The Federation Rehabilitation Act of 1920 provided grants-in-aid for civilian handicapped. It was administered by the Federal Board for Vocational Education in cooperation with state boards of vocational education. See, Reuben D. Cahn, "Civilian Vocational Rehabilitation," *Journal of Political Economy*, 32 (December 1924), 665–689.

23. The original committee included: Edward T. Devine, chairman (social worker, secretary of the New York Charity Organization Society, 1896–1912, and director of the New York School of Philanthropy); Miles M. Dawson (lawyer, actuary, and workmen's compensation expert); Carroll W. Doten (economist, statistician at MIT, member of Massachusetts Employers' Liability Commission); Henry J. Harris (economist, statistician, Library of Congress; formerly, Bureau of Labor); Charles R. Henderson (sociologist, University of Chicago); Frederick L. Hoffman (actuary, Prudential Life Insurance Company); I. M. Rubinow (economist, actuary); Henry R. Seager (political scientist, Columbia University); and John B. Andrews. Hoffman later resigned in opposition to compulsory health insurance. See, "New Committee on Social Insurance," *Survey*, 29 (March 15, 1913), 827.

24. G. R. Miller, *Social Insurance in the United States* (Chicago, 1918), 8, 7; John B. Andrews to Robert Wagner, January 9, 1911, Andrews Papers.

25. John R. Commons to Henry W. Farnam, December 25, 1909, Andrews Papers; Henry W. Farnam, *The Economic Utilization of History and Other Economic Studies* (New Haven, 1913), 193, 94, 121.

26. John R. Commons, "Constructive Investigation and the Industrial Commission of Wisconsin," *Survey*, 29 (January 4, 1913), 440, 441.

27. A. J. Altmeyer, *The Industrial Commission of Wisconsin: A Case Study in Labor Law Administration* (Madison, Wis., 1932), 17.

28. Commons, "Constructive Investigation and the Industrial Commission of Wisconsin," 441, 440.

29. *Ibid.*, 444–445. Commons pointed out that the Industrial Commission was modeled after the law which established the Railroad Commission. Collaboration between the Industrial Commission and businessmen in the area of industrial safety is discussed in Gerd Korman, *Industrialization, Immigrants and Americanizers: The View from Milwaukee, 1866–1921* (Madison, Wis., 1967), 118ff.

30. Miller, *Social Insurance in the United States*, 4.

31. Irwin Yellowitz, *Labor and the Progressive Movement in New York State, 1897–1916* (Ithaca, N.Y., 1965), 138ff.

32. I. M. Rubinow, "Compulsory State Insurance of Workingmen," *Annals* 24 (1904), 341; I. M. Rubinow to Lessing Rosenwald, September 25, 1931, Isaac M. Rubinow Papers (Cornell University), ROA to ROZ, folder. These Papers contain a great deal of biographical information on Rubinow.

33. I. M. Rubinow, *Standards of Health Insurance* (New York, 1916), 138.

34. Rubinow, *Social Insurance.*

35. Rubinow also served as a consultant to the National Association of Workmen's Compensation Boards, and the National Association of Insurance Commissioners.

36. Rubinow, *Health Insurance.*

37. Testifying before a congressional committee in 1916, Rubinow affirmed he had been a member of the Socialist Party of America for nearly twenty years. He claimed that the Socialist Party believed in social insurance as a "practical and effective method of coping with problems of destitution in present-day society." Rubinow, testimony, "Commission to Study Social Insurance and Unemployment," *Hearings before the Committee on Labor*, U.S. Cong., House of Representatives, 64th Cong., 1st session, 1916, 36. The Russian Revolution would upset Rubinow's socialist convictions.

Socialist opinion was not as unanimous as Rubinow implied. According to Morris Hillquit, socialism had "little in common with the modern measures of state relief comprehended within the system of social insurance." It implied no fundamental institutional changes, and sought merely to palliate the "suffering and social injustice" inherent in capitalism. Morris Hillquit, "Socialism and Social Insurance," National Conference of Charities and Correction, *Proceedings* (1917), 525.

38. Rubinow, *Social Insurance*, 481.

39. *Ibid.*, 3.

40. I. M. Rubinow, *The Quest for Security* (New York, 1934), 511.

41. *Ibid.*, 514.

42. Rubinow, *Social Insurance, passim.*

43. *Ibid.;* also I. M. Rubinow, "Subsidized Unemployment Insurance," *Journal of Political Economy*, 21 (May 1913), 412–431.

44. Rubinow, "Compulsory State Insurance of Workingmen," 331; Rubinow, *Social Insurance*, 491, 500. See also I. M. Rubinow, "Labor Insurance," *Journal of Political Economy*, 12 (June 1904), 362–381.

45. Rubinow, *Social Insurance*, 490, 491.

46. *Ibid.*, 490.

47. I. M. Rubinow, "Public and Private Interests in Social Insurance," *American Labor Legislation Review*, 21 (June 1931), 184.

48. Rubinow, *Social Insurance*, 500.

49. Katharine Coman, "Social Insurance, Pensions, and Poor Relief," *Survey*, 32 (May 9, 1914), 187–188. Also Katharine Coman, "Twenty Years of Old Age Pensions in Denmark," *Survey*, 31 (January 17, 1914), 463–465; Katharine Coman, "The Problems of Old Age Pensions in England," *Survey*, 31 (February 21, 1914), 640–642; Katharine Coman, "Insurance for the Superannuated Worker in Spain," *Survey*, 31 (February 28, 1914), 669–671.

50. I. M. Rubinow, "Old-Age Pensions and Moral Values: A Reply to Miss Coman," *Survey*, 31 (February 28, 1914), 671, 672.

51. Rubinow, *Social Insurance*, 314, 315. See State of Massachusetts, *Report of the Commission on Old Age Pensions, Annuities and Insurance*, January 1910 (Boston, 1910).

52. Rubinow, *Standards of Health Insurance*, 121; Rubinow, *Social Insurance*, 275.

53. *Ibid.*, 297.

54. I. M. Rubinow, "Dependency Index of New York City, 1914–1917," *American Economic Review*, 8 (December 1918), 713–740.

55. Along with his contributions to social insurance, Rubinow ranked his work in Palestine as his most important achievement. Under his supervision four hospitals, a rural medicine program, school medical services, and infant welfare stations were organized. He directed a staff which grew from 45 to 500. Rubinow applied his "theories of organized social medicine" in developing a "system of full time medical service by physicians who receive salaries." I. M. Rubinow, "Typed Autobiographical Statement," Rubinow Papers.

56. Rubinow, who devoted considerable thought to problems of anti-semitism and minority group relations during these years, also served as secretary of the Anti-Defamation League of B'nai B'rith.

57. I. M. Rubinow, "Can Private Philanthropy Do It?," *Social Service Review*, 3 (September 1929), 364, 369.

58. I. M. Rubinow, "Needed: A Social Insurance Revival," *Survey*, 56 (May 15, 1926), 233.

59. Isaac M. Rubinow, "Poverty," *Encyclopaedia of the Social Sciences*, vol. 12, 285.

60. Robert Hunter, *Poverty* (Torchbook edition: New York, 1965), 5 (orig. pub., 1904).

61. Rubinow, "Can Private Philanthropy Do It?," 384, 386, 385;

Rubinow, "Needed: A Social Insurance Revival," 283. One beneficial result of the Depression of the 1930's, in Rubinow's opinion, was to burst the "great American bubble of private philanthropy as a basis for social justice — one might say the great American substitute for social policy. . . ." Rubinow never asserted that private philanthropy and social work were of no value; but the concept that they could substitute for a broad public program "dealing with poverty" demanded "exposure and destruction." Rubinow, *Quest for Security*, 339.

62. Progressive social reformers like the Webbs in England condemned social insurance as a relief program which "does not prevent." It did, presumably, increase the danger of malingering, thus having adverse effects on "personal conduct and individual character." Sidney and Beatrice Webb, *The Prevention of Destitution* (London, 1916), 160, 174.

63. John B. Andrews to Olga S. Halsey, January 27, 1915, Andrews Papers. Similarly, Louis Brandeis urged a comprehensive social insurance program as "an incentive to justice." Louis D. Brandeis, "Workingmen's Insurance — The Road to Social Efficiency," National Conference of Charities and Correction, *Proceedings* (1911), 162. Also, Royal Meeker, "Social Insurance in the United States," National Conference of Social Work, *Proceedings* (1917), 534; Rufus M. Potts, *Welfare (Social) Insurance: To What Extent is it Desirable and Feasible in the United States and by What Means can it be Accomplished?* (pamphlet, 1916), 12; Robert M. Woodbury, *Social Insurance: An Economic Analysis* (New York, 1917), 142ff.; Miller, *Social Insurance in the United States*, 53, 60.

64. Commons described his unemployment scheme as "exactly like that of the workman's compensation law of this state." It avoided the socialism and paternalism of Europe and, in the best traditions of American capitalism, induced the "business man to make a profit or avoid a loss by efficient labor management." John R. Commons, "Unemployment: Compensation and Prevention," *Survey*, 47 (October 1, 1921), 8.

65. During the Depression of the 1930's, Rubinow observed a Catholic nun distributing nickels to hundreds of men in downtown New York. Was it not the case, he reflected, that the "mass demoralization of such humiliation and such need is more dangerous to the human soul than that of receiving a regular income from an insurance organization." Nothing, Rubinow concluded, was more demoralizing than the "sense of insecurity, the sense of failure and inability to meet one's family obligations." I. M. Rubinow to Lessing

Rosenwald, September 25, 1931, Rubinow Papers, ROA-ROZ, folder.

66. Rubinow, *Social Insurance*, 494.

67. Rubinow, *Quest for Security*, 572.

68. Rubinow, "Public and Private Interests in Social Insurance," 186.

69. I. M. Rubinow, "Stabilization versus Insurance?," *Social Service Review*, 5 (June 1931), 211. Rubinow noted also that unemployment differed substantially from industrial accidents in that the employer had less control over the situation (p. 210).

70. I. M. Rubinow, "Medical Benefits Under Workmen's Compensation," *Journal of Political Economy*, 25 (July 1917), 723.

*Chapter III   The Origins of Workmen's Compensation*

1. William Hard and Others, *Injured in the Course of Duty* (New York, 1910); Arthur B. Reeve, "Our Industrial Juggernaut," *Everybody's Magazine*, 16 (February 1907), 147–157.

2. I. M. Rubinow, *The Quest for Security* (New York, 1934), 71.

3. Crystal Eastman, *Work-Accidents and the Law* (New York, 1910), 13.

4. *Ibid.*, 85.

5. *Ibid.*, 32, 95, 98.

6. E. H. Downey, *History of Work Accident Indemnity in Iowa* (Iowa City, 1912), 55, 3, 54, 53. See also, Emory S. Bogardus, "The Relation of Fatigue to Industrial Accidents," *American Journal of Sociology*, 17 (September, November 1911, January 1912), 206–222, 351–374, 512–539.

7. Compensation literature was vast. A sample illustrating the theory and principles of workmen's compensation includes: Gilbert L. Campbell, *Industrial Accidents and Their Compensation* (Boston, 1911); James H. Boyd, *Workmen's Compensation and Industrial Insurance Under Modern Conditions* (Indianapolis, 1913), 2 vols.; Robert M. Woodbury, *Social Insurance, An Economic Analysis* (New York, 1917); Ralph H. Blanchard, *Industrial Accidents and Workmen's Compensation* (New York, 1917); James E. Rhodes, 2d, *Workmen's Compensation* (New York, 1917); Durand H. Van Doren, *Workmen's Compensation and Insurance* (New York, 1918). A great deal of information is contained in the successive issues of the *American Labor Legislation Review*, beginning in 1911.

8. Eastman, *Work-Accidents and the Law*, 166.

9. E. H. Downey, *Workmen's Compensation* (New York, 1924), 9.

10. Eastman, *Work-Accidents and the Law,* 127, 128, 136. Miss Eastman estimated that about 23 percent of the killed and injured belonged to a relief association.

11. *Ibid.,* 110, 114.

12. Howell Cheney, "Work, Accidents, and the Law," *Yale Review,* 19 (November 1910), 259.

13. Downey, *History of Work Accident Indemnity in Iowa,* 20, 21.

14. *Ibid.,* 48, 51. For a defense of the common law in the light of traditional American doctrines of individualism and freedom of contract see Walter S. Nichols, "An Argument Against Liability," American Academy of Political and Social Science, *Annals,* 38 (July 1911), 159–165.

15. I. M. Rubinow, "Medical Benefits under Workmen's Compensation," *Journal of Political Economy,* 25 (June 1917), 583. H. T. Smith of the Aetna Life Insurance Company substantiated Rubinow's evaluation of the right-to-action: "It is quite universal now to settle cases even where the facts do not disclose apparent liability if a small settlement can be made, particularly so where the injury is severe or a permanent one. Furthermore considerable money can be saved if done in the early stages before the case falls into the hands of an attorney." The change in policy was attributable, in part, to the fact that "juries are naturally sympathetic and do not care for technical defenses, and with the public at large are inclined to take the view that an employee should be compensated when injured no matter what the judge tells them about the law." H. T. Smith, "Liability Investigations and Adjustments," *Liability and Compensation Insurance. A Series of Lectures Delivered before the Insurance Institute of Hartford, 1913* (Hartford, 1913), 66, 67.

16. Changes in employers' liability laws are discussed in Harry Weiss, "The Development of Workmen's Compensation Legislation in the United States," unpublished Ph.D., University of Wisconsin, 1933, ch. I. Also, Boyd, *Workmen's Compensation and Industrial Insurance Under Modern Conditions,* I, ch. I. A detailed study covering their status in a leading industrial state at the turn of the century is Albert S. Boles, *The Legal Relations between the Employed and their Employers in Pennsylvania, Compared with the Relations Existing Between Them in Other States* (Harrisburg, Pa., 1901).

17. W. F. Moore, "Employers' Liability Insurance," in William A. Fricke, *"Insurance: 'A Text-Book'"* ([Milwaukee:] National Conven-

tion of Insurance Commissioners, 1898), 929–971; L. N. Denniston, "Historical Review," *Liability and Compensation Insurance,* 3–12.

18. Harold G. Villard, *Workmen's Accident Insurance in Germany* (Workmen's Compensation Publicity Bureau, n.d.), 18.

19. Denniston, "Historical Review," 10; J. E. Rhodes, 2d, "The Liability Contract," *Liability and Compensation Insurance,* 25–38.

20. Rhodes, *Workmen's Compensation,* 89; Irwin Yellowitz, *Labor and the Progressive Movement in New York State, 1897–1916* (Ithaca, N.Y., 1965), 107–108.

21. George E. Barnett, "The End of the Maryland Workmen's Compensation Act," *Quarterly Journal of Economics,* 19 (February 1905), 320–322; Malcolm H. Lauchheimer, *The Labor Law of Maryland* (Baltimore, 1919), 46ff.

22. Massachusetts, *Report of Committee on Relations between Employer and Employee, Submitted in Accordance with Resolve Approved June 5, 1903* (Boston, 1904), 43. The optional law of 1908 authorized employers to establish compensation schemes subject to approval by the State Board of Conciliation and Arbitration.

23. The unconstitutionality of the act was based upon the double liability of the employer.

24. I. M. Rubinow, "Accident Compensation for Federal Employes," *American Labor Legislation Review,* 2 (February 1912), 35. The measure applied to some 80,000 federal employees. It provided full wages for temporary disability up to a year, and up to one year's wages for fatal injuries. Among the precedents for the federal act, Rubinow cited the compensation beginning in 1882 for disabilities incurred by members of the United States Life Saving Service, and an "obscure item" in the Post Office Department appropriation act of 1901 which authorized compensation for railway mail clerks.

25. The measure was first introduced in 1913 by Representative William B. Wilson, subsequently Secretary of Labor, at the request of the AALL. Later known as the Kern-McGillicuddy bill, it was prepared by Henry Seager, Isaac Rubinow, and John B. Andrews, assisted by Middleton Beaman. It covered all civil employees of the federal government; authorized benefits on the fourth rather than the sixteenth day; provided for medical services; established a benefit schedule up to 66⅔ percent of wages if a married employee was killed; 66⅔ percent for total disability for the full period of disability; 66⅔ percent of loss of earning power for partial disability, a condition ignored by the original act; and established a United States Employes'

Compensation Commission to administer the measure. John B. Andrews, "New Federal Workmen's Compensation Law," *Survey*, 36 (September 23, 1916), 617–618.

26. The employers' liability commissions established in 1909 and 1910 held a series of national conferences to discuss issues of common interest. See National Conference on Workmen's Compensation for Industrial Accidents, *Proceedings* (1909); Third National Conference, Workmen's Compensation for Industrial Accidents, *Proceedings* (1910), Including a Brief Report of the Second National Conference, Washington, January 20, 1910; Conference of Commissions on Compensation for Industrial Accidents, *Proceedings* (1910).

27. These details can be traced in the successive issues of the *American Labor Legislation Review*. For the status of workmen's compensation by the late 1920's, see John R. Commons and John B. Andrews, *Principles of Labor Legislation* (rev. ed., New York, 1927).

28. *Report to the Legislature of the State of New York by the Commission Appointed under Chapter 518 of the Laws of 1909 to inquire into the question of employers' liability and other matters,* first Report, March 19, 1910 (Albany, 1910), app. V, 15, Minutes of Evidence, 180, 207; *Report to the Legislature of Ohio of the Commission Appointed under Senate Bill No. 250 of the Laws of 1910* (Columbus, 1911), app. XLIII, 355. Another Ohio employer frankly admitted that an advantage of a compensation law would be to "define and limit the possible cost of accidents to the employer. This cost is now unlimited, depending only upon the caprice of juries and prudence requires the employer to make a larger reserve to pay a great deal for insurance to meet this" (*ibid.,* 358). According to the Connecticut Commission, there existed a "demand on the part of both employer and employe that they shall be relieved from the expense and friction of litigation." *Report of the Connecticut State Commission on Compensation for Industrial Accidents* (1912), 3. Similarly, an Iowa employer testified "heartily in favor of a liability law that will take care of the injured employe without court costs, attorney fees, etc.," and the Iowa Commission noted that "from the standpoint of the employer it can be said that his business and all of his earnings and investments are under constant menace and liable to be swept away, only awaiting a catastrophe that is likely to occur that will subject him to a series of law suits." *Report of the Employers' Liability Commission to the Governor of Iowa, 1912* (Des Moines, 1912), 203, 17.

29. New York State, *Employers' Liability Commission,* app. V, 152, Minutes of Evidence, 172, 188.

30. Willard C. Fisher, "American Experience with Workmen's Compensation," *American Economic Review,* 10 (March 1920), 20; *Report of the Employers' Liability Commission of the State of Illinois* (Chicago, 1910), 194.

31. Ferd C. Schwedtman and James A. Emery, *Accident Prevention and Relief: An Investigation of the Subject in Europe with Special Attention to England and Germany Together with Recommendations for Action in the United States* (New York, 1911). The resolution adopted at the annual meeting was as follows: "Be It Resolved, that the present system of determining employers' liability is unsatisfactory, wasteful, slow in operation and antagonistic to harmonious relations between employers and wage-workers; that an equitable, mutually contributory indemnity system, automatically providing relief for victims of industrial accidents and their dependents, is required to reduce waste, litigation and friction, and to meet the demands of an enlightened nation" (*ibid.,* xiv). The role of the National Civic Federation in promoting compensation legislation is discussed in, James Weinstein, "Big Business and the Origins of Workmen's Compensation," *Labor History,* 8 (Spring 1967), 156–174.

32. Schwedtman and Emery, *Accident Prevention and Relief,* xiii, 259. For the NAM viewpoint, see also F. C. Schwedtman, "Principles of Sound Employers' Liability Legislation," American Academy of Political and Social Science, *Annals,* 38 (July 1911), 202–204, and F. C. Schwedtman, "Voluntary Indemnity for Injured Workmen," *American Labor Legislation Review,* I (January 1911), 49–54.

33. Schwedtman and Emery, *Accident Prevention and Relief,* 20. Also F. C. Schwedtman, "Nation Wide Movement for Industrial Safety," *Survey,* 30 (April 19, 1913), 102–104.

34. Schwedtman and Emery, *Accident Prevention and Relief,* 250, 251, 255.

35. State of New York, *Employers' Liability Commission,* Minutes of Evidence, 103, 412; *Report to the Legislature of Ohio of the Commission,* Minutes of Evidence, 84, 99, 107. Railroad workers, "to whose highly paid members the modest maxima of the ordinary compensation awards appear particularly unjust," remained opposed to compensation. Fisher, "American Experience with Workmen's Compensation," 20. The Chicago Federation of Labor explicitly charged that workmen's compensation was designed to protect employers against

prospective liberalization of the liability laws: "The Chicago Federation of Labor has declared itself opposed to any kind of compensation until such time as we have an Employers' Liability Law enacted, and the wisdom of this stand is shown in the attitude of the employers themselves. They have come to realize that on account of public opinion it is possible that the Legislature will be compelled to enact a law which will deprive them of the so-called defenses, and before the so-called defenses are taken away from them by law they want us to barter away our rights to compensation by agreeing to a much less compensation than we are entitled to, they agreeing to forego the use of the so-called defenses." *Report of the Employers' Liability Commission of the State of Illinois* (Chicago, 1910), 34.

36. Victor DeWitt Brannon, *Employers' Liability and Workmen's Compensation in Arizona*, University of Arizona, Bulletin V, no. 8, November 15, 1934 (Tuscon, 1934), 28.

37. *Ibid.,* 33, 43–44.

38. Rubinow, *Quest for Security*, 102.

39. E. H. Downey, "The Present Status of Workmen's Compensation in the United States," *American Economic Review*, 12 (March 1922), supplement, 130, 132.

40. Adding to the bitter denunciation of the Ives decision was the fact that within a day of the decision occurred the disastrous Triangle Waist Company fire in New York City. Rhodes, *Workmen's Compensation*, 228ff. According to the opinion of the Court, delivered by Justice Werner, the compensation statute was "plainly revolutionary" in terms of the "letter or spirit of our written constitutions." It was specifically challenged as incompatible with the Fourteenth Amendment, and the provisions of the New York State Constitution, which guaranteed persons against deprivation of life, liberty, or property without due process of law. The Court denied that the statute could be justified as the exercise of a police power as it did "nothing to conserve the health, safety or morals" of the worker; its sole purpose was to make the employer liable without fault, a principle whose extension implied the right of the legislature to expropriate wealth at will. See, Boyd, *Workmen's Compensation and Industrial Insurance,* I, 83ff.

The commission which prepared the Pennsylvania compensation act frankly conceded that under an elective measure costs could not exceed what employers were willing to pay: "The scale of compensation represents about that given in the elective Acts now in force throughout the United States. In an elective Act the scale of compensation is inevitably limited by the necessity of providing a free election. To insure this it is essential that the cost of compensation, and so of insurance against it, shall be, as near as possible, identical with the cost of the enlarged common law liability. . . . Any increase in the scale of compensation to a point which would make its cost the greater . . . would necessarily result in its rejection by many employers." State of Pennsylvania, *Report of Industrial Accidents Commission,* 1915 (Philadelphia, 1915), 5. The constraining influence of interstate competition was noted by another commission: "The act adopts as the basis of liability the fifty percent rule. . . . This corresponds with the rule generally adopted in the states, and it seems wise that the burden on the industries of Connecticut should not be greater than that upon the surrounding states, otherwise our manufacturers are put to a disadvantage in competition." *Report of the Connecticut State Commission on Compensation for Industrial Accidents,* 1912, 15.

41. The original New Jersey measure of 1911 authorized the following benefit schedule: *Death.* 25 percent to 60 percent of wages, according to number of dependents, for 300 weeks; $5 minimum, $10 maximum per week; *Total Disability.* 50 percent of weekly wages; $5 minimum, $10 maximum — 300 weeks if temporary, 400 weeks if permanent; *Partial Disability.* 50 percent of daily wages, if permanent, during number of weeks specified in a schedule; 300 week limit; $10 maximum per week.

42. John B. Andrews, "Workmen's Compensation in New Jersey — The Wrong Way," *Survey,* 33 (March 27, 1915), 696.

43. *Ibid.,* 696. Also "Three Years under the New Jersey Workmen's Compensation Law: Report of an Investigation Under the Direction of the Social Insurance Committee of the American Association for Labor Legislation," *American Labor Legislation Review,* 5 (March 1915), 33–102. For a detailed evaluation of the Pennsylvania compensation law, see John B. Andrews, *et al., The Accident Compensation Law of Pennsylvania and Its Administration: A Survey Submitted to the Citizens' Committee on the Finances of the State of Pennsylvania* (December 1922).

44. I. M. Rubinow, "American Methods of Compensating Permanent Partial Disabilities," Casualty Actuarial and Statistical Society of America, *Proceedings,* II, part II, 237, 242 (reprint, n.d.).

45. Downey, "The Present Status of Workmen's Compensation in the United States," 132.

46. Commons and Andrews, *Principles of Labor Legislation,* 434ff.

47. Harry Weiss, "Employers' Liability and Workmen's Compensa-

tion," in John R. Commons, *et al.*, *History of Labor in the United States, 1896–1932* (New York, 1935), III, 610. A good general survey of workmen's compensation in the 1930's is Walter F. Dodd, *Administration of Workmen's Compensation* (New York, 1936).

48. John Perry Horlacher, *The Results of Workmen's Compensation in Pennsylvania: A Study of the Pennsylvania System from the Point of View of the Injured Worker* (Philadelphia, 1934), 23.

49. *Ibid.*, 25. These agreements were signed "on the basis of misrepresentation in more than two out of every five cases."

50. Herman M. Somers and Anne R. Somers, *Workmen's Compensation: Prevention, Insurance, and Rehabilitation of Occupational Disability* (New York, 1954), 44.

51. *Ibid.*, 12. Unlimited medical care was provided in 36 jurisdictions, and medical assistance accounted for one-third of benefits (*Ibid.*, 87).

52. *Ibid.*, 72. Permanent partial disabilities are classified as scheduled (readily identifiable body member) and nonscheduled. The benefit formula is similar to total disability except that "in the case of the scheduled injuries, the total award is further modified by a special schedule which states the total length of time for which benefits may be paid for different types of injuries." Permanent partial disability benefits averaged $629 in New Jersey, $1,089 in New York, and $1,589 in Wisconsin for cases settled in 1951 (*ibid.*, 71, 74).

53. S. H. Wolfe, "Is the State to Compensate Injured Workmen?," *Addresses Made at the Fifth Annual Meeting of the Liability Insurance Association on State Insurance of Workmen's Compensation for Accidents* (New York: Globe Indemnity Company of New York, 1911), 51.

54. Conspicuous in the defense of monopoly state funds were the American Association for Labor Legislation, and labor groups. The position of the insurance companies is described in, Paul Kennaday, "Big Business and Workmen's Compensation," *Survey*, 29 (March 8, 1913), 809–810.

55. See, for example, Dr. Ferdinand Friedensburg, *The Practical Results of Workingmen's Insurance in Germany* (Workmen's Compensation Service and Information Bureau, New York, 1911). The author, former president of the Senate of the German Imperial Insurance Office, charged that one could "feel only deep and bitter pain when he sees that insurance has been the very factor which has led to universal degeneration and demoralization" (p. 46). In a review of this pamphlet, I. M. Rubinow observed that it had "created almost

a sensation in this country, serving as a weapon for many who oppose the movement for social legislation and intimidating some of those who would further it." It was given "wide publicity by some militant representatives of American liability insurance companies"; *Political Science Quarterly*, 27 (June 1912), 312, 314.

56. Frank E. Law, "State Insurance of Workmen's Compensation for Accidents," *Addresses Made at the Fifth Annual Meeting of the Liability Insurance Association*, 22.

57. *Ibid.*, 24, 25; J. Scofield Rowe, "Compensation for Accidents to Workpeople — Should it be Administered by the State?," *ibid.*, 63, 64.

58. Law, "State Insurance of Workmen's Compensation for Accidents, 26, 23; Edson S. Lott, "Different Methods of Workmen's Compensation Insurance," *Proceedings of the Conference on Social Insurance* (Called by the International Association of Industrial Accident Boards and Commissions), Washington, D.C., December 5–9, 1916, U.S. Department of Labor, Bureau of Labor Statistics, Bulletin No. 212 (Washington, 1917), 104.

59. Workmen's Compensation Publicity Bureau, *Some Points about Monopolistic State Insurance of Workmen's Compensation* (rev. ed., New York, 1923), 42.

60. William C. Archer, "Criticism of Prof. A. W. Whitney's Paper," *National Compensation Journal*, I (May 1914), 30.

61. F. Spencer Baldwin, "Competitive State Funds," *Proceedings of the Conference on Social Insurance*, 131.

62. A. W. Whitney, "Standardization of Rates and its Effect Upon Accident Prevention," *National Compensation Journal*, I (May 1914), 11.

63. Baldwin, "Competitive State Funds," 132, 133. A particularly bitter war raged in Ohio between the state fund and the insurance companies. A member of the Ohio Industrial Commission charged that there was "no justification for the conduct of those who willfully and persistently misrepresent the facts as to the Ohio State insurance fund in order to prevent its introduction into other States." On the question of state insurance, he complained, "many business men are allowing their judgment to be warped by an appeal to the prejudice against State ownership"; T. J. Duffy, "State Monopoly of Compensation Insurance," *Proceedings of the Conference on Social Insurance*, 145, 144.

Among the leading critics of competitive compensation insurance were Miles Dawson and E. H. Downey. See Miles M. Dawson, "The System Best Adapted to the United States," American Academy of

Political and Social Science, *Annals,* 38 (July 1911), 175–183; Miles
M. Dawson, "Superiority of Compulsory Mutual Insurance," *American
Labor Legislation Review,* 3 (June 1913), 259–265; Miles M. Dawson,
"State Accident Insurance in America a Demonstrated Success," *American Labor Legislation Review,* 10 (March 1920), 8–14. Competition,
according to Downey, had undesirable effects by every criterion of
compensation insurance: security of payments; prompt settlement of
claims; equitable cost distribution; accident prevention; and economy
in administration. E. H. Downey, "The Organization of Workmen's
Compensation Insurance," *Journal of Political Economy,* 24 (December
1916), 951–984; E. H. Downey, "The Making of Rates for Workmen's
Compensation Insurance," *Journal of Political Economy,* 25 (December
1917), 961–983. Downey argued that competition was reducing security of payments because of rate-cutting and extravagant selling costs.
State insurance regulations were ineffective because they permitted
companies to operate on insufficient reserves and allowed the organization of small, insecure carriers. State reserve requirements were based
upon percentages of premium income, but this presumed that carriers
would maintain adequate rates, and that no carriers would experience
above average loss ratios.

The problems resulting from the "open cutting of book rates" were
reinforced by "mis-classification and by competitive merit rating."
Some eight stock casualty companies failed in 1915–16 "mainly on
account of rate cutting." "Workmen's Compensation," Pennsylvania,
Insurance Department, *44th Annual Report of the Insurance Commissioner,* part II: Life and Accident Insurance, 1916 (Harrisburg, 1917),
iii. Other state insurance commissions complained of the competitive
cutting and manipulation of rates by private insurance companies.
See "Workmen's Compensation Matters," *Sixty-Second Annual Report
of the Insurance Commissioner of the Commonwealth of Massachusetts, January 1, 1917,* part II: Life, Miscellaneous, Assessment and
Fraternal Insurance (Boston, 1917), xvii ff; "Workmen's Compensation," *Bulletin of the Industrial Commission of Wisconsin,* I (July 20,
1912), 69ff.

64. The states with monopolistic state funds were Nevada, North
Dakota, Ohio, Oregon, Washington, West Virginia, and Wyoming.
Competitive state funds had been established in Arizona, California,
Colorado, Idaho, Maryland, Michigan, Montana, New York, Pennsylvania, and Utah.

A detailed comparative study is Carl Hookstadt, "Comparison of
Workmen's Compensation Insurance and Administration," U.S. De-

partment of Labor, Bureau of Labor Statistics, *Bulletin* No. 301 (April 1922). The investigation covered twenty states and two Canadian provinces. Private insurance companies in 1919 acquired 60 percent of premium dollars; mutuals, 18 percent; and state funds, 22 percent. Expense ratios of stock companies were 35 to 40 percent; mutuals, 15 to 20 percent; competitive state funds, 6 and 7 to 15 percent; and monopoly state funds, 3 to 7 or 8 percent. Throughout the controversy over the relative superiority of state and private insurance funds, there were two points of agreement — that the state funds were more economical in administrative overhead, and that the state funds performed "little safety and inspection work in comparison with private companies." The private companies maintained, of course, that included in their overhead was the cost of safety inspection and other services to the employer.

65. C. W. Price, "The Wisconsin Idea of Promoting Safety," *National Compensation Journal*, I (February 1914), 9; John R. Commons, "Constructive Investigation and the Industrial Commission of Wisconsin," *Survey*, 29 (January 4, 1913), 440–448.

66. John B. Andrews to Arthur T. Morey, June 5, 1916, American Association for Labor Legislation (John B. Andrews) Papers.

67. The Council was an outgrowth of the safety congress held in 1912. See *Proceedings of the First Co-operative Safety Congress (held under the auspices of the Ass'n of Iron and Steel Electrical Engineers)*, Milwaukee, Wisconsin, Sept. 30th to Oct. 5th, 1912. The organized safety movement is discussed in Don D. Lescohier, "The Campaigns for Health and Safety in Industry," in John R. Commons, *et al.*, *History of Labor in the United States, 1896–1932* (New York, 1935), III, 366ff. The beginnings of the movement are dated around 1907, when the American Museum of Safety was established by the American Institute of Social Sciences, and the Association of Iron and Steel Electrical Engineers was organized. The Association was one of the first technical groups to appoint a safety committee. At about the same time, the U.S. Steel Corporation launched its Safety-first program.

Other treatments of the subject include Sydney W. Ashe, *Organization in Accident Prevention* (New York, 1917); and Sydney W. Ashe, "Industrial Safety," American Academy of Political and Social Science, *Annals*, 123 (January 1926), entire issue. The subject was frequently discussed in the *Proceedings of the International Association of Industrial Accidents Boards and Commissions*, organized in 1914.

68. Charles T. Cutting, "The Conservative Element in the Work-

men's Compensation Problem," *National Compensation Journal,* I (November 1914), 3.

69. John R. Commons, "Unemployment Prevention," *American Labor Legislation Review,* 12 (March 1922), 21.

70. Dodd, *Administration of Workmen's Compensation,* 698.

71. Somers and Somers, *Workmen's Compensation,* 202–203, 210.

72. Downey, "The Present Status of Workmen's Compensation in the United States," 132, 133.

73. Somers and Somers, *Workmen's Compensation,* 229.

74. The most significant improvements, in the last quarter-century, have occurred in the area of medical and occupational disease benefits. Only thirteen laws provided medical benefits without limit of time or amount in 1940; by 1965 the number had risen to forty-two. Twenty-six jurisdictions compensated for industrial disease in 1940; all but one did by 1965.

Workmen's compensation still remains faulty in terms of the proportion of wage-loss covered. The Social Security Administration estimates that the proportion has actually dropped in the last quarter-century, reaching a nadir in the early 1950's. As of December 1965, nominal benefits in laws covering 95 percent of protected workers ranged from 60 to 66⅔ percent of wages, but effective rates were much lower. This was particularly true in the case of death or long-term disability. Only twenty jurisdictions provided benefits to widows for life or until remarriage (but eight of these limited the total amount payable). Calculating on the basis of permanent total disability provisions effective in October 1963, the Social Security Administration estimated that a disabled worker (aged forty, with a dependent wife and child) would receive compensation benefits equal to less than 35 percent of projected wages in twenty-nine states; and less than 15 percent in eighteen states.

The number of monopoly state funds dropped to six as of January 1, 1966, when the Oregon law was amended to permit private companies to serve as carriers. See, Alfred M. Skolnik, "Twenty-Five Years of Workmen's Compensation Statistics," *Social Security Bulletin,* 29 (October 1966), *passim.*

Arthur J. Altmeyer, former Commissioner of Social Security, maintains that workmen's compensation represents a "discouraging record of failure to live up to its high purpose of providing prompt and adequate compensation to injured workers. . . . Indeed, in many states benefits today are even less adequate in terms of the wage loss sustained. Litigation has delayed prompt payment, and administrators have failed to protect the rights of injured workers." Arthur J. Alt-meyer, "The Development and Status of Social Security in America," in Gerald G. Somers, ed., *Labor, Management, and Social Policy: Essays in the John R. Commons Tradition* (Madison, 1963), 140.

*Chapter IV   Health Insurance: "Made in Germany"*

1. The AALL's Committee on Workmen's Compensation was incorporated into the Committee on Social Insurance in 1913. The First National Conference on Social Insurance, held in Chicago in June 1913 "as a result of the efforts of this committee was one of the chief means of rousing a more general American interest in plans for compulsory sickness insurance." AALL, "Report of the Committee on Social Insurance," 1914 (typed), American Association for Labor Legislation (John B. Andrews) Papers, 1.

2. Another early program for compulsory health insurance came from the Progressive National Service. See *Sickness Insurance: Prepared for the Committee on Social and Industrial Justice of the Progressive National Service* (New York, 1914?).

3. The commission was never appointed in New Hampshire. A New Jersey Commission on Old Age, Insurance and Pensions, appointed in 1911, also turned its attention to health insurance in 1917. As in Massachusetts, a second commission was created in California in 1917. The governors of California, Massachusetts, and Nevada had endorsed health insurance in their inaugural messages in 1916. In March of that year the first legislative hearings on health insurance were held in Massachusetts. Dorothy Ketcham, "Health Insurance," *American Political Science Review*, 13 (February 1919), 89–92; Margaret A. Hobbs, "History of the Health Insurance Movement in America" (typed memorandum), Andrews Papers.

4. The following details on German and English health insurance are drawn largely from I. M. Rubinow, *Social Insurance: With Special Reference to American Conditions* (New York, 1913).

5. Membership in the guild and building funds was always insignificant. The number insured in the aid funds declined sharply from 20 percent of the total to less than 10 percent by 1911. Next to the local funds, the most important were the establishment and communal funds. The latter, however, were abolished in 1911, and replaced by the *Landkrankenkasse*, or rural sick-fund, which included both agricultural workers and miscellaneous urban wage-earners.

6. Employee contributions beyond 4½ percent were required in less than 1 percent of the funds. Since the lowest rates prevailed in the smallest societies, more than 50 percent of the total membership contributed 2–3 percent.

7. Technically, the cash benefits were calculated as half the average wages of the class of workers belonging to the fund.

8. An act of 1906 authorized local authorities to levy rates for the feeding of schoolchildren. In 1907 they were required to provide for medical inspection of schoolchildren, and the Children's Act of 1908 dealt with neglected and dependent children. In 1908 a national, tax-supported system of old-age pensions was established. The Town and Country Planning Act of 1909 provided local authorities with additional powers to control building and subdivision. Other Liberal measures included a Trade Boards Act which established trade boards to deal with wages and working conditions in a number of "sweated" industries; and the Labour Bureau Act of 1909 which established a national system of employment exchanges.

9. Harold Spender, "A National Health-Charter," *Contemporary Review,* 99 (June 1911), 654–655; Sydney Brooks, "Lloyd George and His Policies," *Forum,* 46 (September 1911), 332. A lengthy account of the origins of the National Insurance Act of 1911 can be found in Bentley B. Gilbert, *The Evolution of National Insurance in Great Britain: The Origins of the Welfare State* (London, 1966).

10. For women, the contribution was 3d., the rates for the employer and state remaining the same. If a worker earned less than 15s. ($3.75) a week, his rate of contribution declined.

11. The sanatorium benefit was removed from the health insurance system in 1921 and transferred to local authorities.

12. By the mid-1920's, there were 1,192 approved societies; 31 had branches totaling 7,226. Hermann Levy, *National Health Insurance: A Critical Study* (Cambridge, 1944), 6, 7, 9, 14, 26, 27. According to an American study, "the use of the approved societies as carriers of cash benefits has been an expedient but in many ways unfortunate procedure. Certainly no other country seeing the extra expense, duplication and over-lapping caused by the present system should think of resorting to this method of handling the cash benefits." William T. Ramsey and Ordway Tead, *Report of Investigation into the Operation of the British Health Insurance Act* (Pennsylvania Health Insurance Commission, 1920), 33.

13. Richard M. Titmuss, "Health," in Morris Ginsberg, ed., *Law*

*and Opinion in England in the 20th Century* (Berkeley, Calif., 1959), 308.

14. Hermann Levy, "The Economic History of Sickness and Medical Benefit Since the Puritan Revolution," *Economic History Review,* 14 (1944), 156. See also W. H. McNamara, "The Medical Profession and the Insurance Act," *Westminster Review,* 180 (November 1913), 477–484.

15. Titmuss, "Health," 312.

16. Responsibility for National Health Insurance was transferred in 1919 to the newly established Ministry of Health.

17. "Health Insurance Standards," *American Labor Legislation Review,* 6 (June 1916), 238.

18. *Health Insurance. Standards and Tentative Draft of an Act. Submitted for Criticism and Discussion by the Committee on Social Insurance of the American Association for Labor Legislation* (2nd ed., December 1915); Henry Seager, "Plan for a Health Insurance Act," *American Labor Legislation Review,* 6 (March 1916), 21–25; "Health Insurance. Tentative Draft of an Act. Submitted for Criticism and Discussion by the Committee on Social Insurance of the American Association for Labor Legislation," *American Labor Legislation Review,* 6 (June 1916), 239–268; *Medical Provisions of the Tentative Draft of an Act for Health Insurance. Developed in Conference with Physicians and Submitted for Criticism and Discussion by the Committee on Social Insurance of the American Association for Labor Legislation* (December 1916).

19. "Brief for Health Insurance," *American Labor Legislation Review,* 6 (June 1916), 155–236. Also, "Health Insurance: A Positive Statement in Answer to Opponents," *American Labor Legislation Review,* 7 (December 1917), entire issue.

20. "Brief for Health Insurance," 155, 157, 161, 163. Also, B. S. Warren and Edgar Sydenstricker, "Health Insurance: Its Relation to Public Health," Treasury Department, United States Public Health Service, *Public Health Bulletin,* No. 76, March 1916 (2nd ed., Washington, D.C., 1916), 6ff. Warren, a surgeon in the U.S. Public Health Service, was an outstanding publicist for health insurance. He placed special emphasis upon its potentialities for prevention. See B. S. Warren, "Sickness Insurance: A Preventive of Charity Practice," *Journal of the American Medical Association,* 65 (December 11, 1915), 2056–2059.

21. "Brief for Health Insurance," 174; Eugene T. Lies, "Sickness,

Dependency and Health Insurance," National Conference of Social Work, *Proceedings* (1917), 550–553; Francis King Carey, "Compulsory Health Insurance for Maryland. A Letter to the Members of the City Club of Baltimore," City Club of Baltimore, *Bulletin*, V, May 1917, 7, 10. According to Frederick R. Johnson, general secretary of the Boston Associated Charities, illness was responsible for one-third of charitable applications. Mary Beard, director of the District Nursing Association of Boston, maintained that nearly half the clients of the Association were unable to afford medical care. Massachusetts Health Insurance Hearing, Before the Special Commission on Social Insurance, 1916 (typed stenographic record), Andrews Papers, 4, 11.

22. "Brief for Health Insurance," 186, 187.

23. *Ibid.*, 195, 196.

24. John A. Lapp, "Health Insurance as a Means of Providing Medical Care," National Conference of Social Work, *Proceedings* (1919), 193; J. P. Chamberlain, "Sickness Insurance and Its Possibilities in Mining and Railroading," *Survey*, 33 (January 16, 1915), 423–426. Dr. W. A. Sawyer, secretary of the California State Board of Health, maintained that "in some of our communities, particularly in the lumber camps, the mining communities, and in connection with the railroads," a system approximating compulsory insurance existed. One found "fine hospitals," "trained nurses," and other facilities. Testimony, "Before the Social Insurance Commission of the State of California. Public Hearing to Investigate and Examine into the Question of Public Health Insurance for the State of California, San Francisco, November 20, 21, 22, 1916 (typed, Library, New York State School of Industrial and Labor Relations), 152. For a general survey of the evolution of industrial medicine see, Pierce Williams, *The Purchase of Medical Care Through Fixed Periodic Payment* (New York, 1932).

25. Robert T. Legge, "Students' Health Insurance at the University of California," U.S. Department of Labor, Bureau of Labor Statistics, *Bulletin*, 212, entire issue, *Proceedings of the Conference on Social Insurance* (Washington, D.C., 1917), 505; Edith Shatto King, "Health Insurance in a Student Community," *Survey*, 36 (September 23, 1916), 619–620; Richard C. Cabot, "Better Doctoring for Less Money," part I, *American Magazine*, 81 (April 1916), 8.

26. "Brief for Health Insurance," 196. Prior to National Health Insurance, the Contract Practice Committee of the British Medical Association had been working on a plan to establish a provident-medical service run by doctors. Levy, *National Health Insurance*, 16, 17.

The Majority of the Royal Poor Law Commission of 1909, on the other hand, sought an expansion of contract practice, while the Minority urged a medical service administered by local health authorities.

A major American precedent for compulsory health insurance, rarely cited, was that established by Congress for merchant seamen in 1798. The masters of American ships arriving from foreign ports had to transfer to customs collectors a sum equal to 20 cents a month deducted from each seaman's wage. The law applied also to vessels in the coastal trade. The money collected in each district was applied to hospitals and other medical facilities. After 1802 the money was deposited in a general fund. Prior to 1840, Congress made occasional deficiency appropriations, and a regular annual appropriation thereafter. The system was administered by clerks of the Treasury Department's Revenue Marine Division. In 1884, the compulsory program was terminated, and the costs met out of a tonnage tax. This arrangement ended in 1905, when Congress provided for a Marine Hospital Service supported by regular federal appropriations. This account is drawn from, Milton Terris, "An Early System of Compulsory Health Insurance in the United States," *Bulletin of the History of Medicine*, 15 (May 1944), 433–444.

Other experiments in prepaid or cooperative medicine are described in Wilson G. Smillie, "An Early Prepayment Plan for Medical Care: The Thomsonian System of Botanical Medicine," *Journal of the History of Medicine and Allied Sciences*, 6 (Spring 1951), 253–257; and Durward Long, "An Immigrant Co-operative Medicine Program in the South, 1887–1963," *Journal of Southern History*, 31 (November 1965), 417–434.

27. "Group Disability Insurance by Metropolitan," *Survey*, 32 (August 8, 1914), 475. In 1920 Metropolitan wrote a group plan covering health, life, and accident for the 1400 employees of the ten companies of Kingsport, Tennessee. "Every Worker in Town Insured," *Survey*, 43 (January 31, 1920), 482.

The Metropolitan was distinctive among insurance companies for its health and welfare programs. These were identified with Lee Frankel and Louis I. Dublin. A Philadelphia chemist, and University of Pennsylvania Ph.D., Frankel came to New York as director of the United Hebrew Charities. Following an address at the National Civic Federation in December 1908, attended by Haley Fiske of Metropolitan, Frankel was hired as manager of the Industrial Department. Within a year he became assistant secretary in charge of the newly created Welfare Department, and in 1912 was promoted to sixth vice-president. Dublin, a statistician, collaborated with Frankel until the latter's death in 1931.

The Welfare Department devoted considerable attention to tuberculosis, responsible for nearly 20 percent of the Company's death claims. Frankel and Dublin prepared a short pamphlet, *A War Upon Consumption,* which was distributed by Company agents. Metropolitan established a sanatorium for its employees, and in 1917 launched the famous Framingham (Mass.) health demonstration.

An outstanding innovation was the establishment of a visiting nurse service at the suggestion of Lillian Wald. The Company used existing agencies, or created its own nursing service for visits to policyholders. See Marquis James, *The Metropolitan Life: A Study in Business Growth* (New York, 1947), ch. XI.

Frankel and Metropolitan were singled out by the AALL as among the most active, subtle opponents of health insurance. Irene Osgood Andrews to E. B. Beard, July 29, 1919, Andrews Papers. Frankel developed the argument that the proponents of health insurance really meant "universal" rather than "compulsory" insurance. Universal health insurance could be achieved by means of a tax upon employed persons, and the tax remitted to those "who prefer to transmute taxes into insurance premiums." Lee K. Frankel, "Some Fundamental considerations in Health Insurance," *Proceedings of the Conference on Social Insurance,* 598–605.

28. "Brief for Health Insurance," 202, 203.

29. *Report of the Social Insurance Commission of the State of California,* January 25, 1917 (Sacramento, 1917), *passim.* Appointed in 1915, this was the first of the health insurance commissions. Its members included Katharine C. Felton; Dr. Flora W. Smith; George H. Dunlop; Mrs. Frances N. Noel; Paul Herriott, chairman. The advisory members consisted of Chester H. Rowell; Daniel C. Murphy; Ansley K. Salz; Barbara Nachtrieb, executive secretary. Rubinow served as consulting actuary. Both this commission and its successor, appointed in 1917, reported in favor of health insurance. *Report of the Social Insurance Commission of the State of California,* March 1919 (Sacramento, 1919).

30. *Report of the Health Insurance Commission of the State of Illinois,* May 1, 1919, *passim.* The Commission included William Butterworth; Dr. E. B. Coolley; Edna L. Foley; Dr. Alice Hamilton; Mary McEnerney; John E. Ransom; Matthew Woll; M. J. Wright; William Beye, chairman. H. A. Millis was secretary. Despite the

massive evidence collected by the Commission concerning the inadequacy of medical arrangements for the poor, it opposed compulsory
health insurance: governmental guardianship "of the normal adult man
or woman has sooner or later either ended in disaster for the government which attempted it or in the servility of those so governed"
(p. 166). A minority report by Alice Hamilton and John Ransom
favored health insurance.

31. Ohio Health and Old Age Insurance Commission, *Health,
Health Insurance, Old Age Pensions — Report, Recommendations,
Dissenting Opinions* (Columbus, Ohio, February 1919), *passim.* The
members of the Commission were, W. A. Julian; T. J. Donnelly; M. B.
Hammon; A. R. Warner; D. F. Garland; O. B. Chapman; R. E. Lee;
H. R. Mengert, secretary; John A. Lapp, director of investigations.
The Ohio Commission reported in favor of compulsory health insur-
ance.

32. *Report of the Health Insurance Commission of Pennsylvania,*
January 1919 (Harrisburg, 1919), *passim.* The Commission included
Edward E. Beidleman; Charles W. Sones; James B. Weaver, from the
State Senate. House members included William T. Ramsey; John M.
Flynn; Isadore Stern. The governor's appointees were William Flinn;
William Draper Lewis; Dr. J. B. McAlister. Edith Hilles served as
executive secretary. It did not offer a concrete recommendation.

33. A study of voluntary health insurance in New York City arrived
at conclusions similar to those of the commissions. Much of the insurance was carried through fraternals; voluntary agencies infrequently
furnished medical benefits; benefits were small and of short duration.
Anna Kalet, "Voluntary Health Insurance in New York City," *American Labor Legislation Review,* 6 (June 1916), 142–154.

34. "Brief for Health Insurance," 230, 234.

35. I. M. Rubinow, "Health Insurance in Its Relation to Public
Health," *Journal of the American Medical Association,* 67 (September
30, 1916), 1013; I. M. Rubinow, *Standards of Health Insurance* (New
York, 1916), 235.

36. *Ibid.,* 235.

37. *Ibid.,* 237, 238, 242; Rubinow, "Medical Services under Health
Insurance," *Proceedings of the Conference on Social Insurance,* 689.
On the subject of the family doctor, the Illinois Commission reported
that in the larger centers, especially Chicago, the "old-time relation
between the doctor and the family, and especially the wage-earning
family, has pretty much disappeared. Social workers . . . are almost
. . . unanimous in the statement that frequently when sickness comes

there is no family doctor to call, there may be hesitancy to call strange physicians because of inability to pay at once, sometimes payment at once is demanded . . ." *Report of the Health Insurance Commission of the State of Illinois*, 81. The "great majority of families" were equally handicapped in their financial ability to secure specialist services (p. 82).

38. Michael M. Davis, Jr., "Organization of Medical Service," *American Labor Legislation Review*, 6 (March 1916), 19, 20; Davis, "The Medical Organization of Sickness Insurance," *Medical Record*, January 8, 1916 (reprint), 7, 12, 16; Davis, "Existing Conditions of Medical Practice, Forms of Service Under Health Insurance, and Preventive Work," *Proceedings of the Conference on Social Insurance*, 679.

39. Cabot, "Better Doctoring for Less Money," part II (May 1916), 44, 78, 81; part I (April 1916), 78.

On health insurance and the organization of medical care along group or cooperative lines see also Alexander Lambert, "Medical Organization Under Health Insurance," *American Labor Legislation Review*, 7 (March 1917), 36–50. Dr. Andrew R. Warner, a member of the Ohio Health Insurance Commission, proclaimed that "individualistic" medical practice "must go." Just as "it was found convenient to concentrate production in factories, so it would be found convenient to put the modern practice of medicine into institutions and make it available for the use of the people, with a tremendous gain in efficiency." Quoted in "Second National Conference of Health Insurance Commissioners," *American Labor Legislation Review*, 8 (June 1918), 194, 196.

Some persons felt that no satisfactory health insurance system could combine both medical and cash benefits. The physician was inevitably overworked, underpaid, or both. The quality of medical services remained low. Thus, cash benefits should be completely divorced from medical benefits. An attempt was made in the permissive Sage-Machold Health Centre bill, introduced into the New York legislature in 1920, to establish a separate system of state-aided local health centers whose medical benefits would be available to the entire population. Administered by health departments, the proposed centers would serve approximately 50,000 persons and consist of hospitals, clinics, diagnostic facilities, and nursing services. The expense of construction and maintenance would be shared by the state and local district. Service would be free to those unable to pay; others would render partial or full payment. Gerald Morgan, " 'To Conserve the Human

Resources of the State,'" *New Republic*, 26 (March 23, 1921), 102–109; and Morgan, *Public Relief of Sickness* (New York, 1922). This health centre proposal is reminiscent of the health organization recommendation by the Minority of the Royal Poor Law Commission of 1909.

40. Rubinow, *Standards of Health Insurance*, 240–241.

41. Dr. A. C. Burnham to Frederick M. Davenport, February 10, 1920, Andrews Papers. Burnham supported the health center proposal mentioned above.

42. National Industrial Conference Board, *Workmen's Compensation Acts in the United States: The Medical Aspect*, Research Report No. 61 (New York, 1923), 26, 27, 38, 39.

43. New York Academy of Medicine, Public Health Committee, "The Medical Aspects of Workmen's Compensation," *Medical Record*, 100 (October 29, 1921), 769; Edward F. McSweeney, "Medical Men and Workmen's Compensation in Massachusetts," *Survey*, 31 (November 8, 1913), 157; Massachusetts, *Report of the Special Commission on Social Insurance*, January 15, 1918, Senate No. 244 (Boston, 1918), 27; Committee on Social or Health Insurance of the Chicago Medical Society, "Objections to Compulsory Health Insurance," *Illinois Medical Journal*, 31 (March 1917), 189; American Medical Association, "Report of Committee on Social Insurance," *Journal of the American Medical Association*, 68 (June 9, 1917), 1755; Alexander Lambert to Frederick M. Davenport, March 28, 1919, Andrews Papers; Rubinow, "Medical Services Under Health Insurance," 693.

44. New York State Medical Society, "Report of the Committee on Medical Economics," *New York State Journal of Medicine*, 17 (May 1917), 236.

45. Rubinow, "Medical Services under Health Insurance," 694. It was expected that the stand on commercial insurance companies would appease labor groups as well as physicians. Irene Osgood Andrews and Irene Sylvester Chubb to Dr. John Woodruff, July 25, 1919, Andrews Papers.

46. I. M. Rubinow, *The Quest for Security* (New York, 1934), 184, 213.

47. Rubinow, "Medical Services under Health Insurance," 692, 693; Joseph P. Chamberlain to John B. Andrews, March 15, 1916, Andrews Papers. The contrast in viewpoint between medical organizations representing the practicing physician and those representing health officers was quite sharp. See *Health Insurance: Report of the Standing Committee Adopted by the Conference of State and Territorial Health Authorities with the United States Public Health Service*

(Washington, D.C., May 13, 1916). The Committee consisted of Dr. B. S. Warren, U.S. Public Health Service, and Dr. William C. Woodward, Health Officer of the District of Columbia. The hospital administrator favoring health insurance was represented by such figures as Michael M. Davis, Jr., and Dr. S. S. Goldwater, director of Mt. Sinai Hospital, New York. For the industrial physician's viewpoint, see Dr. C. E. McDermid to John B. Andrews, February 27, 1917, Andrews Papers. McDermid, employed by the Utah Fuel Company Hospital, described his delight in being able to make calls with no suspicion in the patient's mind that his motives were mercenary. Contract practice, though an object of derision, established the soundest patient-physician relationship possible. The nursing profession was another institutionally centered group which favored health insurance. "Report of the Committee on Health Insurance," *American Journal of Nursing,* 17 (July 1917), 864–866.

48. Committee on Social or Health Insurance of the Chicago Medical Society, "Objections to Compulsory Health Insurance," 192, 190; John P. Davin, "The Legislative History of Compulsory Health Insurance in the State of New York," *Medical Record,* 97 (January 17, 1920), 106.

49. Committee on Social or Health Insurance of the Chicago Medical Society, "Objections to Compulsory Health Insurance," 191; M. L. Harris, "Effects of Compulsory Health Insurance on the Practice of Medicine," *Journal of the American Medical Association,* 74 (April 10, 1920), 1041. It was even argued by physicians that the impending prohibition law would make health insurance unnecessary. Liquor was the leading cause of poverty; after prohibition people would be affluent enough to pay legitimate bills. Edward H. Ochsner, "Some Objections to Health Insurance Legislation," *Illinois Medical Journal,* 31 (February 1917), 80; and Committee on Social or Health Insurance of the Chicago Medical Society, 189.

50. The amendment proposed by the Social Insurance Commission stated: "It is hereby declared to be the policy of the State of California to make special provision for the health and welfare of those classes of persons, and their dependents, whose incomes, in the determination of the legislature, are not sufficient to meet the hazards of sickness." *Report of the Social Insurance Commission of the State of California* (1917), 17.

51. Ansley K. Salz to John B. Andrews, October 12, 1918; John B. Andrews to Stanley M. Lynk, December 29, 1936, Andrews Papers.

Andrews singled out Frederick Hoffman of Prudential as responsible for the allegations of Berlin sponsorship.

52. Ansley K. Salz to John B. Andrews, October 25, November 12, 1918, Andrews Papers. The Andrews Papers include a typed copy of a deposition by Ernest Jerome Hopkins, sworn before a notary public in San Francisco, February 2, 1920. Hopkins was a journalist, who had been on the journalism faculty of the University of Southern California. According to this deposition, he had been employed as a publicist in 1918 by the California Research Society of Social Economics. He claimed that Babcock told him the Insurance Economics Society had established the Society of Social Economics, and that important backing came from Dr. Milbank Johnson, medical director of the Pacific Mutual Life Insurance Company of Los Angeles. According to Hopkins, Babcock also told him that the Insurance Economics Society planned to engage in similar campaigns in other states.

53. Ansley K. Salz to John B. Andrews, October 25, 1918, November 22, 1918; Ernestine W. Black to John B. Andrews, December 5, 1918, Andrews Papers.

54. They were spurred on by the "commercial insurance interests . . . under the organization of the Insurance Economics Society of Detroit, which sent its secretary, Mr. C. D. Babcock . . . to conduct the campaign." "The Health Insurance Movement in America" (typed memorandum for Dr. Alexander Lambert, January 31, 1919), Andrews Papers, 3, 4; Consumers' League, *Bulletin*, 9 (December 1919), 1.

55. The director of the San Francisco office of the California Social Insurance Commission charged that the majority of Stephen's advisers were Christian Scientists, and had convinced him that health insurance was objectionable. Both the chairman of the State Board of Control and the State Treasurer were Christian Scientists, and the state administration generally was engaged in combating the measure. Ernestine W. Black to John B. Andrews, December 5, 1918, Andrews Papers.

56. *Ibid.*, and Black to Andrews, June 29, 1918.

57. Medical Society of the State of California, "Report of the Committee on Health Insurance," *California State Journal of Medicine*, 16 (July 1918), 348, 349.

58. *Special California Bulletin A-1 by Insurance Economics Society of America* (Detroit, n.d.). The publication singled out Isaac Rubinow as the American alter ego of the "Iron Chancellor," who had "dulled the sensibilities of the German people and destroyed initiative and

self-reliance as to facilitate the growth of autocracy and caste control."
Rubinow's advice "during the period of his employment entirely dominated the activities of the commission, their report was written by him
and in so far as he could influence the recommendations of the commission they have been entirely along the lines of what he describes
in his book as the German system."

59. Medical Society of the State of California, "Report of the Committee on Health Insurance," 349.

60. "Health Insurance Bill as Developed from 'Tentative Drafts,'"
*American Labor Legislation Review*, 9 (June 1919), 209–224; John
B. Andrews to Mildred P. Stewart, February 6, 1919, Andrews Papers.
Senator Davenport introduced the final bill in 1920.

61. Irene Sylvester Chubb to Isaac M. Rubinow, April 25, 1919;
John B. Andrews to John R. Commons, April 29, 1919, Andrews Papers. Sweet's Committee also bottled up minimum wage and women's
eight-hour-day bills in that session.

62. Irene Sylvester Chubb to Isaac M. Rubinow, April 25, 1919;
Irene Osgood Andrews to Dr. Julius Rosenstern, September 23, 1919,
Andrews Papers. Exemption of members of a religious faith was a
concession forced by Christian Scientists.

63. Harry B. Mason, "What Compulsory Health Insurance Would
Mean to the Druggist," *Detroit Bulletin of Pharmacy* (January 1916),
reprint, 14, 15, 17, 18.

64. National Fraternal Congress of America, "Report of Committee
on Social Insurance," *The Fraternal Monitor* (n.d., probably Fall
1920), 11. It was pointed out that "great benefit in the campaign for
the education of the people on this subject resulted from the assistance
given by the New York League for Americanism, with headquarters
at Syracuse, of which Mr. C. D. Babcock was the efficient secretary"
(p. 11); also "Notes on the Hearing of the Davenport Health Insurance Bill, April 7, 1920," typed, Andrews Papers, 1, 2. Mrs. Locke
claimed that "socialistic" and "pro-German" health insurance legislation threatened the life of the fraternals. Confusing the AALL with
the International Association, Mrs. Locke described it as a pro-German
organization with headquarters in Zurich.

65. Chamber of Commerce of the State of New York, *Preamble and
Resolution Presented by Committee on Insurance*, adopted April 1,
1920 (pamphlet, n.d.), 2; *Social Insurance with Special Reference
to Compulsory Health Insurance. A Report Prepared for the Committee
on Insurance of the Chamber of Commerce of the State of New York*,

by John Franklin Crowell (New York, 1917), *passim; Compulsory Health Insurance. Statement issued by Social Insurance Department, The National Civic Federation* (pamphlet, n.d., probably 1917), 5; Dennis C. Pierce to John B. Andrews, April 16, 1920; James A. Loyster to John B. Andrews, April 16, 1920; John B. Andrews to Sam A. Lewisohn, October 3, 1919, Andrews Papers; National Industrial Conference Board, *Sickness Insurance or Sickness Prevention?* Research Report No. 6 (May 1918; pamphlet circulated by Insurance Economics Society).

66. Grant Hamilton, "Proposed Legislation for Health Insurance," *Proceedings of the Conference on Social Insurance*, 563, 568; see also Rubinow, *Quest for Security*, 212.

67. According to a list compiled by the New York State Federation of Labor, the following labor organizations had endorsed health insurance: International Typographical Union; International Union of Steam and Operating Engineers; Spinners' International Union; United Textile Workers of America; International Brotherhood of Pulp, Sulphite and Paper Mill Workers of the United States and Canada; Glass Bottle Blowers' Association of the United States and Canada; International Brotherhood of Foundry Employees; International Glove Workers' Union of America; Brotherhood of Railway Carmen of America; National Women's Trade Union League; Southern Labor Congress. In addition there were the following state federations: California, Connecticut, Illinois, Minnesota, Missouri, Nebraska, New Jersey, New York, Ohio, Wisconsin. New York State Federation of Labor, *Health Insurance — Official Endorsement of the New York State Federation of Labor with report of its Committee on Health* (New York, 1918), 15.

68. *Ibid.*, 10.

69. *Ibid.*, 11; New York State Federation of Labor, Executive Council, "Health Insurance Discussion," January 8, 1918, typed, Andrews papers, 119.

70. Great Eastern Casualty Company, *Circular, To Our New York Agents*, February 17, 1916.

71. The League's headquarters were in Syracuse.

72. John B. Andrews to Stanley M. Lynk, December 29, 1936, Andrews Papers; I. M. Rubinow, "Letter," *Journal of the American Medical Association*, 68 (April 28, 1917), 1279; Irene Osgood Andrews and Irene Sylvester Chubb to Dr. John Woodruff, July 25, 1919; Irene Osgood Andrews to E. B. Beard, July 29, 1919, Andrews Papers. J. R.

Maloney's testimony before the California Social Insurance Commission does suggest that the insurance companies might have accepted health insurance if their terms had been met. Maloney, president of the Insurance Federation of California, interpreted the issue as follows: "That private stock insurance and all other forms of insurance, mutual and otherwise, are asking for only one thing in this whole scheme of things, if you determine that you want social health insurance in California that you retain the State, that you retain the labor unions, that you retain the fraternal orders, and the same with the stock companies . . . and throw the field open . . . and then let your competitive condition take care of the situation." Why should the insurance field alone "be picked out for the elimination of the profit in the caring for the poor and indigent in this country — they all have to eat, they have to sleep, and they have to sleep in houses, too." "Before the Social Insurance Commission of the State of California. Public Hearing," 333, 316–317.

73. John B. Andrews and Olga Halsey to Dr. Frank W. Low, November 6, 1919, Andrews Papers.

74. Edward H. Ochsner, "Further Objections to Compulsory Health Insurance," New York League for Americanism, *Bulletin* No. 5 (Syracuse, n.d., probably 1919), 10. The AALL described Ochsner, a Chicago physician, as the outstanding nemesis of health insurance in Illinois, and one who stressed the pro-German argument. "Memorandum for Dr. Alexander Lambert," 3.

75. John B. Andrews to Josephine Shatz, November 8, 1919; Andrews to Frederick M. Davenport, July 3, 1919, Andrews Papers.

76. John B. Andrews to John A. Lapp, March 21, 1919; Andrews to Joseph P. Chamberlain, March 22, 1919, Andrews Papers. Apparently Rooney was one of several physicians "trying as political doctors to become president of the State Medical Society through their opposition to health insurance." John B. Andrews to Emma B. Beard, April 24, 1919, Andrews Papers. Another of the most vigorous opponents of health insurance was Dr. E. MacD. Stanton, chairman of the Committee on Public Information, Schenectady County Medical Society. John B. Andrews to Caroline O'Day, March 23, 1920, Andrews Papers.

77. Rooney even opposed an investigating commission because the earlier Wainwright Commission on workmen's compensation had proven so detrimental to physicians. New York State Medical Society, "Report of the Committee on Legislation," *New York State Journal of Medicine*, 17 (May 1917), 234, 235. Rooney warned that to save itself

the profession "must organize, as it never has organized before" (p. 235).

78. Irene Sylvester Chubb to Isaac M. Rubinow, April 25, 1919, Andrews Papers.

79. *Rochester Times-Union,* February 27, 1919; Medical Society of the County of Schenectady, Circular (n.d.); *Express* (Buffalo, N.Y.), August 29, 1919; Dentists' Protective Association of Monroe County, paid newspaper advertisement; Dr. C. J. Patterson to John J. Mackrell, February 22, 1919, Andrews Papers; *Albany Journal,* April 30, 1919; *Knickerbocker Press,* July 16, 1919; Medical Society of the County of Erie, Circular (1919); *Syracuse Post-Standard,* October 31, 1919; *Rome Sentinel,* April 9, 1919.

80. Dr. Alexander Lambert to John B. Andrews, May 3, 1920; John B. Andrews and Olga Halsey to Samuel M. Lindsay, December 1, 1919, Andrews Papers.

81. Frederic Almy to John B. Andrews, January 26, 1920, Andrews Papers.

82. *Ibid.;* Almy to Andrews, March 3, 1920, Andrews Papers.

83. *Express* (Buffalo, N.Y.), March 3, 1920; Dr. John Pryor, testimony, "Notes on the Hearing of the Davenport Health Insurance Bill," 4.

84. Professional Guild of Kings County, *Synopsis of the Davenport-Donohue Compulsory Health Insurance Bill* (pamphlet, n.d., probably 1919), *passim.* Members of the Guild included the Medical Society of the County of Kings; Second District Dental Society; Kings County Pharmaceutical Society; Kings County Dental Society; Flatbush Medical Society, and others. The Guild's prime mover was apparently Dr. John J. A. O'Reilly of Brooklyn.

85. Roy Lubove, "The New Deal and National Health," *Current History,* 45 (August 1963), 77–86, 117.

86. Health insurance efforts after 1920 are discussed in: J. F. Follmann, Jr., *Medical Care and Health Insurance: A Study in Social Progress* (Homewood, Ill., 1963); Joseph Hirsh, "The Compulsory Health Insurance Movement in the United States," *Social Forces,* 18 (October 1939), 102–114; Maurice B. Hamovitch, "History of the Movement for Compulsory Health Insurance in the United States," *Social Service Review,* 27 (September 1953), 281–299; Louis S. Reed, "Legislative Proposals for Compulsory Health Insurance," *Law and Contemporary Problems,* 6 (Autumn 1939), 628–644. U.S. Department of Health, Education, and Welfare, Social Security Administration, Division of

Program Research, *Health Insurance and Related Proposals for Financing Personal Health Services: A Digest of Major Legislation and Proposals for Federal Action, 1935–1957,* by Agnes W. Brewster (Washington, D.C., 1958).

## Chapter V   *Mothers' Pensions and the Renaissance of Public Welfare*

1. Eveline M. Burns, *The American Social Security System* (Boston, 1951), 31, 33.

2. I. M. Rubinow, *Social Insurance: With Special Reference to American Conditions* (New York, 1913), 435, 436.

3. An influential episode was the termination of outdoor relief in Brooklyn in 1879. See Robert Treat Paine, "Discussion on Poor Relief," National Conference of Charities and Correction, *Proceedings* (1888), 442–444. It was "wonderful," according to a Buffalo charity organization leader, "how the refusal to give outside the institution develops grit, restores health, and brings relatives and friends from under cover." Frederic Almy, "Public or Private Outdoor Relief," National Conference of Charities and Correction, *Proceedings* (1900), 137. Almy reported that twelve of the twenty-one largest cities gave little or no outdoor relief: New York, Philadelphia, Brooklyn, St. Louis, Baltimore, San Francisco, New Orleans, Washington, Kansas City, Louisville, Jersey City, and Cincinnati. The nine offenders, "in order of lavishness," were: Milwaukee, Detroit, Boston, Buffalo, Minneapolis, Newark, Cleveland, Chicago, and Pittsburgh.

The status of public relief around the turn of the century is discussed in Charles R. Henderson, "Poor Laws of the United States," National Conference of Charities and Correction, *Proceedings* (1897), 256–271; Homer Folks, "Report of the Committee on Municipal and County Charities," National Conference of Charities and Correction, *Proceedings* (1898), 106–183. A later survey, emphasizing improvements in administration, is L. A. Halbert, "The Organization of Municipal Charities and Corrections," National Conference of Charities and Correction, *Proceedings* (1916), 387–396. See, however, the harsh indictment in George A. Warfield, *Outdoor Relief in Missouri: A Study of Its Administration by County Officials* (New York, 1915).

4. C. R. Henderson, "Public Outdoor Relief," National Conference of Charities and Correction, *Proceedings* (1891), 40.

5. *Ibid.,* 40, 41.

6. *Ibid.,* 40.

7. Levi L. Barbour, "Public Outdoor Relief," National Conference of Charities and Correction, *Proceedings* (1891), 44, 43, 45. A further sample of criticism of public outdoor relief, along the lines discussed, includes the following articles in the National Conference of Charities and Corrections, *Proceedings:* C. G. Trusdell, "The History of Public and Private Indoor and Outdoor Relief" (1893), 94–105; George E. M'Gonegal, "The Problem of Out-Door Relief. Report of the Standing Committee" (1888), 141–153; Oscar C. M'Culloch, "The Tribe of Ishmael: A Study in Social Degradation" (1888), 154–159; J. R. Washburn, "Outdoor Relief" (1898), 196–197; George S. Wilson, "Outdoor Relief in Relation to Charity Organization" (1900), 256–265; Thomas J. Riley, "A Discussion of Public Outdoor Relief" (1915), 474–479. Relevant also is Amos G. Warner, *American Charities: A Study in Philanthropy and Economics* (New York, 1894).

8. Homer Folks, "Discussion: Pensions to Widows," National Conference of Charities and Correction, *Proceedings* (1912), 486; see also Almy, "Public or Private Outdoor Relief," 135.

9. Roy Lubove, *The Professional Altruist: The Emergence of Social Work as a Career, 1880–1930* (Cambridge, Mass., 1965).

10. L. A. Halbert, "Boards of Public Welfare: A System of Government Social Work," National Conference of Social Work, *Proceedings* (1918), 220–221.

11. "The National Public Welfare League," *Public Welfare,* 1 (April 1918), 3. Hanson served as General Superintendent of the League. Originally interested in the "problem of the social evil," he had worked as a volunteer investigator for the Kansas City Board of Public Welfare. The National Public Welfare League actually originated in 1911, but was incorporated in 1916.

12. James M. Ford, "The Board of Public Welfare of Kansas City, Missouri," National Conference of Charities and Correction, *Proceedings* (1916), 400.

13. *Ibid.,* 401. For the work of other Boards of Public Welfare see the following articles in the National Conference of Charities and Correction, *Proceedings* (1916): D. Frank Garland, "The Municipality and Public Welfare," 306–316; W. A. Crossland, "The Social Welfare Board of St. Joseph, Missouri," 404–410; Evelyn Gail Gardiner, "Municipal Organization of Social Service in the Proposed New Charter of Grand Rapids," 410–415. A somewhat different effort to improve the administration of public welfare agencies is described in, Bessie A. McClenahan, *The Iowa Plan for the Combination of Public and Private Relief* (Iowa City, 1918).

14. Gardiner, "Municipal Organization of Social Service," 414; L. A. Halbert, "Boards of Public Welfare and Good City Government," National Conference of Charities and Correction, *Proceedings* (1913), 214; Garland, "The Municipality and Public Welfare," 308, 310, 309. This idealized concept of government embodied, to some extent, the "organic" interpretation of society which influenced reform thought in the progressive era. See Roy Lubove, "The Twentieth Century City: The Progressive as Municipal Reformer," *Mid-America*, 41 (October 1959), 195–209.

15. Garland, "The Municipality and Public Welfare," 309, 311.

16. Halbert, "Boards of Public Welfare and Good City Government, 213. The Kansas City School of Social Service, sponsored by the Board, offered a two-year course consisting of lectures and field work. The evolution of its Research Bureau is described in, *Second Annual Report of the Board of Public Welfare of Kansas City, Missouri, April 19, 1910–April 18, 1911*, 17ff.

17. Halbert, "Boards of Public Welfare and Good City Government," 213, 216.

18. These developments are described in detail in Homer Folks, *The Care of Destitute, Neglected, and Delinquent Children* (New York, 1902). See also: National Conference of Charities and Correction, *History of Child Saving in the United States at the Twentieth National Conference of Charities and Correction in Chicago: Report of the Committee on the History of Child-Saving Work* (June 1893); William H. Slingerland, *Child Welfare Work in Oregon: A Study of Public and Private Agencies and Institutions for the Care of Dependent, Delinquent and Defective Children for the Oregon Child Welfare Commission* (Salem, 1918); William H. Slingerland, *Child Welfare Work in California: A Study of Agencies and Institutions* (New York, 1915); William H. Slingerland, *Child Welfare Work in Pennsylvania: A Co-Operative Study of Child-Helping Agencies and Institutions* (New York, 1915); Jeffrey R. Brackett, "Tendencies in Care of Destitute and Neglected Children in Massachusetts," National Conference of Charities and Correction, *Proceedings* (1911), 93–98; Henry W. Thurston, *The Dependent Child: A Story of Changing Aims and Methods in the Care of Dependent Children* (New York, 1930); Emma O. Lundberg, *Unto the Least of These: Social Services for Children* (New York, 1947).

19. The origins of the Conference are examined in Harold A. Jambor, "Theodore Dreiser, *The Delineator Magazine*, and Dependent Children: A Background Note on the Calling of the 1909 White

House Conference," *Social Service Review,* 32 (March 1958), 33–40.

20. Homer Folks confirms that the idea for a Conference originated with West, who had grown up in an institution. Homer Folks, "Reminiscences," Columbia University Oral History Project, 52. The formal request was presented to Roosevelt by Homer Folks, secretary, New York State Charities Aid Association; Hastings H. Hart, superintendent, Illinois Children's Home and Aid Society; John M. Glenn, director, Russell Sage Foundation; Thomas M. Mulry, president, St. Vincent de Paul Society; Edward T. Devine, secretary, New York Charity Organization Society; Julian W. Mack, judge, Circuit Court, Chicago; Charles W. Birtwell, secretary, Boston Children's Aid Society; Theodore Dreiser, editor, *Delineator;* and James E. West, secretary, National Child-Rescue League.

21. *Proceedings of the Conference on the Care of Dependent Children, held at Washington, D.C., January 25, 26, 1909* (Washington, D.C., 1909), 9.

22. Theodore Roosevelt, "Special Message to Congress, February 15, 1909," *ibid.,* 5.

23. As might be expected, those associated with children's institutions protested against the wholesale condemnation of their work. See the remarks of Right Rev. D. J. McMahon, supervisor, Catholic Charities Archdiocese of New York, *ibid.,* 97; Ludwig B. Bernstein, superintendent, Hebrew Sheltering Guardian Orphan Asylum, *ibid.,* 129, 147; George B. Robinson, president, New York Catholic Protectory, *ibid.,* 148; Simon Wolf, president, Hebrew Orphan's Home, Atlanta, *ibid.,* 150; Solomon Lowenstein, superintendent, Hebrew Orphan Asylum, *ibid.,* 151.

24. *Ibid.,* 10, 11. The recommendations also included an endorsement of preventive social legislation and a plea for enactment of the bill pending in Congress for the establishment of a federal children's bureau.

25. C. C. Carstens, *Public Pensions to Widows with Children: A Study of their Administration in Several American Cities* (New York, 1913), 7ff.; Emma O. Lundberg, "Aid to Mothers with Dependent Children," American Academy of Political and Social Science, *Annals,* 98 (November 1921), 97–98; Lundberg, *Public Aid to Mothers with Dependent Children,* U.S. Department of Labor, Children's Bureau, Publication No. 162 (Washington, D.C., 1926), 2–3.

26. Hannah Einstein, the organizer of the Fund, had been on the governing board of the United Hebrew Charities. She discovered "how very inadequately widowed mothers and their young and dependent

children were being cared for." Mrs. William Einstein, "Survey of the Operation and Needs of Child Welfare Boards in the State of New York," Eighteenth New York State Conference of Charities and Correction, *Proceedings* (1917), 253.

27. By 1930, mothers' pensions laws had been enacted in all states but Alabama, Georgia, New Mexico, and South Carolina. On their administration, see: Carstens, *Public Pensions to Widows with Children;* Lundberg, "Aid to Mothers with Dependent Children"; Lundberg, "Public Aid to Mothers with Dependent Children"; Laura A. Thompson, *Laws Relating to "Mothers' Pensions" in the United States, Canada, Denmark, and New Zealand,* U.S. Department of Labor, Children's Bureau, Legal Series No. 4, Bureau Publication No. 63 (Washington, D.C., 1919); Emma O. Lundberg, "Progress of Mothers' Aid Administration," *Social Service Review,* 2 (September 1928), 435–458; Emma O. Lundberg, "Mothers' Aid," *Social Work Year Book,* I, 1929 (New York, 1930), 273–279.

28. On the link between poverty, dependent motherhood, and delinquency see Sophonisba P. Breckinridge, "Neglected Widowhood in the Juvenile Court," *American Journal of Sociology,* 16 (July 1910), 53–87.

29. Porterfield was also president of the Juvenile Improvement Club, which provided scholarships to enable boys of working age to remain in school. He had been aware of the widows' pensions program inaugurated by the United Jewish Charities of Kansas City. L. A. Halbert, "The Widows' Allowance Act in Kansas City," *Survey,* 31 (February 28, 1914), 675–676.

30. Sherman M. Craiger, "Mothers on the Pay-Roll in Many States," *Review of Reviews,* 52 (July 1915), 82; E. E. Porterfield, "How the Widow's Allowance Operates," *Child-Welfare Magazine,* 7 (February 1913), 208. Also E. L. Mathias, "The Widowed Mother and Children — How to Help Them," *The Child,* 1 (April 1912), 20–22. At the White House Conference of 1909 it was a juvenile court judge, William H. De Lacy of Washington, D.C., who argued that "needy and lone mother" should be the exception "in enforcing the rule against outdoor relief." *Proceedings of the Conference on the Care of Dependent Children,* 56.

31. Merritt W. Pinckney, "Experiences and Observations which Lead Me to Favor such a Law," National Conference of Charities and Correction, *Proceedings* (1912), 473. Those close to the situation "from probation officer to judge felt the need of some measure to prevent the kind of separations that were daily taking place in the Chi-

cago Juvenile Court and to a much greater extent proportionately in the other counties of the state where private charity is not so well supported." John W. Witter, "The Illinois Funds to Parents Act," *The Child,* 1 (March 1912), 29.

32. Gertrude Vaile to William H. Matthews, January 29, 1915, AICP, folder 15–7, Archives, Community Service Society (hereafter, ACSS); Ben B. Lindsey, "The Mothers' Compensation Law of Colorado," *Survey,* 29 (February 15, 1913), 714–716.

33. *Child Welfare in Tennessee: An Inquiry by the National Child Labor Committee for the Tennessee Child Welfare Commission* (1920), 511.

34. Commonwealth of Massachusetts, *Report of the Commission on the Support of Dependent Minor Children of Widowed Mothers, January, 1913,* House No. 2075 (Boston, 1913). The other members were Robert F. Foerster, chairman, and David F. Tilley. Tilley dissented from the majority report favoring a mothers' pension law.

35. Clara C. Park, "Widows' Pension in Massachusetts," *Child-Welfare Magazine,* 6 (June 1912), 343; Clara C. Park, "Motherhood and Pensions," *Survey,* 30 (April 12, 1913), 74. For an example of the sentimental tributes to the home typical of the mothers' pensions movement see Mrs. David O. Mears, "The Home," *First International Congress in America on the Welfare of the Child, Under the Auspices of National Congress of Mothers,* Washington, D.C., March 10–17, 1908. According to Mrs. Mears, president of the National Congress of Mothers, the home was the "most sacred spot known to the human heart. Even the beauty of Eden was not perfected until there was a home in it." The parental heart was possessed by "love, deep, tender, sacred . . . at the coming of the new treasure" (p. 147).

36. *Report of Mothers' Pension League of Allegheny County, 1915–16* (n.p., n.d.). Mothers' Pensions were endorsed by the General Federation of Women's Clubs in 1912. Mabel P. Daggett, "The City as a Mother," *World's Work,* 25 (November 1912), 114.

37. The Brooklyn Bureau of Charities and its secretary, Thomas J. Riley, also strongly opposed mothers' pensions.

38. John D. Lindsay to William F. Colne, February 2, 1912, COS, folder, Widow's Pensions, Apr. 1899–Mar. 1912, ACSS. The measure was introduced by State Senator John F. Ahearn. The initiative in opposing the bill seems to have been taken by the Society for the Prevention of Cruelty to Children, and the New York State Charities Aid Association.

39. "Hearing before Senate Cities' Committee on Senate Bill No.

1135, introduced by Mr. Ahearn, being an act in relation to children committed to charitable and public institutions in the city of New York, in the Boroughs of Manhattan and the Bronx — April 6, 1899," COS, folder, Widows' Pensions, Apr. 1899–Mar. 1912, ACSS, 2, 3, 4, 10, 14.

40. Mary E. Richmond, "Motherhood and Pensions," *Survey*, 29 (March 1, 1913), 775, 776. See also Mary E. Richmond, " 'Pensions' and the Social Worker," *Survey*, 29 (February 15, 1913), 665–666.

41. Richmond, "Motherhood and Pensions," 780.

42. Charity Organization Society of New York, "Memorandum: In re the Assembly Bill to amend the Greater New York Charter in relation to creating a board of trustees of home assistance in the City of New York for dependent widows with children — No. 146. Introduced by Mr. Schifferdecker and referred to the Committee on Affairs of Cities" (1912?), AICP, folder 15–7, ACSS, 3; Robert W. de Forest and Otto T. Bannard to William W. Colne, February 14, 1912, *ibid.*

43. Roy Lubove, "The Welfare Industry: Social Work and the Life of the Poor," *The Nation* (May 23, 1966), 609–611.

44. State of New York, *Report of the New York State Commission on Relief for Widowed Mothers, transmitted to the Legislature March 27, 1914* (Albany, 1914), 151.

45. *Ibid.* 131, 132. See also Otto T. Bannard to W. Frank Persons, January 9, 1913, COS, folder, Widows' Pensions, 1913–1914, ACSS.

46. Lee K. Frankel, "Discussion: Mothers' Pensions," Eighteenth New York State Conference of Charities and Correction, *Proceedings* (1917), 274.

47. Ansley Wilcox to John A. Kingsbury, March 5, 1915, COS, folder, Widows' Pensions, Feb. 1913–Oct. 1920, ACSS.

48. Mrs. William Einstein, "Pensions for Widowed Mothers as a Means of Securing for Dependent Children the Benefits of Home Training and Influence," Eleventh New York State Conference of Charities and Correction, *Proceedings* (1910), 224; Mrs. William Einstein, "The Keeping Together of Families," Second New York City Conference of Charities and Correction, *Proceedings* (1911), 76; Mrs. William Einstein, "The Keeping Together of Families," Third New York City Conference of Charities and Correction, *Proceedings* (1912), 62; Mrs. William Einstein, "Discussion," Fifth New York City Conference of Charities and Correction, *Proceedings* (1914), 241, 242.

Long after the mothers' pensions struggle had ended, Sophie Loeb, Mrs. Einstein's associate on the New York State Commission and later the New York City Board of Child Welfare, remained "publicly antagonistic to private agencies and wants to wipe them out." "Minutes of Central Office Committee Meeting, November 23, 1928," COS, folder, Board of Child Welfare, 1915–29, ACSS, 3. Nor did Mrs. Einstein prove forgiving. See, Mrs. William Einstein, *Foster Father Knickerbocker's 39,000 Dependent Children* (Child Welfare Committee of America, Publication No. 48, Series, 1928).

49. The Commission paid tribute to Aaron J. Levy, a member of the New York State Assembly, as the individual most responsible both for the Commission and the emergence of the mothers' pensions' movement in New York State: "It was not . . . until the Hon. Aaron J. Levy . . . championed this cause that the movement took a real hold in this State. Year after year Mr. Levy introduced and fought for the passage of several bills looking towards this end, and finally when these efforts were unavailing, he succeeded in passing the law creating this Commission." *New York State Commission on Relief for Widowed Mothers*, 3–4.

Anthony J. Griffin, Henry W. Pollock, and Ralph W. Thomas were appointed to the Commission from the New York State Senate. The State Assemblymen were Frederick S. Burr, Aaron J. Levy, Martin G. McCue, James W. Rozan, and Thomas K. Smith. The Governor appointed Mrs. Hannah Einstein, Sophie Irene Loeb, E. Frank Brewster, William Hard, John D. Lindsay, and Ansley Wilcox. Levy served as permanent chairman. The Commission appointed Richard M. Neustadt as secretary, and Robert W. Hebberd, secretary of the State Board of Charities, as director of investigations.

For a detailed legislative history of Mothers' Pension legislation in New York State for 1911 to 1915 see William E. Hannan, *Mothers' Pension Legislation in New York and Other States*, New York State Library, Bulletin, Legislation, 41 (Albany, 1916).

50. *New York State Commission on Relief for Widowed Mothers*, 7.

51. *Ibid.*, 9, 91, 107, 115.

52. *Ibid.*, 7, 8.

53. *Ibid.*, 15, 9.

54. *Ibid.*, 51, 79, 93. From the viewpoint of the private societies, they were less guilty of supplying inadequate assistance than of failure to provide casework and related services to the degree required. For a self-evaluation see *Report of an Investigation of Matters Relating to the Care, Treatment and Relief of Dependent Widows with Dependent Children in the City of New York. Made for the Executive Committee of the Conference called by Mr. O. F. Lewis and held in the Office of Mr. Thomas M. Mulry on January 4, 1913* (The report was

prepared by Edward T. Devine, and was based upon material gathered by Francis H. McLean and a staff of social workers). However, William H. Matthews, director of the Department of Family Welfare, New York Association for Improving the Condition of the Poor, and later chairman, New York City Board of Child Welfare, concluded after a period of uncertainty that the private charities had failed and that a state assistance program was needed. "In spite of the large amount of money raised by private societies in New York City," he charged, "they were quite unable to meet the plain needs of the families under discussion. Their own records are proof of that fact." William H. Matthews, "Experiences in Administration," U.S. Department of Labor, Bureau of Labor Statistics, *Proceedings of the Conference on Social Insurance*, Bulletin 212, entire issue (Washington, D.C., 1917), 816. Matthews' own organization, the AICP, had instituted a pension program in 1912; but while 43 families were assisted, another 431 under the Society's care did not receive comparable allowances. William H. Matthews, "Widows' Families: Pensioned and Otherwise," *Survey*, 32 (June 6, 1914), 270–275. In light of the AICP experience, its acting general director concluded that, unless private agencies raised sufficient funds to cope with widowed mothers, there would be no alternative to a state program. Bailey B. Burritt to Board of Managers, April 10, 1914, AICP, folder 37–10, ACSS. Matthews agreed that if the private agencies did not do better they would be brushed aside. Wm. H. Matthews to Charles L. Taylor, April 10, 1914, *ibid.*

A split apparently developed between the COS and AICP over the mothers' pension issue by 1914. The COS insisted to the end that private charity, as represented by its own pension program, was sufficient. W. Frank Persons to Peter E. Alliot, June 2, 1914, COS, folder, Widows' Pensions, 1913–1914, ACSS; W. Frank Persons to Bailey B. Burritt, January 9, 1915, AICP, folder, 15–7, ACSS. But Burritt informed Devine of the COS that although he preferred private action, it was time to stop giving the public the impression that voluntary agencies had the situation under control. It was known to social workers that widows and their children were suffering because of arduous work combined with inadequate wages. Bailey B. Burritt to Edward T. Devine, February 25, 1914, AICP, folder, 15–7, ACSS. By the beginning of 1915, the AICP had determined not to oppose any satisfactory mothers' pension proposal. W. Frank Persons to Bailey B. Burritt, January 9, 1915, *ibid.*

55. *New York State Commission on Relief for Widowed Mothers*, 115, 126, 116.

56. Porter R. Lee, "The Administrative Basis of Public Outdoor Relief," National Conference of Social Work, *Proceedings* (1917), 151, 152.

57. Helen G. Tyson, "The Fatherless Family," American Academy of Political and Social Science, *Annals*, 77 (May 1918), 82, 90. The belief that mothers' pensions might be the instrument through which public agencies would be modernized along the lines of the private case work agency was fairly widespread. See Ada E. Sheffield, "The Influence of Mothers' Aid Upon Family Life," *Survey*, 34 (July 24, 1915), 378–379; Jeffrey R. Brackett, "Public Outdoor Relief in the United States," National Conference of Charities and Correction, *Proceedings* (1915), 448–449.

58. Gertrude Vaile, "Public Administration of Charity in Denver," National Conference of Charities and Correction, *Proceedings* (1916), 418, 417; Vaile, "Administering Mothers' Pensions in Denver," *Survey*, 31 (February 28, 1914), 673. "The only possible way that I can see to safeguard either the public fund or the people who must turn to it for help," Miss Vaile maintained, "is just thoughtful, sympathetic case work, which studies each individual's need and tries to lift him out of it by personal service. . . . This is the principle laid down by the charity organization society for the work of private charities." Gertrude Vaile, "Principles and Methods of Outdoor Relief," National Conference of Charities and Correction, *Proceedings* (1915), 480.

59. Among the more useful services were the arrangements made for physical examinations of children and for vocational guidance.

60. *First Annual Report of the Board of Child Welfare of the City of New York, October 1, 1915 to October 1, 1916*, 12.

61. *Third Annual Report of the Board of Child Welfare of the City of New York, January 1, 1918 to December 31, 1918*, 18. "The main interest of our Board," in a word, "is to encourage the mother at all times to promote better conditions in the home, in the interest of cleanliness, sanitation and better healthful surroundings, as well as to inspire thrifty habits and social betterment in the interest of her children for better citizenship"; *ibid.*, 16.

62. Mary F. Bogue, *Administration of Mothers Aid in Ten Localities, with Special Reference to Health, Housing, Education, and Recreation*, U.S. Department of Labor, Children's Bureau, Publication No. 184 (Washington, D.C., 1928), 25. Under the COS pension policy, church attendance had been required for continuance of the allowance. W. Frank Persons to W. H. McClain, October 28, 1910, COS, folder, Widows' Pensions, 1907–1919, ACSS.

63. Lundberg, "Public Aid to Mothers with Dependent Children," 24.

64. Edith Abbott and Sophonisba P. Breckinridge, *The Administration of the Aid-to-Mothers Law in Illinois,* U.S. Department of Labor, Children's Bureau, Legal Series No. 7, Bureau Publication No. 82 (Washington, D.C., 1921), 167.

65. *Ibid.,* 6, 170. In some counties the allowance per month per child was as low as $2.00 to $2.50. Edith Abbott, "The Experimental Period of Widows' Pension Legislation," National Conference of Social Work, *Proceedings* (1917), 161. For further details see "One Year of Mothers' Pensions in Illinois," *Institution Quarterly,* 5 (December 31, 1914), 8–16; "Is the Mothers' Pension Failing?" *Institution Quarterly,* 6 (December 31, 1915), 10–14; W. Morland Graham, "Mothers' Pensions and Their Failure in Illinois, *Institution Quarterly,* 7 (September 30, 1916), 7–21.

66. "Widows' Pension Legislation," *Municipal Research,* 85 (May 1917), 77.

67. Mary F. Bogue, "The Greater Economy of Adequate Grants," National Conference of Social Work, *Proceedings* (1919), 304; Bogue, "Problems in the Administration of Mothers' Aid," National Conference of Social Work, *Proceedings* (1918), 350, 351.

68. The consequences of combining economic assistance and behavioral objectives in the same program are examined in, Winifred Bell, *Aid to Dependent Children* (New York, 1965), and Gilbert Y. Steiner, *Social Insecurity: The Politics of Welfare* (Chicago, 1966). Also pertinent are Richard M. Elman, *The Poorhouse State: The American Way of Life on Public Assistance* (New York, 1966), and Joseph P. Ritz, *The Despised Poor: Newburgh's War on Welfare* (Boston, 1966). Bureaucratic harrassment and deprivation of constitutional rights of welfare clients are stressed in Richard A. Cloward and Richard M. Elman, "Poverty, Injustice and the Welfare State, Part I: An Ombudsman for the Poor?" *Nation* (February 28, 1966), 1–6; "Part II: How Rights Can be Secured," *ibid.* (March 7, 1966), 1–5.

*Chapter VI   The Aged and the State*

1. John B. Andrews to Dr. John George O'Meara, May 31, 1921, American Association for Labor Legislation (John B. Andrews) Papers.

2. Leifur Magnusson, "Significant Advances in Social Insurance

Since the War," *American Labor Legislation Review,* 18 (June 1928), 189.

3. Eight additional countries enacted workmen's compensation legislation between the end of World War I and 1928; more important, existing legislation in numerous countries was improved in coverage and benefits. Up to 1914, health insurance acts were in effect in ten countries: Germany, Austria, Hungary, Luxembourg, Norway, Yugoslavia, Russia, Great Britain, Rumania, and Czechoslavakia. As in compensation, liberalization in coverage and benefits took place in the 1920's, and by 1928 eight additional nations established a compulsory health insurance program: Bulgaria, Greece, Chile, Estonia, Japan, Lithuania, Poland, and Portugal.

Of the twenty-six countries with old-age insurance or pensions in 1928, about half enacted their legislation since World War I. New pension programs included the federal legislation of Canada in 1927, Norway, 1923 and Uruguay, 1919. New compulsory laws included: Argentina, 1923; Belgium, 1920; Bulgaria, 1924; Greece, 1922; Portugal, 1919; Russia, 1922; Serb-Croat Kingdom, 1922; Cuba, 1923; Italy, 1923; Spain, 1919. Magnusson, *ibid, passim.*

4. John B. Andrews to Jeffrey R. Brackett, December 6, 1921, Andrews Papers.

5. Ernest W. Burgess, "Aging in Western Culture," and Philip M. Hauser and Raul Vargas, "Population Structure and Trends," in Ernest W. Burgess, ed., *Aging in Western Societies: A Comparative Survey* (Chicago, 1960), 15, 35, 39, 42.

6. I. M. Rubinow, *Social Insurance: With Special Reference to American Conditions* (New York, 1913), 302, 304, 305.

7. Abraham Epstein, *The Challenge of the Aged* (New York, 1928), 10.

8. The status of the aged in preindustrial societies is discussed by Leo W. Simmons, "Aging in Preindustrial Societies," in Clark Tibbitts, ed., *Handbook of Social Gerontology: Societal Aspects of Aging* (Chicago, 1960), 62–91. According to Simmons, "perhaps the most significan range of contrast to be observed in the adjustments of aging from very primitive to highly industrialized societies is that in the former the 'terms' or conditions for aging were imbedded in the cultural developments as by-products of broad societal interests, while in the latter the trend has been toward a breakdown of the traditional types of adaptations to aging and the growth of planned and legislated forms of old age security as specific objectives and through the instrumentality of group-action programs" (pp. 66–67).

Long-term institutional developments affecting the aged — urbanization, family structure, the pace of social change, economic organization, and government — are discussed by Philip M. Hauser, "Facing the Implications of an Aging Population," *Social Service Review*, 27 (June 1953), 162–176. An analysis of the aged and Huttite culture, useful for comparative purposes, is, Joseph W. Eaton, "The Art of Aging and Dying," *Gerontologist*, 4 (June 1964), 94–100, 103, 112.

9. Rubinow, *Social Insurance*, 302, 313.

10. See Albert U. Romasco, *The Poverty of Abundance: Hoover, the Nation, the Depression* (New York, 1965), for a discussion of Hoover's social thought.

11. Frederick L. Hoffman, "The Problem of Poverty and Pensions in Old Age," *American Journal of Sociology*, 14 (September 1908), 185, 186, 190; Frederick L. Hoffman, "State Pensions and Annuities in Old Age," American Statistical Association, *Quarterly Publications*, 11 (March 1909), n.s., 367.

12. Hoffman, "State Pensions and Annuities in Old Age," 368, 367, 389, 383, 370.

13. Hoffman, "The Problem of Poverty and Pensions in Old Age," 190; Hoffman, "State Pensions and Annuities in Old Age," 381, 369, 389.

14. Massachusetts, *Report of the Commission on Old Age Pensions, Annuities and Insurance*, January, 1910, House No. 1400 (Boston, 1910), 21, 22. Categories of aged dependents, besides those in almshouses or recipients of charitable relief, included those in correctional and mental institutions, in benevolent homes, and in receipt of some form of military pension. Members of the Commission included: Magnus W. Alexander, chairman; James T. Buckley; Mrs. M. R. Hodder; Arthur M. Huddell; Walter G. Chase; F. Spencer Baldwin, executive secretary. Baldwin, a Boston University professor, was author of the Commission report.

15. F. Spencer Baldwin, "Old Age Pension Schemes: A Criticism and a Program," *Quarterly Journal of Economics*, 24 (August 1910), 728, 727.

16. *Massachusetts Commission on Old Age Pensions*, 310; Baldwin, "Old Age Pension Schemes," 732. Within a few years, apparently, Baldwin changed his mind and favored compulsory old-age insurance. F. Spencer Baldwin, "Old Age Insurance," *American Labor Legislation Review*, 3 (June 1913), 202–212.

17. (Compulsion apparently did not always exercise an "enervating

influence.") Baldwin, "Old Age Pension Schemes, 737; *Massachusetts Commission on Old Age Pensions,* 324.

18. *Ibid.,* 323. The Commission noted that "experience with voluntary contributory schemes points to the inevitable conclusion that such a system never could become universal in its application" (p. 315).

19. Louis D. Brandeis, "Our New Peonage: Discretionary Pensions," *Independent,* 73 (July 25, 1912), 189, 190.

20. The postal savings banks had been established in 1861.

21. The Massachusetts Savings Bank Insurance plan was promoted by the Massachusetts Savings Insurance League as well as by Brandeis. It offered a wide range of policies: straight life; endowment; simple annuity; returnable premium annuity; insurance and annuity; immediate annuity. As of October 31, 1909, 2,575 policies were in force; by October 1, 1911, 5,130 policies. Only 88,000 policies were in force by 1930. On the establishment and growth of the Massachusetts savings bank insurance system see, *Massachusetts Commission on Old Age Pensions,* 190ff.; Rubinow, *Social Insurance,* 428ff; Alice H. Grady, "A Massachusetts Experiment in Savings Bank Life Insurance," National Conference of Social Work, *Proceedings* (1930), 273–278. Louis D. Brandeis, "Massachusetts Savings-Bank Insurance and Pension System," American Statistical Association, *Publications,* 11 (March 1909), 409–416.

22. Benjamin S. Beecher, "State Insurance in Wisconsin," *Review of Reviews,* 47 (January 1913), 79–82. As in Massachusetts, the basic idea was "taking over of the best insurance practice of the day reduced to its simplest terms and offering it to the people at cost, with a large part of the cost eliminated through the fact that no agents are employed and that there is no 'overhead' charge to maintain offices and high salaried officials" (*ibid.,* 79). The Wisconsin insurance fund was originally limited to $1000 on a single life.

23. A Bureau of War Risk Insurance had been established in the Treasury Department in 1914. The War Risk Insurance Act of 1917 provided for voluntary, contributory life and disability insurance for members of the armed forces. By the fall of 1918, the federal government had written some $40,000,000,000 worth of insurance for 4,000,000 members of the armed forces. The policies and amount of insurance dropped sharply after the Armistice. See Samuel McCune Lindsay, "The Soldiers' and Sailors' Insurance Acts," National Conference of Social Work, *Proceedings* (1918), 392–395; William F.

Gephart, *Effects of the War Upon Insurance, With Special Reference to the Substitution of Insurance for Pensions* (New York, 1918), ch. III; Benjamin M. Price, "Uncle Sam's Insurance," *Survey,* 45 (November 20, 1920), 281–282.

24. Rubinow, *Social Insurance,* 335–338. The Spanish program is discussed by Katharine Coman, "Insurance for the Superannuated Worker in Spain," *Survey,* 31 (February 28, 1914), 669–671.

25. The Austrian act was limited to salaried employees. On Sweden see Katharine Coman, "Old Age and Invalidity Insurance in Sweden," *Survey,* 31 (December 20, 1913), 318–319.

26. The French system is examined in, I. M. Rubinow, "Compulsory Old-Age Insurance in France," *Political Science Quarterly,* 26 (September 1911), 500–529. The German subsidy to each matured pension was 50 marks ($11.90) a year; the French, 60 francs ($11.58), increased to 100 francs (19.30) in 1912. The French employed a system of uniform premiums; the Germans used the graded plan based upon five wage classifications. The French benefit program differed from the German in using the practice of individual accounts developed under voluntary, contributory state insurance. The German program was administered by territorial institutions, *Versicherungs-Anstalten,* and by special institutions for railroads, mines, and navigation. In France, numerous institutions served as carriers: the National Old-Age Retirement Fund, unions, mutual benefit societies, new funds comparable to the German territorial funds. Rubinow, *Social Insurance,* 346ff.

27. One American critic of old-age pensions complained that in Denmark the aged "are not regarded as paupers, but as members of the industrial army who are entitled to honorable discharge." Katharine Coman, "Twenty Years of Old Age Pensions in Denmark," *Survey,* 31 (January 17, 1914), 465.

28. The Royal Commission which recommended a national program for Australia urged that it "should be distinctly laid down in the proposed Commonwealth legislation that Old-age Pensions are to be granted as a right and not as a charity." Australia, *Report of the Royal Commission on Old-Age Pensions,* March 1907 (London, 1907), 6.

29. William L. Blackley, "National Insurance: A Cheap, Practical, and Popular Means of Abolishing Poor Rates," *Nineteenth Century,* 4 (November 1878), 834–857.

30. Sir Arnold Wilson and G. S. Mackay, *Old Age Pensions: An Historical and Critical Study* (London, 1941), 16–18. Blackley sub-

sequently dropped the provision for health insurance included in his original proposal.

31. Charles Booth, *Pauperism: A Picture and the Endowment of Old Age, An Argument* (London, 1892), 182, 235, 236, 219. Booth estimated that nearly 30 percent of the aged, nearly 40 percent in London, applied for parish assistance in the course of a year. Booth, *The Aged Poor in England and Wales* (London, 1894), 48.

32. Chamberlain was "kept abreast" of continental social insurance legislation by Sir Charles Dilke. Wilson and Mackay, *Old Age Pensions,* 21.

33. J. A. Spender, *The State and Pensions in Old Age* (2nd ed., London, 1894), 127–128.

34. Report of the Royal Commission on the Aged Poor. . . . (London, 1895), III, 710.

35. Chamberlain served as chairman of an unofficial parliamentary committee appointed in 1891 to explore the pension issue. It was followed by the more important Royal (Aberdare) Commission of 1893, whose report in 1895 largely reflected charity organization views. In 1896 the Liberal Government appointed a Departmental (Treasury) Committee on pensions (Rothschild Committee) which rejected all proposed pension schemes. A Select Committee of Parliament (Chaplin Committee) was appointed in 1899, which rejected the German technique of compulsion in favor of the Danish system. The Conservative Government the same year appointed still another Departmental Committee to determine the financial implications of a pension program.[35]

These various commissions between 1891 and 1899 are described by Wilson and Mackay, *Old Age Pensions,* 24–35; Katharine Coman, "The Problems of Old Age Pensions in England," *Survey,* 31 (February 21, 1914), 640–642; Helen L. Witmer, "The Influence of Old Age Pensions on Public Poor Relief in England and Wales," *Social Service Review,* 4 (December 1930), 594–595; Ronald V. Sires, "The Beginnings of British Legislation for Old-Age Pensions," *Journal of Economic History,* 14 (Summer 1954), 234–236.

36. C. S. Loch, *Old Age Pensions and Pauperism* (London, 1892), 40.

37. *Report of the Royal Commission on the Aged Poor,* I, lxxxvi.

38. *Ibid.,* III, 552, 558.

39. William H. Lecky, "Why I oppose Old-Age Pensions," *Forum,* 28 (February 1900), 694.

40. Bentley B. Gilbert, "Winston Churchill versus the Webbs: The

Origins of British Unemployment Insurance," *American Historical Review,* 71 (April 1966), 847.

41. Sires, "The Beginnings of British Legislation for Old-Age Pensions," 237. The following discussion of friendly society and union advocacy of old-age pensions is drawn from this useful account.

42. *Ibid.,* 242. Charles Booth and F. Herbert Stead were instrumental in the establishment of the Committee.

43. It was charged, in the course of debate, that pensions would undermine the "inheritance of a sturdy, strong, self-reliant manhood, that will take upon itself the responsibilities of life and be equal, therefore, to the responsibilities of Empire." In response, a labor representative described the aged as "veterans of industry, people of almost endless toil, who have fought for and won the industrial and commercial supremacy of Great Britain. Is their lot and end to be the Bastille of the overlasting slur of pauperism? We claim these pensions as a right." Bishop of Ripon, House of Lords, July 20, 1908; William Crooks, House of Commons, July 9, 1908, in Carlton Hayes, *British Social Politics: Materials Illustrating Contemporary State Action for the Solution of Social Problems* (Boston, 1913), 166, 159.

44. Among the reasons cited by Lloyd George in favor of noncontributory pensions were the exclusion of most women from contributry schemes and the fact that most workers did not earn enough to provide for old age in addition to sickness, infirmity and unemployment, *ibid.,* 142–143. Most pension acts disqualified applicants on the grounds of criminal record, habitual inebriety, or desertion. More generally, pensions were contingent upon evidence of "moral character." Rubinow, *Social Insurance,* 373, 374.

45. John B. Andrews, "Progress in Old Age Pension Legislation," *American Labor Legislation Review,* 13 (March 1923), 48.

46. Robert B. Irwin and Evelyn C. McKay, *Blind Relief Laws: Their Theory and Practice* (New York: American Foundation for the Blind, 1929), 7, 28. In New York City the municipality assumed the expense; elsewhere assistance for the blind was financed by the state, the county, or the two jurisdictions combined. As was often the case in social insurance or public assistance legislation, here also "when one state has copied the law of another, there has been little discrimination between desirable and undesirable features" (p. 11).

47. Eugene T. Lies, "Public Outdoor Relief in Chicago," National Conference of Charities and Correction, *Proceedings* (1916), 346, 347.

48. Rubinow, *Social Insurance,* 404. Sharp increases in expenditures occurred after 1879 when an arrears act was passed, and after 1890,

when a generous ninety-day service act was passed. The number of pensioners increased from about 200,000 in 1870 to nearly 1,000,000 by 1902. It dropped to 860,000 by 1912. Nearly 40 percent of the pensioners were women and children.

49. *Ibid.*, 408.

50. Franklin MacVeagh, "Civil Service Pensions," American Academy of Political and Social Science, *Annals*, 38 (July 1911), 4.

51. Lewis Meriam, *Principles Governing the Retirement of Public Employees* (New York, 1918), 3.

52. Frederick MacKenzie, "Old Age Insurance Legislation Now up to the States," *American Labor Legislation Review*, 10 (December 1920), 254. This was a contributory plan based upon a salary deduction of 2½ percent, raised to 3½ percent after 1926. Federal appropriations were added after 1929.

53. John B. Andrews, "Old Age Pensions for Federal Employes," *Survey*, 44 (May 22, 1920), 271.

54. "It must be noted that in this country retirement systems have been generally established without actuarial estimates of their future liabilities and the adequacy of the income provided to meet them; they have, therefore, either approached insolvency or, if a clause has been provided compelling the government to cover any deficiency that might develop, they have become an increasingly heavy burden on the community." Paul Studensky, *The Pension Problem and the Philosophy of Contributions* (New York, 1917), 3. The Carnegie Foundation complained of pension funds "made up of odds and ends that come under the headings of gifts, legacies, bequests, devises, and income from investments." "Too many of the plans adopted," it added, "appear to be inspired by a desire to launch a system somehow, relying on a secret and indefinable hope that Providence or the public treasury or the wealthy philanthropist will not permit the poor pensioners to suffer." Thus the New York City Public School Teachers' Retirement Fund was declared insolvent in 1915 and pensions reduced by two-thirds. It seems that pensions were calculated in part on the basis of absence deductions or fines, but these were often refunded if good cause could be established. Advance borrowing from municipal excise money and postponement of absence deduction refunds had kept the fund alive for several years. The Carnegie Foundation for the Advancement of Teaching: *Tenth Annual Report of the President and the Treasurer* (October 1915), 51, 59.

55. *Massachusetts Commission on Old Age Pensions*, 272.

56. Florence E. Parker, *et al.*, *Care of Aged Persons in the United*

*States,* U.S. Bureau of Labor Statistics, Bulletin, No. 489, October 1929, 233. The cities were: Philadelphia and Pittsburgh (1915); New York (1920); Chicago, Minneapolis, and San Francisco (1922); Boston and Detroit (1923); Baltimore (1926).

57. *Ibid.,* 227. Apart from provision for special groups like teachers, judges, or veterans employed in the public service, the six states with comprehensive retirement systems were: Massachusetts (1911); Connecticut and Maine (1919); New York (1920); New Jersey (1921); Pennsylvania (1923).

As of 1927, twenty-one state-wide teacher retirement systems existed. The Carnegie Foundation for the Advancement of Teaching, established in 1905, provided pensions for college teachers. On pensions for public school and college teachers see Burton J. Hendrick, " 'The Superannuated Man': Labor Pensions and the Carnegie Foundation," *McClure's Magazine,* 32 (December 1908), 124–127.

58. F. Spencer Baldwin, "Retirement Systems for Municipal Employees," American Academy of Political and Social Science, *Annals,* 38 (July 1911), 8.

59. *Massachusetts Commission on Old Age Pensions,* 155.

60. Murray Webb Latimer, *Industrial Pension Systems in the United States and Canada* (New York: Industrial Relations Counselors, Inc., 1932), I, 42. Besides these 397 pension systems, another twenty-four had been established but discontinued. The first three formal pension programs were established by transportation companies: Grand Trunk Railway of Canada, 1874; American Express Company, 1875; Baltimore and Ohio Railroad, 1880. By 1905, twelve railway pension systems, covering 35.4 percent of employees, had been established.

Alfred Dolge, the New York State felt manufacturer, established the first pension plan in a manufacturing establishment in 1882, but his firm failed in 1898. Important in this area were the pension programs launched for the Carnegie Steel employees in 1901, and by Standard Oil of New Jersey in 1903. Public utilities were also significant in the development of early industrial pension programs. The first was that established by the Consolidated Gas Company of New York in 1892. Of the eleven public utilities plans up to 1910, seven were established by street railway companies. Of the major pension groups, contributory plans predominated only in banking. Latimer, *Industrial Pension Systems,* I, *passim.*

61. *Ibid.,* 54, 55, 56.

62. *Ibid.,* II, 842, 843, 846, 848, 893. The discontinued plans, con-

centrated in smaller enterprises, affected some 3 percent of employees covered.

63. The Merchants Association of New York, *Industrial Pensions: Report of Special Committee on Industrial Pensions and Report of a Survey of Industrial Pension Systems* (New York, 1920), 18.

64. Abraham Epstein, *The Problem of Old Age Pensions in Industry: An Up-to-Date Summary of the Facts and Figures Developed in the Further Study of Old Age Pensions* (Harrisburg: Pennsylvania Old Age Pension Commission, 1926), 18, 19, 20, 22, 33.

65. *Ibid.*, 56.

66. *Ibid.*, 43, 45.

67. The majority of contributory plans established between 1926 and 1929 were reinsured; all but one of the pension plans established between 1929 and 1932 were underwritten. Latimer, *Industrial Pension Systems*, II, 850, 869.

68. National Industrial Conference Board, *Industrial Pensions in the United States* (New York, 1925), 101. The NICB's estimate of the number of existing pension plans was much lower than Epstein's. Whereas Epstein calculated 370 formal plans, the NICB figure was 248 operated by 245 firms. As usual, metal industries, railroads, and public utilities dominated. Of the 248 plans, 168 were formal-discretionary, 43 formal-limited-contractual, and 28 contributory on an optional or compulsory basis. Most of the latter were found in banking.

69. *Ibid.*, 63.

70. Albert de Roode, "Pensions as Wages," *American Economic Review*, 3 (June 1913), 287. But as de Roode recognized, "one striking fact stands out which is of the utmost importance in the treatment of pensions as a form of wages. This fact is that the employee has no contractual right in the pension fund." In other words, the worker "foregoes an increase in his wage for the establishment of a pension, but he gets no right to that pension" (pp. 287, 288). The deferred wage theory was criticized on similar grounds by Luther Conant, Jr., *A Critical Analysis of Industrial Pension Systems* (New York, 1922), 91.

71. National Industrial Conference Board, *Industrial Pensions*, 64.

72. Edward S. Cowdrick, *Pensions: A Problem of Management*, American Management Association, Annual Convention Series: No. 75 (New York, 1928), 11.

73. *Ibid.*, 22; National Industrial Conference Board, *Industrial Pensions*, 27.

74. *Ibid.*, 16, 17; Merchants' Association of New York, *Report of Special Committee on Industrial Pensions,* 14. See also Conant, Critical Analysis of *Industrial Pension Systems,* 18; and Latimer, *Industrial Pension Systems,* II, 758.

75. Merchants' Association of New York, *Report of Special Committee on Industrial Pensions,* 28.

76. Latimer, *Industrial Pension Systems,* II, 785.

77. *Ibid.,* 894, 895, 774.

78. National Industrial Conference Board, *Industrial Pensions,* 2. See also Boston Chamber of Commerce, *Report of the Special Committee on Social Insurance, Non-Contributory Old Age Pensions and Health Insurance,* February 6, 1917, 4; and Pennsylvania State Chamber of Commerce, Legislative and Research Bureau, *Special Report on Old Age Pensions* (Philadelphia, 1919), i, ii.

79. John A. Lapp, "Do Prosperity and Welfare Work in America Make Unnecessary the Establishment of Protective Labor Standards?" *American Labor Legislation Review,* 17 (September 1927), 226.

80. Leo Wolman, "The Frontiers of Social Control," *American Labor Legislation Review,* 17 (September 1927), 239.

81. Mabel Louise Nassau, *Old Age Poverty in Greenwich Village: A Neighborhood Study,* Greenwich House Series No. 6 (New York, 1915), 17, 18, 35, 70, 84.

82. *Ibid.,* 60.

83. Industrial Commission of Wisconsin, *Report on Old Age Relief* (March 1, 1915), 11, 10, 26.

84. Estelle M. Stewart, *The Cost of American Almshouses,* U.S. Bureau of Labor Statistics, Bulletin, 386 (June 1925), 41. Almshouses existed in all states but New Mexico; they were all county institutions except in seven states. Poor relief in Connecticut, Maine, Massachusetts, Rhode Island, and Vermont was a township responsibility; in Pennsylvania and New Jersey responsibility was assumed by counties, towns, and townships. Some 88 percent of the almshouses were managed by county officials or poor-law officials through a superintendent. The remainder were managed under a contract system.

85. *Report of the Pennsylvania Commission on Old Age Assistance, January, 1925,* 91. See also Lee W. Squier, *Old Age Dependency in the United States: A Complete Survey of the Pension Movement* (New York, 1912), 54; John A. Lapp, "The Growing Insistence upon Pensions Instead of Institutional Care for Aged Dependents," *American Labor Legislation Review,* 15 (March 1925), 23–29, and John B. Andrews, "The Significance of the Pennsylvania Old Age Assistance

Act in the United States," in *Report of the Pennsylvania Commission.*

86. Massachusetts, Senate, *Report on Old-Age Pensions by the Commission on Pensions* (Boston, 1925), 13, 75, 76.

87. National Civic Federation, Industrial Welfare Department, *Extent of Old Age Dependency* (New York, 1928), 13, 32, 35.

88. *Ibid.*, 12, 17, 33.

89. Abraham Epstein, *Insecurity: A Challenge to America: A Study of Social Insurance in the United States and Abroad* (2nd. rev. ed., New York, 1938), 499. See pp. 491–506 of this book for a summary of investigations and data concerning old-age dependency. Squier had estimated that 1,250,000 persons aged sixty-five and over, were dependent on public and private charity. Squier, *Old Age Dependency in the United States,* 324.

90. *Massachusetts Commission on Old Age Pensions,* 339–340. Arthur M. Huddell, dissenting from the report of the Commission, supported this bill. The aged, in the terminology of Edward Bellamy, were sometimes referred to as veterans of the industrial army, and thus entitled to pensions. For example, "to the superannuated soldier in the industrial army . . . the doling out of charity by the operation of poor laws is humiliating, degrading and debasing." Squier, *Old Age Dependency in the United States,* 54.

91. Epstein, *Insecurity,* 532. Other pension bills were introduced by Congressman M. Clyde Kelly of Pennsylvania, in 1913, and Congressman Isaac Sherwood of Ohio, in 1917. Abraham Epstein, *The Challenge of the Aged* (New York, 1928), 260–261.

92. *Massachusetts Commission on Old Age Pensions,* 204–206. Massachusetts' initiative was attributable in part to the prodding of Edward Everett Hale who advocated the Booth idea of the universal endowment of old age. Edward Everett Hale, "Old-Age Pensions," *Cosmopolitan,* 35 (June 1903), 168–172; Edward Everett Hale, "Old Age Pensions," *Charities and the Commons,* 18 (June 1, 1907), 275–278. See also *Massachusetts Commission on Old Age Pensions,* 224.

93. For the development of pension legislation between 1923 and 1929 see: "Progress Toward Old Age Pensions," *American Labor Legislation Review,* 17 (March 1927), 34–35; Louise Y. Gottschall, "Progress in Old Age Pensions," *American Labor Legislation Review,* 19 (June 1929), 151–152; Murray W. Latimer, "Old Age Pensions in America," *American Labor Legislation Review,* 19 (March 1929), 57–58; Elizabeth Brandeis, "Old Age Pensions and Unemployment Compensation," in John R. Commons, *et al., History of Labor in the United States, 1896–1932* (New York, 1935), III, 611–615.

94. For developments between 1929 and 1933, see Epstein, *Insecurity,* 533–537.

95. Latimer, "Old Age Pensions in America," 58; Brandeis, "Old Age Pensions and Unemployment Compensation," 614, 615.

96. Epstein, *Challenge of the Aged,* 261–262; and Epstein, *Insecurity,* 533.

97. Fraternal Order of Eagles, The Old Age Pension Commission, *The Times Demand Old Age Pensions: The Past, Present and Future of the Movement* (South Bend, Ind., 1922), 23.

98. Frank E. Hering, "Awakening Interest in Old Age Protection," *American Labor Legislation Review,* 13 (June 1923), 143, 141.

99. *Report of the Old Age Commission of the Fraternal Order of Eagles,* August 11, 1925, 4–5; *Labor World,* March 10, 1923; Frank E. Hering to Samuel Gompers, February 20, 1923, Andrews Papers; Fraternal Order of Eagles, *Old Age Pension Bulletin,* 1 (June, 1922), 3; *ibid.,* 1 (September 1922), 3; *ibid.,* 1 (October 1922), 2; *ibid.,* 1 (January 1923), 3; *ibid.,* 1 (February 1923), 1.

100. *Report of the Pennsylvania Commission on Old Age Assistance, January, 1925,* 21, 22. The Eagles were active in the campaign for the 1923 bill. See *The Eagle Magazine,* 11 (June 1923), 5–7, 37–39.

101. *Report of the Pennsylvania Commission on Old Age Assistance, January, 1925,* 24, 25.

102. Pennsylvania State Chamber of Commerce, *Mimeographed Newspaper Release* (n.d., probably 1926), 1, 4.

103. Pennsylvania Manufacturers' Association, *Monthly Bulletin* (July 1926), 1; *ibid.* (May 1927), 1.

104. Abraham Epstein to W. J. Brennan, March 6, 1924, Andrews Papers.

105. John B. Andrews to Abraham Epstein, March 8, 1923, Andrews Papers.

106. Executive Council of the National Civic Federation, Printed Circular, signed by Ralph M. Easley, chairman (March 1923).

107. Owen D. Young to Bishop J. McConnell, February 11, 1928, American Association for Social Security (Abraham Epstein) Papers, Cornell University, Old Age Pensions–Industrial Plans, folder. Bishop McConnell was president of Epstein's American Association for Old Age Security.

108. Frank E. Hering to John B. Andrews, April 2, 1923, Andrews Papers. At this same time, Andrews had nothing but the highest praise for Epstein. He lauded Epstein's presentation of the pension case at a

hearing before the Pennsylvania legislature in March 1923, congratulated Hering on having so well equipped an assistant, described the reports of the Pennsylvania Commission as the best produced in America, and urged Governor Pinchot to keep Epstein active in the work. John B. Andrews to Frank Hering, March 31, 1923; John B. Andrews to Gifford Pinchot, April 25, 1923 and July 11, 1923, Andrews Papers.

109. Abraham Epstein to John B. Andrews, April 26, 1923, and April 28, 1923, Andrews Papers.

110. James H. Maurer to John B. Andrews, April 27, 1923, Andrews Papers.

111. Frank E. Hering to John B. Andrews, May 26, 1923, Andrews Papers; Frank E. Hering to Abraham Epstein, May 16, 1923, Abraham Epstein Papers, Columbia University, Box 13.

112. The Eagles, for example, complained that they were not "properly consulted" after passage of the Pennsylvania old-age pension bill in 1923, a charge which Epstein denied. John B. Andrews to Abraham Epstein, April 25, 1924; Abraham Epstein to John B. Andrews, April 30, 1924, Andrews Papers.

113. I. M. Rubinow, *The Quest for Security* (New York, 1934), 278.

114. John B. Andrews to Frank E. Hering, August 1, 1927, Andrews Papers.

115. Frank E. Hering, "We Are on the Fighting Line," *The Eagle Magazine* (March 1923), 26, 27.

116. Abraham Epstein to John B. Andrews, October 9, 1925; I. M. Rubinow to John B. Andrews, November 8, 1925, Andrews Papers. Rubinow, along with Epstein, John Lapp, and Miles Dawson met with Andrews but the latter saw no hope for a social insurance revival. I. M. Rubinow to N. I. Stone, August 24, 1933, I. M. Rubinow Papers, Cornell, Correspondence, SA-TZ, folder.

117. All concerned, including Andrews, were discouraged over the indifference of social workers in the 1920's to social insurance or pension legislation. Abraham Epstein to John B. Andrews, February 16, 1924, Andrews Papers. Andrews found the lack of interest in pension legislation on the part of charity societies "baffling"; they appeared to be "suffering from lethargy in reference to the care of the dependent aged population that is almost heartbreaking to the proponents of old age assistance laws." John B. Andrews to Mary A. Mack, April 17, 1924, Andrews Papers.

118. John B. Andrews to Paul H. Douglas, February 15, 1927, Andrews Papers.

119. *Ibid.*

120. John B. Andrews to Paul Douglas, April 5, 1928, Andrews Papers.

121. Abraham Epstein to Paul Douglas, February 27, 1928; John B. Andrews to Frank E. Hering, April 2, 1927; John B. Andrews to Paul Douglas, May 27, 1927, Andrews Papers.

122. John B. Andrews to John A. Lapp, April 7, 1927 (marked "not sent"), Andrews Papers.

123. I. M. Rubinow to John B. Andrews, March 12, 1928, Andrews Papers.

124. Paul Douglas to John B. Andrews, March 14, 1928, Andrews Papers.

125. John B. Andrews to Florence Kelley, March 27, 1928, Andrews Papers. See also Paul H. Douglas to John B. Andrews, March 14, 1928; Henry R. Seager to John B. Andrews, March 20, 1928, Andrews Papers.

*Chapter VII　Unemployment — Prevention or Insurance?*

1. Sidney Fine, *Laissez Faire and the General-Welfare State: A Study of Conflict in American Thought, 1865–1901* (Ann Arbor, Mich., 1956), 322–323.

2. Donald L. McMurry, "The Industrial Armies and the Commonweal," *Mississippi Valley Historical Review,* 10 (December 1923), 216–217.

3. Samuel Rezneck, "Unemployment, Unrest, and Relief in the United States during the Depression of 1893–97," *Journal of Political Economy,* 61 (August 1953), 332. Referring to proposals for workshops and public works, the Board argued that "our climate apparently condemns such propositions at the outset, however willing the community might be to be taxed for such a purpose." Massachusetts, "Report of the Massachusetts Board to Investigate the Subject of the Unemployed," *House Document No. 50,* March 13, 1895 (Boston, 1895), V, xi.

4. John Graham Brooks, "The Future Problem of Charity and the Unemployed," American Academy of Political and Social Science, *Annals,* 5 (July 1894), 10.

5. B. O. Flower, "How to Increase National Wealth by the Employment of Paralyzed Industry," *Arena,* 18 (August 1897), 201, 202, 204.

6. Relief programs during the depression of the 1890's are discussed

in Leah Hannah Feder, *Unemployment Relief in Periods of Depressions: A Study of Measures Adopted in Certain American Cities, 1857 through 1922* (New York, 1936), chs. IV–VII. This depression "marked the first extensive use of work relief . . . as an unemployment relief measure" (p. 169).

7. Mrs. C. R. Lowell, "The Unemployed in New York City, 1893–94," *Journal of Social Science*, 32 (November 1894), 23; Josephine Shaw Lowell, "Methods of Relief for the Unemployed," *Forum*, 16 (February 1894), 660.

8. Charles O. Burgess, "The Newspaper as Charity Worker: Poor Relief in New York City, 1893–1894," *New York History*, 43 (July 1962), 249–268.

9. Lowell, "The Unemployed in New York City, 1893–94," 20, 21; Lowell, "Methods of Relief for the Unemployed," 657.

10. J. J. M'Cook, "The Tramp Problem: What It Is and What to Do with It," National Conference of Charities and Correction, *Proceedings* (1895), 295.

11. On hereditarianism and the feebleminded in the early twentieth century see Mark H. Haller, *Eugenics: Hereditarian Attitudes in American Thought* (New Brunswick, N.J., 1963).

12. Amos G. Warner, "Some Experiments on Behalf of the Unemployed," *Quarterly Journal of Economics*, 5 (October 1890), 3. See also Edmond Kelly, *The Elimination of the Tramp (by the Introduction into America of the Labour Colony System Already Proved Effective in Holland, Belgium, and Switzerland . . .)* (New York, 1908); and W. D. P. Bliss, *What is Done for the Unemployed in European Countries*, Bureau of Labor, Bulletin No. 76 (May 1908). The need for discrimination is emphasized in Washington Gladden. "What to Do with the Workless Man," National Conference of Charities and Correction, *Proceedings* (1899), 141–152. A sharp distinction between biological and social causes of poverty was made by Edward Devine: "If we think of pauperism as mental disease or mental defect, and of poverty which is not pauperism as an economic and social condition, the former to be eliminated or relieved by eugenic and sanitary measures acting on the individual, the latter to be eliminated or mitigated by economic progress and social reform, resulting in greater efficiency and more just relations, we are at least thinking in scientific terms, and relying upon remedies which science can examine and assess." Edward T. Devine, *Pauperism: An Analysis*, Studies in Social Work, No. 9, New York School of Philanthropy (January 1916), 5.

13. John B. Andrews, "A Practical Program for the Prevention of

Unemployment in America," *American Labor Legislation Review,* 5 (4th ed. rev., June 1915), 173–192. All quotations in this section are drawn from this document, pp. 173, 176, 178, 184, 189, 192.

14. William Henry (Lord) Beveridge, *Power and Influence* (New York, 1955), 24.

15. William Henry Beveridge, *Unemployment: A Problem of Industry, 1909 and 1930* (London, 1930), 2.

16. Beveridge, *Power and Influence,* 56, 69.

17. Beveridge, *Unemployment,* 189, 191.

18. *Ibid.,* 1, 12.

19. *Ibid.,* 37, 67, 111. Beveridge listed four sources of change in "industrial quality": the decline of particular industries, the most striking example in England being agriculture; introduction of new machinery or processes as in the lace trade; substitution of one type of labor for another, as in boot-making; geographical relocation. As far as the "personal factor" and unemployment was concerned, Beveridge devoted a chapter to the subject but his primary concern was with conditions "lying outside the character and beyond the control of individuals" (p. 133).

20. *Ibid.,* 13, 70, 101, 198, 201.

21. *Ibid.,* 189.

22. Beveridge, *Power and Influence,* 74.

23. William M. Leiserson, "The Problem of Unemployment Today," *Political Science Quarterly,* 31 (March 1916), 10.

24. Don D. Lescohier, *The Labor Market* (New York, 1923), vii.

25. Leiserson, "The Problem of Unemployment Today," 17.

26. J. E. Conner, *Free Public Employment Offices in the United States,* U.S. Bureau of Labor, Bulletin No. 68 (January 1907), 3. At the time of the investigation, thirty-seven offices were in operation in the fifteen states: California, Connecticut, Illinois, Kansas, Maryland, Michigan, Minnesota, Missouri, Montana, Nebraska, New York, Ohio, Washington, West Virginia, and Wisconsin.

27. Henry G. Hodges, "Statutory Provisions for and Achievements of Public Employment Bureaus," American Academy of Political and Social Science, *Annals,* 59 (May 1915), 166. Laws providing for employment bureaus were in effect in nineteen states by 1915: Ohio (1890); Missouri and Illinois (1899); Connecticut, Maryland, Michigan, Minnesota, West Virginia, Kansas, Wisconsin (1900–1905); Massachusetts (1906); Colorado and Nebraska (1907); Oklahoma and Rhode Island (1908); Indiana (1909); Kentucky, South Dakota, New York (1910–1914). Independent municipal bureaus existed in

Arizona, California, Missouri, Montana, New Jersey, Oregon, and Washington.

28. E. L. Bogart, "Public Employment Offices in the United States and Germany," *Quarterly Journal of Economics*, 14 (May 1900), 345–346.

29. Grace Abbott, "The Chicago Employment Agency and the Immigrant Worker," *American Journal of Sociology*, 14 (November 1908), 289. There were 289 licensed private employment agencies in Chicago as of June 1908; of the 178 investigated, 110 specialized in the placement of foreigners. Some 25 percent were managed by steamship agents or foreign banks, suggesting the "probable existence of the padrone system" (p. 295). On the immigrant and the private employment agency, see also Chicago, *Report of the Mayor's Commission on Unemployment* (Chicago, March 1914).

30. There was little or no cooperation among the public bureaus despite the establishment of a few interstate associations. Two of these dealt with migratory farm labor — a Western Association of Free Employment Bureaus, established in 1904 and consisting of the labor commissioners of the wheat-belt states, and a National Farm Labor Exchange, established in 1914, also located in the wheat states. The major attempt at organization was the American Association of Public Employment Offices (later the International Association of Public Employment Services), established in 1913. Shelby M. Harrison, *et al.*, *Public Employment Offices: Their Purpose, Structure and Methods* (New York, 1924), 126.

31. On employer placement associations see, Andrew J. Allen, "Policies and Methods of Employment Agencies Maintained by Employers' Associations," in *Proceedings of the American Association of Public Employment Offices, Annual Meetings: First — Chicago, December, 1913; Second, Indianapolis, Sept., 1914; Third — Detroit, July, 1915,* Bureau of Labor Statistics, Bulletin No. 192 (May 1916), 52–60.

32. Frances A. Kellor, *Out of Work: A Study of Unemployment* (New York, 1915), 333.

33. Unions were concerned with labor market organization, but not through the public employment bureau. The union theory of unemployment was based on the "work fund" idea. Control would be achieved through "regulation of the number of workmen among whom the employment is to be divided," and by increasing the "total amount of employment"; D. P. Smelser, *Unemployment and American Trade Unions* (Baltimore, 1919), 34.

34. Charles B. Barnes, "Public Bureaus of Employment," American

Academy of Political and Social Science, *Annals,* 59 (May 1915), 186. Barnes was author of *The Longshoremen* (New York, 1915), a Beveridge-type analysis of casual labor on the New York docks.

35. This was still true by the 1920's. A public employment service consisting of "an office in the State Bureau of Labor Statistics usually entailing a mail order system," existed in Montana, Nebraska, Kansas, West Virginia, Maryland, South Dakota, Arkansas, Georgia, New Hampshire, and Iowa. Harrison, *et al., Public Employment Offices,* 118.

36. Margaret Nash, "Municipal Employment Bureaus in the United States," *National Municipal Review,* 4 (July 1915), 434.

37. Leiserson, "The Problem of Employment Today," 23.

38. Lescohier, *The Labor Market,* 165; Charles B. Barnes, "A Report of the Condition and Management of Public Employment Offices in the United States, Together with some Account of the Private Employment Agencies of the Country," in "Proceedings of the American Association of Public Employment Offices . . . ," 68.

39. *Ibid.,* 63. Barnes cited the offices at Milwaukee, Cleveland, Tacoma, and East St. Louis as exceptions, and described the Boston public employment office as probably the best in the country. Employees of the Boston office were under civil service, the record system was efficient, and special divisions existed for men, women, skilled, unskilled, and juvenile workers.

40. *Ibid.,* 66.

41. Paul H. Douglas and Aaron Director, *The Problem of Unemployment* (New York, 1931), 341.

42. John B. Densmore, "Lessons of the War in Shifting Labor," American Academy of Political and Social Science, *Annals,* 81 (January 1919), 28–37; M. B. Hammon, "Lessons from English War Experience in the Employment of Labor," *American Economic Review,* 8 (March 1918), supplement, 147–157; L. C. Marshall, "The War Labor Program and Its Administration," *Journal of Political Economy,* 26 (May 1918), 425–460; Don D. Lescohier, "Employment of Labor and the War — Discussion," *American Economic Review,* 8 (March 1918), supplement, 189–193; William M. Leiserson, "The Shortage of Labor and the Waste of Labor," *Survey,* 39 (March 30, 1918), 701–703.

43. The origins of the federal employment services are described in, Darrell H. Smith, *The United States Employment Service: Its History, Activities and Organization* (Baltimore, 1923); Harrison, *et. al., Public Employment Offices;* Ruth M. Kellogg, *The United States Employment Service* (Chicago, 1933); Edward T. Devine, "The Federal

Employment Service: Analysis and Forecast," *Survey*, 42 (April 5, 1919), 9–17; Lescohier, *The Labor Market*.

44. The specialized divisions included the United States Boys' Working Reserve, United States Public Service Reserve, Stevedores and Marine Workers' Division, Mining Division, and others for returned veterans, handicapped, farm labor, professional, and technical workers. Harrison, *et al., Public Employment Offices*, 132.

45. Don D. Lescohier, "Immigration and the Labor-Supply," *Atlantic Monthly*, 123 (April 1919), 487.

46. George E. Barnett, "Employment of Labor and the War — Discussion," *American Economic Review*, 8 (March 1918), supplement, 184–186.

47. Henry R. Seager, "Coordination of Federal, State, and Municipal Employment Bureaus," *ibid.*, 141–146.

48. William M. Leiserson, "A Federal Labor Reserve Board for the Unemployed. Outlines of a Plan for Administering the Remedies for Unemployment," American Academy of Political and Social Science, *Annals*, 69 (January 1917), 103–117.

49. On the Kenyon-Nolan and Wagner bills see, Kellogg, *United States Employment Service*, 62–65. The United States Employment Service after 1933 is discussed in Leonard P. Adams, "The Public Employment Service," in Joseph M. Becker, ed., *In Aid of the Unemployed* (Baltimore, 1965), 193–226.

50. Beveridge, *Unemployment*, 401, 312.

51. Alvin H. Hansen, *Business-Cycle Theory: Its Development and Present Status* (New York, 1927); Wesley C. Mitchell, *Business Cycles: The Problem and its Setting* (New York, 1927). See also Harry E. Miller, "Earlier Theories of Crises and Cycles in the United States," *Quarterly Journal of Economics*, 38 (February 1924), 294–329.

52. Herbert Hoover, Secretary of Commerce, served as chairman of the Conference. The emphasis upon voluntary and local action, which characterized his response to the Depression which struck in 1929, was foreshadowed in his address to the Conference: "It is not consonant with the spirit or institutions of the American people that a demand should be made upon the public treasury for the solution of every difficulty. The Administration has felt that a large degree of solution could be expected through the mobilization of the fine cooperative action of our manufacturers and employers, of our public bodies and local authorities, and that if solution could be found in these directions we should have accomplished even more than the care of our unemployed, that we will have again demonstrated that independence and

ability of action amongst our own people that saves our Government from that ultimate paternalism that will undermine our whole political system." "Secretary Hoover's Address, September 26, 1921," in *Report of the President's Conference on Unemployment, September 26 to October 13, 1921* (Washington, D.C., 1921), appendix D, 29.

53. "Unemployment and Business Cycles — Recommendation of the Conference on Unemployment on the Necessity of Exhaustive Investigation into the Causes and Remedies of Periodic Business Depressions," *ibid.*, 160.

54. *Ibid.*, 160; Otto T. Mallery, "A National Policy — Public Works to Stabilize Employment," American Academy of Political and Social Science, *Annals*, 81 (January 1919), 57. The Pennsylvania Act, instigated by Mallery, appropriated $50,000 for the Emergency Public Works Fund. The California measure authorized the State Board of Control to explore the possibilities of expanded public works programs during economic emergencies. Similar legislation was enacted by Wisconsin in 1923. Sam A. Lewisohn, *et al.*, *Can Business Prevent Unemployment* (New York, 1925), 137–140.

55. John B. Andrews, "Reducing Unemployment by Planning Public Works," *National Municipal Review*, 10 (April 1921), 216, 219; also Andrews, "Public Works as an Agency of Control," in Lionel D. Edie, ed., *The Stabilization of Business* (New York, 1924).

56. *Planning and Control of Public Works: Report of the Committee on Recent Economic Changes of the President's Conference on Unemployment* (New York, 1930), xxiii.

57. *Ibid.*, 2. Road-building, representing an expenditure of more than $1,500,000,000 in 1928, represented the largest category of public construction.

58. Otto T. Mallery, " 'Prosperity Reserve' of Public Works Needed to Combat Unemployment," *American Labor Legislation Review*, 18 (March 1928), 80. Mallery was also a member of a sub-committee of the Industrial Relations Committee of the Philadelphia Chamber of Commerce, which urged that public works be considered as a means of stabilizing employment. Report of a Sub-Committee to the Industrial Relations Committee of the Philadelphia Chamber of Commerce, *Program for the Regularization of Employment and the Decrease of Unemployment in Philadelphia* (Philadelphia, 1929), 21.

59. Douglas and Director, *The Problem of Unemployment*, 195.

60. Joseph H. Willits, "War's Challenge to Employment Managers," American Academy of Political and Social Science, *Annals*, 81 (January 1919), 47; Ernest Fox Nichols, "The Employment Manager,"

American Academy of Political and Social Science, *Annals*, 65 (May 1916), 6; Ernest Martin Hopkins, "A Functionalized Employment Department as a Factor in Industrial Efficiency," *ibid.*, 68.

61. Philip J. Reilly, "The Work of the Employment Department of Dennison Manufacturing Company, Framingham, Massachusetts," *ibid.*, 93; Magnus W. Alexander, "Hiring and Firing: Its Economic Waste and How to Avoid It," *ibid.*, 128; also R. C. Clothier, "The Function of the Employment Department," in *Proceedings* of Employment Managers' Conference (held under the Auspices of the National Society for the Promotion of Industrial Education and the Minneapolis Civic and Commerce Association, January 19 and 20, 1916), Bureau of Labor Statistics, Bulletin No. 196, May 1916 (Washington, 1916), 12.

Beginning in 1911, Employment Managers' Associations were established in Boston, New York, Philadelphia, Detroit, and Chicago. See Meyer Bloomfield, "The Aim and Work of Employment Managers' Associations," *Annals* (May 1916), 76–87.

62. Herman Feldman, *The Regularization of Employment: A Study in the Prevention of Unemployment* (New York, 1925), 47–48, 49, 51. See also Herman Feldman, "Newer Methods in the Stabilization of Employment, *American Labor Legislation Review*, 16 (March 1926), 47–56.

63. Lewisohn was a president of the AALL, vice-president of Miami Copper Company, and chairman of the board of directors of the American Management Association. Draper was treasurer of Hills Brothers Co., and president of the American Creosoting Company. For their interpretation of the modern businessman's social responsibilities, see Ernest G. Draper, "Unemployment," *New York Times*, September 11, 1921; "Laboratories of Unemployment Insurance," *American Labor Legislation Review*, 14 (June 1924), 131; and by Lewisohn, *The New Leadership in Industry* (New York, 1926); "Unemployment — The Price of Progress or the Sign of Decay," *American Labor Legislation Review*, 19 (March 1929), 81–87; "Labor Legislation and the Business Mind," *American Labor Legislation Review*, 18 (March 1928), 51–60; *Can Business Prevent Unemployment*.

64. Feldman, *Regularization of Employment*, 175.

65. National Industrial Conference Board, *The Unemployment Problem*, Research Report Number 43, November 1921 (New York, 1922), 41, 79.

66. Bryce M. Stewart, *et al.*, *Unemployment Benefits in the United States: The Plans and Their Setting* (New York, 1930), 95.

67. *Unemployment Benefit Plans in the United States and Unem-*

*ployment Insurance in Foreign Countries,* Bureau of Labor Statistics, Bulletin No. 544, July 1931 (Washington, D.C., 1931).

68. Three of the sixteen were guaranteed-employment plans.

69. For details of the Cleveland and Chicago joint plans, see William J. Mack, "Safeguarding Employment: The 'Cleveland Plan' of Unemployment Compensation," *American Labor Legislation Review,* 12 (March 1922), 25–30; Earl Dean Howard, "Unemployment Insurance in the Chicago Clothing Industry," *American Labor Legislation Review,* 14 (June 1924), 135–136; Fred C. Butler, "Guaranteed Employment in the Cleveland Garment Industry," *ibid.,* 137–142; William J. Mack, "Reducing Unemployment and Improving Industrial Relations," *ibid.,* 143–145. See also Lewisohn, *et al., Can Business Prevent Unemployment,* 200ff.

70. John R. Commons, "Unemployment — Prevention and Insurance," in Edie, ed., *Stabilization of Business,* 185.

71. Paul H. Douglas, "Can Management Prevent Unemployment?" National Conference of Social Work, *Proceedings* (1930), 266; Douglas and Director, *The Problem of Unemployment,* 109. See also Paul H. Douglas, "The Partial Stabilization of Workers' Incomes Through Unemployment Insurance," American Academy of Political and Social Science, *Annals,* 154 (March 1931), 94–103.

72. I. M. Rubinow, "Stabilization versus Insurance?, "*Social Service Review,* 5 (June 1931), 203, 204, 205.

73. *Ibid.,* 210.

74. Sidney and Beatrice Webb, *The Prevention of Destitution* (London, 1912), 160, 174.

75. Beveridge, *Unemployment,* 219.

76. The account of Churchill's role is drawn from, Bentley B. Gilbert, "Winston Churchill versus the Webbs: The Origins of British Unemployment Insurance," *American Historical Review,* 71 (April 1966), 846–862.

77. Beveridge, *Unemployment,* 262.

78. Beveridge, *Power and Influence,* 84.

79. Gilbert, "Winston Churchill versus the Webbs," 853.

80. Beveridge, *Power and Influence,* 82.

81. Cyril Jackson, *Unemployment and Trade Unions* (London, 1910).

82. William H. Beveridge, *The Past and Present of Unemployment Insurance* (London, 1930), and Beveridge, *Unemployment,* outline the changes made in the British compulsory unemployment insurance

program. The additional benefits were termed "uncovenanted" benefits (1921–1924), "extended" benefits (1924–1928) and "transitional"
benefits (1928–1931). In 1931 expenditures for transitional benefits
were curtailed, and the Unemployment Act of 1934 abolished them
entirely. They were replaced by an Unemployment Assistance program
for unemployed in need but not drawing insurance benefits.

83. *Ibid.*, 282, 409; Beveridge, *The Past and Present of Unemployment Insurance*, 36. Other accounts of the evolution of British compulsory unemployment insurance include, Katharine Coman, "Great
Britain's Experiment in Compulsory Unemployment Insurance," *Survey*, 31 (March 28, 1914), 799–802; Olga S. Halsey, "Compulsory
Unemployment Insurance in Great Britain," *American Labor Legislation Review*, 5 (June 1915), 265–278; Joseph L. Cohen, *Insurance
Against Unemployment: With Special Reference to British and American Conditions* (London, 1921); Mary B. Gilson, *Unemployment Insurance in Great Britain: The National System and Additional Benefit
Plans* (New York, 1931).

84. National Industrial Conference Board, *Unemployment Benefits and Insurance* (New York, 1931), 43, 44, vi. The Metropolitan Life
Insurance Company, in the mid-1920's, expressed an interest in the
possibilities of writing unemployment insurance. Enabling legislation
was passed by the New York State legislature in 1931, but was vetoed
by Governor Roosevelt. See Reinhard A. Hohaus, *A Practical Phase
of Unemployment Insurance* (pamphlet, 1925?). The Metropolitan
insisted that compulsory unemployment insurance presented almost
insurmountable actuarial obstacles in terms of predictability, verifi-
cation of occurrence, and limits on the number of individuals affected
at one time. It was necessary, therefore, to limit experimentation to
the private field. See Frederick H. Ecker, *Is Unemployment Insurable?*
(pamphlet, 1931); Leroy A. Lincoln, *Practicability of Unemployment
Insurance* (pamphlet, 1931).

85. John B. Andrews to Charles E. Pellow, March 24, 1922, American Association for Labor Legislation (John B. Andrews) Papers.

86. The bill was prepared by the AALL's Social Insurance Committee early in 1915, with assistance of Joseph Cohen, and was sponsored
by an AALL-affiliate, the Massachusetts Committee on Unemployment. John B. Andrews to Edward T. Devine, February 18, 1916,
Andrews Papers. After the Social Insurance Committee had prepared
a tentative draft based on memoranda prepared by Cohen, the latter
acted as its representative in discussions with the Massachusetts Com-

mittee on Unemployment. The Committee included Robert G. Valen-
tine, Arthur D. Hill, Felix Frankfurter, Ordway Tead, and Olga Halsey.
Cohen, *Insurance Against Unemployment,* 492.

The bill provided for compulsory insurance in selected trades and
the subsidization of voluntary insurance. Contributions and benefits
were calculated for three wage groups. Contributions were estimated
at 36 cents, 60 cents, and 75 cents a week, divided equally among
employers, employees, and the state. Benefits totaled $3.50, $5.25, and
$7.00 a week respectively up to ten weeks in a year (further limited
to one week's benefit for every six weeks contribution). Cohen, *ibid.,*
475–476.

87. Stewart, *et al., Unemployment Benefits in the United States,*
570ff.; National Industrial Conference Board, *Unemployment Benefits
and Insurance,* 81ff.; "Typed Memorandum by John B. Andrews,
8–18–30," Andrews Papers.

On the federal level, Representative Meyer London in 1916 introduced a resolution providing for a commission to study insurance and
unemployment. The measure was tabled after hearings by the House
Committee on Labor. Representative Victor Berger introduced a bill
in 1928 to establish a Bureau of Unemployment Insurance. Benefits
equal to 50 percent of wages up to six months would be provided,
based on contributions from employers, employees and the state. This
was never reported out of the Judiciary Committee. Stewart, *et al.,
Unemployment Benefits in the United States,* 570, 571, 573. In 1931
Senator Wagner introduced a bill providing for federal grants to state
unemployment funds, and a bill prepared by Representative La
Guardia required each employed individual to pay a tax of 5 cents a
week, supplemented by a 10-cent employer tax. Revenues would be
placed in an Unemployment Insurance Fund. National Industrial
Conference Board, *Unemployment Benefits and Insurance,* 79ff.

88. John R. Commons, "Unemployment: Compensation and Prevention," *Survey,* 47 (October 1, 1921), 8.

89. "An American Plan for Unemployment Reserve Funds. Tentative
Draft of an Act. Submitted as a Basis for State Legislation by the
American Association for Labor Legislation," *American Labor Legislation Review* 20 (December 1930), 349–356. Benefits were limited
to $10 a week up to thirteen weeks a year.

90. John R. Commons, "The Groves Unemployment Reserves Law,"
*American Labor Legislation Review,* 22 (March 1932), 8. John B.
Andrews to Dr. Louis Bloch, September 22, 1931, Andrews Papers.

91. Paul A. Raushenbush, "Wisconsin's Unemployment Compensa-

tion Act," *American Labor Legislation Review,* 22 (March 1932), 12; Elizabeth Brandeis, "Old Age Pensions and Unemployment Compensation," in John R. Commons, *et al., History of Labor in the United States, 1896–1932* (New York, 1935), III, 618–619; William Haber and Merrill G. Murray, *Unemployment Insurance in the American Economy: An Historical Review and Analysis* (Homewood, Ill., 1966), 67. A second bill, based on the AALL "American plan," had also been introduced in the Wisconsin legislature of 1931. In contrast to the Grove system of individual reserves, it provided for a state fund and flat employer contributions of 1.5 percent of payroll (although industry mutual funds could be established). Wisconsin labor organizations initially were unenthusiastic about the Groves bill on the grounds that it did not protect employees of firms with the largest amounts of unemployment, but they eventually supported it. Edwin Witte to John B. Andrews, February 28, 1931, April 16, 1931, January 16, 1932, Andrews Papers.

92. "An American Plan for Unemployment Reserve Funds. Revised Draft of an Act," *American Labor Legislation Review,* 23 (June 1933), 79–95; John B. Andrews to Paul Raushenbush, January 15, 1931, Andrews Papers.

93. Haber and Murray, *Unemployment Insurance in the American Economy,* 67–68.

94. The Conference was called in 1931 through the initiative of Governor Roosevelt of New York.

95. Commons, "The Groves Unemployment Reserves Law," 9; John R. Commons, "Unemployment Insurance versus Unemployment Reserves," broadcast, April 9, 1932, typed, Andrews Papers, 2.

96. "An American Plan for Unemployment Reserve Funds," (December, 1932), 349.

97. *Ibid.*

98. Commons, "Unemployment Insurance versus Unemployment Reserves," 3.

99. John B. Andrews to Walter Lippmann, November 11, 1932; John B. Andrews to William H. Woodwin, April 14, 1932, Andrews Papers.

100. Paul A. Raushenbush, to John B. Andrews, October 30, 1933, Andrews Papers.

101. I. M. Rubinow to N. I. Stone, August 24, 1933, Isaac Rubinow Papers (Cornell), Correspondence SA-TZ.

102. *Report of the Ohio Commission on Unemployment Insurance, November, 1932* (Part I, Conclusions and Recommended Bill), 52, 13.

The Commission consisted of William Leiserson, chairman; Thomas J. Donnelly, secretary; Edwin S. Burdell; Gordon Hayes; Amy G. Maher; Stanley B. Mathewson; I. M. Rubinow; A. H. Silver; Stephen M. Young; Elizabeth Magee, executive secretary.

103. I. M. Rubinow, "The Movement Toward Unemployment Insurance in Ohio," *Social Service Review*, 7 (June 1933), 211.

104. *Ibid.*, 201.

105. I. M. Rubinow to John B. Andrews, December 16, 1932, Andrews Papers.

106. Ohio Chamber of Commerce, *Critical Analysis of the Report of the Ohio Commission on Unemployment Insurance. Prepared by the Committee on Stabilization and Unemployment . . .* (2nd. ed., Columbus, December 1932), 5, 6, 24.

107. Abraham Epstein to Abraham Lefkowitz, December 2, 1933, American Association for Social Security (Abraham Epstein) Papers, Cornell, Unemployment Insurance–New York State, folder; Abraham Epstein to Paul A. Raushenbush, October 27, 1932, *ibid.*, Unemployment Insurance–Wisconsin, folder. An excellent critique of the Wisconsin plan is Walter A. Morton, "The Aims of Unemployment Insurance with Especial Reference to the Wisconsin Act," *American Economic Review*, 23 (September 1933), 395–412. See also Roger Sherman Hoar, *Wisconsin Unemployment Insurance* (South Milwaukee, 1934); and Harry Malisoff, "The Emergence of Unemployment Compensation," *Political Science Quarterly*, 54 (June, September, December 1939), 237–258, 391–420, 577–599.

108. John B. Andrews to Paul A. Raushenbush, December 20, 1932, Andrews Papers. Less doctrinaire and obstinate than Epstein, Rubinow preferred in the interests of unity to support the Wisconsin plan in states where it had already gained support. I. M. Rubinow to Paul Douglas, June 14, 1933, Rubinow Papers, Rubinow–Douglas Correspondence, 1930–1936.

109. I. M. Rubinow, "State Pool Plans and Merit Rating," *Law and Contemporary Problems*, 3 (January 1936), 66–67.

110. Haber and Murray, *Unemployment Insurance in the American Economy*, 69, 120.

*Chapter VIII Conclusion*

1. Edwin E. Witte, "Social Security: A Wild Dream or a Practical Plan?" in Robert J. Lampman, ed., *Social Security Perspectives: Essays by Edwin E. Witte* (Madison, 1962), 11. Witte, of Wisconsin, was director of the technical staff of the Committee on Economic Security.

2. Abraham Epstein to Rev. Glenford W. Lawrence, November 12, 1935, Epstein Papers (Cornell), Unemployment Insurance–Illinois, folder.

3. Abraham Epstein to Barbara N. Armstrong, January 3, 1935, Epstein Papers (Cornell), Committee on Economic Security, folder; Abraham Epstein to J. Douglas Brown, May 1, 1935, *ibid.;* Abraham Epstein to I. M. Rubinow, October 16, 1934, Rubinow Papers, Abraham Epstein, folder. Miss Perkins was chairman of the Committee on Economic Security.

4. I. M. Rubinow to Simon E. Sobeloff, November 13, 1935, Rubinow Papers, Sobeloff, Simon E., folder; I. M. Rubinow to Paul Douglas, February 24, 1936, Rubinow Papers, Rubinow–Douglas Correspondence, folder; Abraham Epstein to I. M. Rubinow, October 4, 1935, Rubinow Papers, Abraham Epstein, 1934–35, folder.

5. I. M. Rubinow to Simon E. Sobeloff, November 13, 1935, Sobeloff, Simon E., folder.

6. *Ibid.*

7. I. M. Rubinow to Abraham Epstein, October 8, 1935, Rubinow Papers, Abraham Epstein, 1934–35, folder.

8. I. M. Rubinow to Simon E. Sobeloff, November 13, 1935, Rubinow Papers, Sobeloff, Simon E., folder.

9. Abraham Epstein, *Insecurity: A Challenge to America: A Study of Social Insurance in the United States and Abroad* (2nd rev. ed., New York, 1938), 762, 793.

10. Abraham Epstein to I. M. Rubinow, October 15, 1935, Abraham Epstein Papers (Columbia), Dr. I. M. Rubinow, from 1928 to 1933, folder; Abraham Epstein, "Our Social Insecurity Act," *Harper's Magazine,* 172 (December 1935), 65; Abraham Epstein, "Financing Social Security," American Academy of Political and Social Science, *Annals,* 183 (January 1936), 214, 213, 215. In fairness to the Committee on Economic Security, it must be noted that the Committee favored a small subsidy out of general revenues in the contributory old-age program. Secretary of the Treasury Morgenthau and President Roosevelt,

however, adamantly "insisted that the system be completely self-sustaining for all time to come." Arthur J. Altmeyer, "The Development and Status of Social Security in America," in Gerald G. Somers, ed., *Labor, Management, and Social Policy: Essays in the John R. Commons Tradition* (Madison, Wis., 1963), 128; and Arthur J. Altmeyer, *The Formative Years of Social Security* (Madison, Wisconsin, 1966), 29.

11. Abraham Epstein, "Social Security — Where are We Now?" *Harper's Magazine*, 181 (June 1940), 38. Altmeyer, who served as chairman of the technical board of the Committee on Economic Security in 1934–35, later regretted the failure to establish a minimum benefit in unemployment compensation. Averaging 41 percent of the wage-loss in 1939, benefits had dropped to 35 percent by the early 1960's. A student of Commons, he ultimately conceded that "there is no statistical evidence that employer experience rating has had any general effect in stabilizing employment." As in workmen's compensation, it has exerted a downward pressure upon benefit levels. In 1960 the average employer contribution rate varied from 0.54 percent to 2.96 percent despite the minimum 2.7 percent federal offset tax. The offset was allowed not only against employer contributions to state unemployment funds, but for exemptions based upon favorable employment experience; Altmeyer, "The Development and Status of Social Security in America," 142, 144, 143. Altmeyer concludes that the Social Security Act should have made provision for employee contributions in order to minimize the "adverse effect" of experience rating; Altmeyer, *Formative Years of Social Security*, 258, 259.

12. The spectacular expansion of private employee benefit plans since 1950 is surveyed in Walter W. Kolodrubetz, "Growth in Employee-Benefit Plans, 1950–1965," *Social Security Bulletin*, 30 (April 1967), 10–27. Total contributions to these plans approximated $20 billion in 1965, and expenditures were estimated at $13 billion (up from $1.8 billion in 1950).

13. For background on the guaranteed income see Robert Theobald, ed., *The Guaranteed Income: Next Step in Economic Evolution?* (Garden City, N.Y., 1966), and James Tobin, "The Case for an Income Guarantee," *The Public Interest* (Summer 1966), 31–41. Alvin L. Schorr, *Poor Kids: A Report on Children in Poverty* (New York, 1966) discusses alternatives to public assistance for this dependency group. The case for a national assistance minimum is presented in Advisory Council on Public Welfare, *"Having the Power, We Have the Duty,"* Report of the Secretary of Health, Education and Welfare

(Washington, D.C., 1966). A survey of proposals for a negative income tax appears in, George H. Hildebrand, *Poverty, Income Maintenance and the Negative Income Tax,* New York State School of
Industrial and Labor Relations, Paperback no. 1 (Ithaca, N.Y., 1967).

14. "Before the fifteenth anniversary of the Social Security Act,"
Gilbert Steiner points out, "business, labor, and government spokesmen
were all envisioning a more and more limited role for public assistance
in the social welfare picture." Gilbert Y. Steiner, *Social Insecurity: The
Politics of Welfare* (Chicago, 1966), 22. At present, expenditures for
public assistance total more than $5 billion, and are distributed among
8,000,000 persons. Steiner attributes the growth of public assistance in
the post-World War II period to inflation and its consequences for
social security benefits; illegitimacy, desertion and a rise in the AFDC
category; the inability of unemployment compensation to deal with
automation and the obsolescence of skills; the migration of Southern
Negroes to the North; the absence or inadequacy of social insurance
programs dealing with long-term illness and disability.

ance, 73–74; mentioned, 35, 82
California State Board of Health, 83
California State Medical Society,
condemns health insurance, 83–84
California, University of, 72, 78
Carnegie, Andrew, 13
Carsey, William A., 144
Casualty Actuarial and Statistical
Society of America, 35
Central Unemployed Body (Great
Britain), 150
Chamberlain, Joseph: advocates old-
age pensions, 121; work relief in
Great Britain, 149–150
Chamberlain, Joseph P., 30
Charity, compared to social insur-
ance, 36. *See also* Public assist-
ance; Public welfare
Charity organization: and attitudes
toward public welfare, 92–93,
103, 145–146; mentioned, 32
Chicago, Illinois: clothing industry,
unemployment insurance in, 162;
mentioned, 74, 87, 94, 97
Chicago, Burlington and Quincy
Railroad, 12
Chicago Medical Society, 80
Child guidance, 97
Child Rescue League, 97
Child welfare, innovations in, 96–
97. *See also* Mothers' pensions
Christian Scientists, oppose health
insurance in California, 81, 83
Churchill, Sir Winston: favors so-
cial insurance, 123; and unem-
ployment insurance, 165; men-
tioned, 150, 153
Cigarmakers' Union, benefit fund of,
18
Cincinnati, Ohio, 95, 161, 164
Cleveland, Ohio: clothing industry,
unemployment insurance in, 162;
mentioned, 95
Cohen, Nathaniel, 150
Colonial Office (Great Britain), 165
Colorado, 53, 99, 100, 136
Columbia University, 29, 34
Columbia University Legislative
Drafting Service, 30

Coman, Katherine, 38–39
Commercial insurance companies:
and fraternal societies, 22; development of industrial insurance,
22–23; views on workmen's compensation, 51–52, 62–64; and
health insurance in New York
State, 86–87
Commons, John R.: formation and
role of American Association for
Labor Legislation, 29, 30, 32; on
Industrial Commission, 33; and
preventive goals in social insurance, 42; on unemployment insurance, 43, 163, 170; on workmen's
compensation and accident prevention, 64; mentioned, 44, 113,
114, 143, 149, 160. *See also*
American Association for Labor
Legislation
Commonweal of Christ, 144
Community Chest, 42
Connecticut: workmen's compensa-
tion in, 53; mentioned, 67, 96,
134, 168, 173
Connery, William, Jr., 137
Cook County, Chicago, administra-
tion of mothers' pensions, 110
Cooper, Peter, 144
Cooperative Congress (Great Brit-
ain), 124
Cornell University, 29
Coxey, Jacob, 144

Dallas, Texas, 95
Daly, Mark, 88
Dauphin County Court, Pennsyl-
vania, 139
Davenport-Donohue bill, 88
Davis, Michael M., Jr., 78
Dawson, Miles M., 52
Dayton, Ohio, 95
Delaware, 53, 136
*Delineator, The,* and mothers' pen-
sions, 97
Denmark, 28, 37, 120
Dennison Manufacturing Company,
161, 162, 164

ployed, 158; mentioned, 11, 20, 21, 53, 67, 110, 134, 135, 136, 168

Pennsylvania Bureau of Workmen's Compensation, 60

Pennsylvania Children's Aid Society, 97

Pennsylvania Commission on Old Age Pensions, 138, 139

Pennsylvania Health Insurance Commission, 75

Pennsylvania Manufacturers' Association, 139, 140

Pennsylvania Mothers' Assistance Fund, 108

Pennsylvania Railroad, 12

Pennsylvania State Chamber of Commerce, 139, 140

Pennsylvania State Federation of Labor, 138

Pensions, for blind, 124, 125

Pensions, for government employees, 125–127

Pensions, industrial, 127–132, 144

Pensions, military, 125

Pensions, old-age: moral issues in, 38–40; favored over insurance, 120; foreign legislation, 120–124; American legislation, 133–137. *See also* Aged; Epstein, Abraham; Fraternal Order of Eagles

Perkins, Frances, 176

Philadelphia, Pennsylvania, 41, 158, 161

Philadelphia and Reading Railroad, 12

Phossy Jaw, 30

Physicians' Protective Association (Buffalo, N.Y.), 87

Pinckney, Merritt W., 100

Pittsburgh, 138

Pittsburgh, University of, 138

*Pittsburgh Survey, The*, 14, 21, 46

Poland, 167

*Political Science Quarterly, The*, 34

Porterfield, E. E., 100

Postal Savings Bank Act (Great Britain), 119, 120

President's Conference on Unemployment, 158

Prevention: and social insurance, 42–44; and workmen's compensation, 55, 64–65; in health insurance, 70. *See also* Health insurance; Safety-first

Procter and Gamble, 161, 164

Professional Guild of Kings County, 88–89

Professionalization, in social work, 3

Prudential Insurance Company (Great Britain), 22

Prudential Life Insurance Company (Newark, N.J.), 22, 83, 86, 116

Pryor, Dr. John H., 88

Public assistance: contrasted to social insurance, 91; historic status of, 92–93. *See also* Charity; Mothers' pensions; Public welfare

Public employment exchanges: advocated by American Association for Labor Legislation, 147–148; growth in United States, 154; and labor market stabilization, 154–155; failure of, 155, 157; in World War I, 156–157. *See also* Unemployment; Unemployment insurance

Public welfare: function of, 25; and private social agencies, 94; and community relief policy, 102, 103; influence of mothers' pensions on, 106–107; defects of, 179–180. *See also* Board of Public Welfare; Mothers' pensions; Public assistance

Queensland (Australia), 167

Quincy (Massachusetts) Report, 92

Railroad brotherhoods, 18

Railroad establishment funds, 12–13

Raushenbush, Paul, 169–170

Rensselaer County, New York, 87

Rhode Island, 138

Richmond, Mary, 102

Robinson-Keating bill, 157

Rochester, New York, 161, 162

Rooney, Dr. James F., 87

Roosevelt, Theodore: and White